THE

YOUNG

HOUSEKEEPER'S FRIEND.

BY

MRS. CORNELIUS.

REVISED AND ENLARGED.

BOSTON:
PUBLISHED BY TAGGARD AND THOMPSON.
M DCCC LXVIII.

PREFACE.

In preparing this little volume, my aim has been to furnish to young housekeepers the best aid that a book can give in the departments of which it treats. No printed guide can perfectly supply the place of that experience which is gained by early and habitual attention to domestic concerns. But the directions here given are designed to be so minute, and of so practical a character, that the observance of them shall prevent very many of the perplexities which most young people suffer during their first years of married life.

The receipts, with the exception of about twenty which are copied from books, are furnished from my own experience, or that of my immediate friends. An ample variety is given for furnishing the table of any American family; but especial reference has been had to those who have neither poverty nor riches; and such directions have been given as will enable a housekeeper to provide a good and healthful table, or, if desired, a handsome one, at a moderate expense.

To save repetition, very minute directions are given at the head of every chapter, by attending to which, the least experienced cook will learn how to proceed in making each article for which a receipt is given.

I do not attempt to give directions in regard to the best methods of taking care of all sorts of furniture, and performing all the various kinds of household labor, because there are works already published which furnish copious and judicious instructions on these subjects.

It may be asked, "Why then publish a book of counsels and receipts, for there surely are many receipt-books?" This is true; but while some of them are not ample guides on the subjects of which they treat, others are based upon a plan both expensive and unhealthy, and all of them that I have seen, leave an inexperienced housekeeper at a loss in regard to many of the things most necessary to economy and comfort.

I have seen many a young lady, just entered upon the duties of married life, perplexed and prematurely care-worn, for want of experience, or a little good instruction, in regard to the simplest domestic processes; and often have felt, with the sincerest sympathy, an earnest wish to render her some effectual aid. If I succeed in affording it through this little book, I shall esteem myself happy; and I have only to ask, in conclusion, that my numerous young friends, and all the youthful housekeepers into whose hands it may fall, will receive it as a token of my friendly interest and best wishes.

M. H. C.

ANDOVER 1845.

PREFACE

TO THE REVISED EDITION.

My aim in the revision of this little book has been to make the arrangement of the receipts and of the index more convenient, the directions more simple and clear, and the entire collection more select and reliable. In place of some of the old receipts many choice new ones are substituted, which, so far as I know, have not been in print before. All of them have been attested by experience, either my own, or of friends in whose judgment in such matters I have entire confidence. The last chapter, written long since in compliance with frequent requests from young friends, is appended in the hope that it will increase the usefulness of the book to those for whose benefit it was originally designed.

I trust it is not improper for me to add, that among the motives which have led to the present revision, is the favor with which many ladies have regarded this book in its original form, notwithstanding its confessed imperfections. It has been my earnest wish for years to make it more worthy of such estimation; and hoping that it will prove a better Friend to Young Housekeepers than it has hitherto been, I ask for the continued patronage of those who have so long and so kindly overlooked its faults.

M. H. C.

March, 1859.

THE

YOUNG HOUSEKEEPER'S FRIEND.

COUNSELS AND SUGGESTIONS

Good housekeeping compatible with intellectual culture.—Persevering attention rewarded.—Effects of unhealthy diet.—Responsibleness of women.—Application of the principles of religion to the duties of domestic life.

A SYMMETRICAL education is extremely rare in this country. Nothing is more common than to see young ladies, whose intellectual attainments are of a high order, profoundly ignorant of the duties which all acknowledge to belong peculiarly to women. Consequently many have to learn, after marriage, how to take care of a family; and thus their housekeeping is, frequently, little else than a series of experiments; often unsuccessful, resulting in mortification and discomfort in the parlor, and waste and ill temper in the kitchen.

So numerous are these instances, that excellence in housekeeping has come to be considered as incompatible with superior intellectual culture. But it is not so. The most elevated minds fulfil best the every-day duties of life. If young women would resolve, let the effort cost what it will, to perfect themselves in their appropriate duties, a defective domestic education would soon be remedied. Observation and persevering attention would give the requisite knowledge, and their efforts would bring a speedy and ample reward. It were far better, when they enter upon the station of a mistress of a family, to be already possessed of such experience as would enable them easily to regulate the expenditures, and so to systematize the work of every day, as to secure economy, comfort, neatness, and order. But if this knowledge has not been previously acquired, let not the learner be discouraged, or for a moment yield to the idea of "letting things take their course." No woman can innocently or safely settle down upon this conclusion. The good to be lost, and the evils incurred, are too great to admit of such a decision. The result will certainly be uncomfortable; and it would not be strange if the dearest domestic affections were thus chilled, and the most valuable family interests sacrificed.

How often do we see the happiness of a husband abridged by the absence of skill, neatness, and economy in the wife! Perhaps he is not able to fix upon the cause, for he does not understand minutely enough the processes upon which domestic order depends, to analyze the difficulty; but he is conscious of discomfort. However improbable it may seem, the health of many a professional man is undermined, and his usefulness curtailed, if not sacrificed, because he habitually eats *bad bread.*

How frequently, in case of students in the various professions, is the brightest promise of future attainment and honor overshadowed by a total loss of health; and the young scholar, in whom the choicest hopes were garnered up, is compelled to relinquish his studies, and turn his unwilling thoughts to other pursuits; or, worse than this, he becomes a helpless invalid for life. Yet even this is an enviable lot, compared with his, whose noble intellectual powers have become like the broken chords of an instrument that shall never again utter its melody. But are such evils as these to be traced to the use of unwholesome food? Every intelligent physician, every superintendent of our insane hospitals, testifies that in very many instances, this is the prominent cause.

We often see the most pious Christians heavy-hearted, and doubting their share in the great salvation; mistaking the salutary discipline of their Heavenly Father for the rod of an offended judge; forgetting the freeness of the mercy offered, looking only at their own unworthiness, and refusing to be comforted. Instances of this sort, resulting in incurable melancholy, may frequently be traced to the same cause. The human body and mind are so intimately associated, that the functions of the one cannot be disturbed without deranging the action of the other; and it is doubtless true, that many a hopeless heart and feeble body would be more benefited by a wholesome diet, than by the instructions of the minister, or the prescriptions of the physician. To say the least, the good offices of these will avail little while counteracted by the want of the other.

If this subject has a direct bearing upon the health of families, so also does it exert an immediate influence upon their virtue. There are numerous instances of worthy merchants and mechanics whose efforts are paralyzed, and their hopes chilled by the total failure of the wife in her sphere of duty; and who seek solace under their disappointment in the wine-party, or the late convivial supper. Many a day-laborer, on his return at evening from his hard toil, is repelled by the sight of a disorderly house and a comfortless supper; and perhaps is met by a cold eye instead of "the thriftie wifie's smile;" and he makes his escape to the grog-shop or the underground gambling-room. Can any human agency hinder the series of calamities entailed by these things? No! the most active philanthropy, the best schemes of organized benevolence, cannot furnish a remedy, unless the springs of society are rectified. The domestic influence of woman is certainly one of these. Every woman is invested with a great degree of power over the happiness and virtue of others. She cannot escape using it, and she cannot innocently pervert it. There is no avenue or channel of society through which it may not send a salutary influence; and when rightly directed, it is unsurpassed by any human instrumentality in its purifying and restoring efficacy.

The Bible sanctions this view of female obligation and influence, in the description it gives of the virtuous woman. "Her price is far above rubies. The heart of her husband doth safely trust in her, so that he shall have no need of spoil. She will do him good, and not evil, all the days of her life. She seeketh wool and flax, and worketh diligently with her hands. She is like the merchant's ships, she bringeth her food from afar. She riseth also while it is yet night, and giveth meat to her household, and a portion to her maidens. She considereth a field and buyeth it; with the fruit of her hands she planteth a vineyard. She girdeth her loins with strength, and strengtheneth her arms. She perceiveth that her merchandise is good, and her candle goeth not out by night. She layeth her hands to the spindle, and her hands hold the distaff. She stretcheth out her hand to the poor; yea, she reacheth forth her hands to the needy. She is not afraid of the snow for her household; for all her household are clothed in scarlet. She maketh herself coverings of tapestry; her clothing is silk and purple. Her husband is known in the gates, when he sitteth among the elders of the land. She maketh fine linen and selleth it; and delivereth girdles unto the merchant. Strength and honor are her clothing; and she shall rejoice in time to come. She openeth her mouth with wisdom; and in her tongue is the law of kindness. She looketh well to the ways of her household, and eateth not the bread of idleness. Her children arise up and call her blessed; her husband also, and he praiseth her. Many daughters have done virtuously, but thou excellest them all. Favor is deceitful, and beauty is vain; but a woman that feareth the Lord she shall be praised. Give her of the fruit of her hands, and let her own works praise her in the gates."

Like the paintings of the old artists, the beauty of this exquisite picture is enhanced by the "softened hue of years," and like them it must be studied long ere its finest touches will be revealed. Female virtue is the same now that it was in the days of the wise man, and this portraiture is, in its outlines, still true to the life. Energy, industry, economy, order, skill, vigilance, cheerfulness, kindness, charity, discretion, and the fear of God, are as essential to the character of a good wife now, as they were then; and the effects of these are still the same in the embellishments of her house, the abundance of her stores, the happiness of her household, her husband's confidence in her, his honorable rank among the elders of the land, the virtues of her children, and her own felicity. To estimate the truth of the picture, we need only observe in society around us, that the happiest families are those in which the wife and mother most resembles it.

In connection with this subject, the inquiry suggests itself whether, in the "excessive externalism of the times," due prominence is given to the practice of home-duties as a part of religion? Whether the spirit of the New Testament is carried, as it should be, into the every-day concerns of life? Is not the giving largely to public objects of benevolence sometimes suffered to supersede the duty of "considering the poor," and "bringing him that is cast out to our house?" Are not the claims of a popular charity readily allowed, while the inevitable ills of life, of which every family must have its share, are sometimes permitted to remain unsoothed by the voice of sympathy, and the gentle ministry of skilful hands and a loving heart? We may even go to church, when we should offer purer incense to Him who sees the heart, by performing the humblest domestic labors at home. Let me not be misunderstood. The public institutions of religion have claims upon us which we cannot innocently set aside; but alas, erring mortals that we are! our piety is seldom symmetrical and consistent. We are prone to love publicity. We find it easier to give money, to enlist our energies in behalf of benevolent societies, to go with the multitude to the house of God, than to practise, in the retirement of home, the "charity which suffereth long and is kind, which envieth not, vaunteth not itself, doth not behave itself unseemly, seeketh not her own, is not easily provoked, thinketh no evil, beareth all things, believeth all things, hopeth all things, endureth all things, and never faileth." Can we not learn, while we do the one, not to leave the other undone?

Style of living. — Consistency. — Economy. — Neatness. — Habits of regular attention to family concerns. — Perplexing days. — Company. — Arrangement of family work for a week. — First instructions to domestics. — Patience. — Good temper. — Observance of the Golden Rule. — Self-government when accidents happen. — Sunday privileges.

CONSIDER in the outset what mode of living best befits your station, resources, and obligations to others; and so adjust your plan that consistency * and appropriateness shall appear throughout. It is much better to adopt a style of expenditure below your means than above them. Of the unhappy effects of this last we have many examples in our country. A very little advance in the style of living, creates an additional expense greater than would at first be believed. That little sentence, "*I can do without it,*" has saved thousands of dollars for future exigencies. Prodigality is as fruitful of mischief as Pandora's box, and no amount of wealth can justify it. Habits of wasteful expenditure are almost always accompanied with selfishness and a cold heart towards the claims of the poor. Be conscientious, therefore, in the practice of economy. Family comfort can hardly be found without it. Neatness is essential to it; for though there may be neatness without economy, there cannot be economy without neatness.

Accustom yourself to take good care of every thing you pos-

---

* The writer has heard of more than one lady who furnished but two dish-towels, fearing that a more ample supply would lead to waste in the use of them. But in one instance, when a superb dinner was given to a large party, the cook was reduced to the necessity of tearing up a sheet to wipe the dishes.

sess. The best managers probably have, at first, a few disagreeable lessons to learn, in the loss of things forgotten or neglected for want of experience in having the entire care of a family. But it is to be hoped there are not many who lose five or six hams eaten by the rats, or forty yards of Russia linen laid upon the snow to whiten, and forgotten till reduced to a pulp fit only for the paper-mill.

Be economical without parsimony, liberal without waste, and practise the best methods of using your possessions without having your mind wholly absorbed by them.

In your arrangements for the table, have reference to the work which is in hand, so that dishes which are easily cooked shall be provided for those days when most work is to be done. A want of consideration in this particular often provokes ill temper, and may even occasion the loss of a good domestic. This is one of the errors which those are liable to commit who are unaccustomed to household labor. Provide a variety of food; a frugal table, with frequent change, is much more agreeable and healthy than a more expensive one, where nearly the same things are served up every day.

If you are subject to uninvited company, and your means do not allow you to set before your guests as good a table as they keep at home, do not distress yourself or them with apologies. If they are real friends, they will cheerfully sit down with you to such a table as is appropriate to your circumstances, and would be made uncomfortable by an effort on your part to provide a better one than you can afford. If your resources are ample, live in such a way that an unexpected visitor shall occasion no difference. The less alteration made in family arrangements on account of visitors, the happier for them as well as for you.

Never treat the subject of having company as if it were a great affair. Your doing this will excite your domestics, and lead them to imagine the addition to their usual work much greater than it is; your own cares, too, will be greatly magnified. A calm and quiet way of meeting all sorts of domestic vicissitudes, and of doing the work of each day, be it more or less, equalizes the pressure of care, and prevents its becoming oppressive.

Be composed when accidents happen to your furniture. The most careful hand is sometimes unsteady. Angry words will not mend broken glass or china, but they will teach your domestics to conceal such occurrences from you, and the only explanation ever given you will be, that they *came apart.* Encourage those whom you employ to come immediately and tell you, when they have been so unfortunate as to break or injure any thing belonging to you. The cases are very rare, in which it is best to deduct the value from their wages.

In the best regulated families there will be some laborious, perplexing days. Adverse and inconvenient circumstances will cluster together. At those times, guard against two things, — discouragement and irritability. If others look on the dark side, find something cheering to say; if they fret, sympathize in their share of the trial, while you set them the example of bearing your part in it well.

Miss Hamilton's three maxims, so often quoted, are worthy of an indelible inscription in every house: —

"Do every thing in its proper time.

"Keep every thing to its proper use.

"Put every thing in its proper place."

She should have added, Do every thing in the best manner; for the habit of aiming at a perfect standard, is not only of the highest importance in our moral interests, but also proportionately so in reference to the common affairs of life.

Accustom yourself, each evening, to arrange in your own mind the meals for the next day, and also the extra work to be done by others, and what you will do yourself. This habit promotes order and system, and gives quietness and ease to the movement of the whole family machinery. When you see defects, such as irregularity, confusion, waste, or want of cleanliness in any part of your household concerns, consider what is the best remedy, and be willing to attend to the subject till the evil is cured.

Visit all the rooms and closets that are in constant use, every day. You will thus acquire that habit of attention to minutiæ, upon which neatness and order so much depend, and it will cost a less expenditure of time and effort to secure these ends, than if a great many little things requiring attention are suffered to accumulate. This habit will also have the best effect upon those who serve you. They will not be tempted to negligence or waste, by the idea that you will never discover it. They will anticipate your daily inspection, and soon find themselves so much benefited by your habits of system and order, that their own convenience will dictate obedience to your directions and suggestions. Endeavor so to perfect your plan, that when you have given the necessary time, be it longer or shorter, to domestic concerns each morning, you can dismiss them from your mind and attend to other things, giving to these no further thought, except that which results from a habit of observing whatever passes in the family.

When a new domestic enters your service, observe whether she seems to understand her business; if not, teach her your methods. Nothing can be more unreasonable than to expect a stranger to remember, and at once practise, a series of directions given all at once, and perhaps in a hurried manner. And yet, this is an injustice of which many a girl has to complain. What wonder if mutual dissatisfaction and a speedy separation is the result? * She is in a new situation, unacquainted with the various parts of your house, and the arrangements of your family. Therefore, duty and self-interest dictate, that you cheerfully instruct her, so far as is necessary; and a few days' attention to her manner of doing her work, will probably be rewarded by a much more skilful and willing service, than if no such care were bestowed. She will discover that you are

* Probably a lady, known to the writer, who had twenty-three girls in the course of six weeks, pursued this inconsiderate course.

kindly disposed, ready to appreciate her efforts, and capable of judging when her work is well done. Confidence is thus inspired, and she will be far more likely to become a faithful and permanent member of your household, than if left in the beginning to pursue her own course, and to be frowned upon if she does not happen to please.

Refrain from severity and too much frequency in finding fault, and be careful not to speak to domestics of their errors at a time when they are perplexed or very busy. To choose a good time, is as necessary to success as to avoid needless severity. If the dinner is not properly done, it is usually best to say nothing at the time; your cook will doubtless be conscious of her failure, and your silence will have a much better effect upon her than any thing you can *then* say; but the next time the same articles are to be cooked, remind her of the previous failure, point out the defect, and give her minute instructions how to avoid its repetition.

Good temper, decision, and reasonable requisitions will secure the confidence and respect of your domestics; while fretfulness, lack of good judgment, and unreasonable demands will alienate them from you, and involve you in endless perplexities. Nothing gives the mistress of a family such power as blended decision and gentleness; they are truly irresistible. You need not, *you must not*, if you regard the best welfare of your household, utter one impatient word from the beginning to the end of the year.

Study the dispositions of those whom you employ. If you keep several domestics, arrange their work so that there shall be as little collision with one another, as possible. Be as considerate of their comfort, as you could reasonably wish others to be of yours in like circumstances. A universal obedience to the Golden Rule would make this world a paradise, and perhaps it is more liable to be forgotten in this relation than in most others. The best management on your part, cannot always save those who serve you from weariness and vexation; but a well-timed word of kindness and sympathy does good like a medicine.

Learn so to systematize your concerns, that each day of the week shall have its appropriate work, and every domestic know, without being prompted, what she is to do on that day. Observe whether all do their appropriate work; but do not prompt them, unless you see that they are likely to forget. They should learn to feel the responsibility to be on their own memory — not yours.

In the morning, soon after breakfast, give all your directions about the dinner, and tea, and specify all the work you wish to have done in addition to the regular routine of the day. If you think of any thing more afterwards, defer it, if you can, till another day; nothing disturbs the temper of domestics more than to have additional work assigned them after the business of the day has been laid out.

The two following modes of arranging the work of a week, are designed for families whose pecuniary means allow an entirely comfortable, but not a costly mode of living; yet they may contain useful hints for those whose wealth admits of the employment of a number of domestics.

On *Monday* have the house swept and dusted, the clothes for the wash collected, and such articles mended as should be before being washed.

On *Tuesday*, wash; and here it should be observed, that those persons who have never practised washing, are often unreasonable in their requirements on this day. If there is but one domestic, she is of course to do the washing; but, unless the family is small, she could be excused from doing the cooking or other ordinary work of the family.

Every one acquainted with this part of family labor, knows that it is very discouraging to be obliged to leave it and do other things; and the cleaning which must be done after the clothes are upon the line, is a sufficient occupation for the remaining time and strength, without one's being obliged to do any portion of the daily housework. In families where the washings are large, it is better to delay the ironing until the next day but one; this gives time for doing some things necessarily omitted on washing-day; for baking, if the size of the family makes it necessary to bake twice a week, and for folding the clothes; and the girl is better able to do the whole ironing in a day, than if she were to perform this labor immediately after washing. To most persons, both washing and ironing are severe labors, and therefore should not be assigned to successive days, unless the domestic herself prefers it, which is sometimes the case.

Therefore, on *Wednesday*, bake, and fold the clothes. On *Thursday*, iron. On *Friday*, have all parts of the house that are in constant use, swept and dusted again, the brasses rubbed, and if there are windows to be washed, closets or sleeping rooms to be scoured, let it be done on this day.

On *Saturday*, bake, and provide such a supply for the table as shall supersede the necessity of cooking on Sunday.

The chief advantage of this method is, that the mistress of the family has not the Monday's sweeping to do, in addition to getting the washing-day dinner; and if she is subject to incidental company, and has not daughters or a friend to help her, or has slender health, this is an important relief.

The other arrangement is to wash on *Monday;* bake, and do other things necessarily omitted, on *Tuesday;* iron on *Wednesday; Thursday,* do no extra work. *Friday*, sweep and clean; *Saturday*, bake; distribute clean bed linen, and see that every thing is in readiness for the Sabbath.

The practice of rubbing all the silver in common use every week is not necessary, provided it is always washed in clean suds, and rinsed in scalding soft water without soap. If it is washed in the kitchen with other dishes, it will be necessary to rub it once in two or three weeks.

There are several advantages in washing on Monday. It is then easy on Saturday to provide food enough to last until after the washing is done, which cannot easily be accomplished if it is delayed until *Tuesday*. Another is, that if Monday is a pleasant day, the clothes may be dried, and the ironing and mending completed during the first half of the week; but if

Tuesday be the washing-day, and it is rainy, the work of the whole week is delayed. Still another reason is, that after the entire rest of Sunday the frame is invigorated for labor; and lastly, it gives one day in the week of comparative leisure to the domestic. This is a consideration worthy of regard. Some ladies are always uneasy, and appear to think themselves wronged, when they see their domestics quietly seated at their sewing; as if they could not render faithful service without being employed the *whole* time in household labor. But those persons who so arrange their affairs as to secure to their domestics several hours every week for their own employments, and who take an interest in promoting, in every reasonable way, their comfort and happiness, will be amply rewarded in their faithfulness and attachment.

The situation of a waiting-maid is, in some families, one of hard bondage. It seems as if her employers had forgotten that she is made of flesh and blood, and is therefore capable of having an aching head and weary limbs. She must run at the call of the various bells throughout the house, and no matter how tired she becomes, there is no rest for the sole of her foot. If the unfortunate being is a homeless, motherless little girl, or a friendless foreigner, so much the worse. By a little consideration on the part of the lady, or ladies, of a family, such hard requisitions might be avoided without any real sacrifice of comfort. Our happiness is promoted by the cultivation of such habits that we shall not need the constant attendance of another to save us from exertion.

If your domestics cannot read, offer to teach them, and devote several half hours to their instruction during the week, and an additional hour on Sunday. It is a religious duty, a part of every Christian's *mission.* Encourage in them a taste for reading, by keeping useful and entertaining books in the kitchen. A love of rational pleasure will thus be promoted, and the effect be every way beneficial.

Let the least possible amount of labor be required from those who serve you, on Sunday. This ought to be a needless injunction in this country; but many a professor of religion, living on the soil trodden by the puritan pilgrims, provides a better dinner for the Sabbath than for any other day. Religion forbids such a practice; but, aside from this consideration, family comfort is essentially promoted by quietness and freedom from care on the Lord's day. Domestics, whatever be their religious predilections, uniformly regard it a great privilege to be exempt from cooking on that day. It is easy, by a little good management, to provide a dinner, nice enough for any table in the land, without even kindling a fire. In the summer this is done in many families; and in the winter, when a fire is of course always burning, a cup of tea, or a dish of vegetables, can be added to the cold articles already provided, without keeping any one from church for the purpose.

In concluding these suggestions, the writer cannot refrain from adding a few words of sympathy and encouragement for those who, having passed their youth in affluent ease, or in the delights of study, are obliged, by the vicissitudes of life, to spend their time and strength in laborious household occupations. There are many such instances in this country, particularly in the great Western Valley. Adversity succeeds prosperity like a sudden inundation, and sweeps away the possessions and the hopes of multitudes. The poor and uneducated are often rapidly elevated to wealthy independence, while the refined and highly educated are compelled to taste the bitterness of poverty; and minds capable of any attainment, and that would grace any station, are doomed to expend their energies in devising methods for the hands to earn a scanty livelihood.

Let not such persons feel themselves degraded by the performance of the humblest domestic labor.

> "Some kinds of baseness
> Are nobly undergone, and most poor matters
> Point to rich ends."

However lowly the common duties of life may be, a faithful and cheerful discharge of them is always honorable, and God smiles on those who patiently fulfil them.

OVENS, BREAD, &c.

Ovens — and how to heat them.

Stoves and cooking-ranges have so generally taken the place of brick ovens, that the following directions, which were appropriate when this book was first published, will seldom be of use now. Yet, as they may sometimes be needed, they are suffered to remain. It is impossible to give minute directions as to the management of the various kinds of baking apparatus now in use. A few experiments will enable a person of good judgment to succeed with any of them.

A few suggestions in regard to the construction of an oven may be useful. For a family of medium size, an oven holding ten or twelve plates is large enough. There should be two or three bushels of ashes, with dead coals in them, poured over the top, after the first tier of bricks which forms the arch is laid. Then the usual brickwork should be laid over them. The advantage is this, — when the oven is heated, these ashes and coals are heated also, and, being so thick, retain the heat a long time. Five successive bakings have been done in such an oven with one heating; the bread first — then the puddings — afterward pastry — then cake and gingerbread — and lastly custards, which, if made with boiled milk and put into the oven hot, and allowed to stand a considerable time, will bake sufficiently with a very slight heat.

The first time an oven is heated, a large fire should be kept burning in it six or eight hours. Unless this is done it will never bake well.

The size and structure of ovens is so different, that no precise rules for heating them can be given. A lady should attend to this herself, until she perfectly understands what is necessary, and can give minute directions to those she employs. It is easy to find out how many sticks of a given size are necessary for baking articles that require a strong heat; and so for those which are baked with less. To bake brown bread, beans, apples, and other things, all at one time, the oven should be heated with hard wood, and if rather large, so as to be two hours in burning out, it is better. To bake thin cake, and some kinds of puddings, pine wood, split small, answers very well.

After the wood is half burnt, stir the fire equally to all parts of the oven. This is necessary to an equal diffusion of the heat. Do it several times before the oven is cleared. If the oven is to be very full, put in a brick, so that you can have it hot, to set upon it any pan or plate for which there may not be room on the bottom.* Be careful that no doors or windows are open near the oven. Let the coals remain until they are no longer red. They should not look dead, but like hot embers. When you take them out, leave in the back part a few to be put near the pans that require most heat, such as beans, Indian pudding, or jars of fruit. Before putting in the things to be baked, throw in a little flour. If it browns instantly, the oven is too hot, and should stand open three or four minutes. If it browns without burning in the course of half a minute, it will be safe to set in the articles immediately. It is often best not to put in those things which require a moderate heat, till those which need a strong heat have been baking ten or fifteen minutes.

A coal scuttle of peat, with less wood, is economical, and gives an equal and very prolonged heat. Many persons use it with pine wood, for their ordinary baking. It takes a longer time to burn out than wood.

It is well to kindle the fire as far back as possible, because all parts of the wood are much sooner on fire than if it is kindled near the mouth of the oven; and if peat is used, it should not be thrown in until the wood is well kindled.

Directions respecting Bread.

There is no one thing upon which health and comfort in a

* The pan which is set on this brick may need a paper over it to keep the top from burning, and after a while should be set on the oven bottom, and another put on the brick.

family so much depend as *bread.* With good bread the coarsest fare is tolerable; without it, the most luxurious table is not comfortable.

It is best economy to purchase *the best* flour, even at an extra cost. Good flour adheres slightly to the hand, and if pressed in it, shows the impress of the lines of the skin. Dough made of it is a *yellowish white*, and does not stick to the hands after sufficient kneading. There is much bad flour in market, which can in no way be made into nutritious food.

When you find good flour, notice *the brand,* and afterwards purchase the same kind. The writer knows a family that for eleven years purchased flour in this way, without once having a poor barrel; then the mills passed to another owner, and though the brand was the same, the flour was good no more.

If you raise wheat, or buy it in the grain, always wash it before sending it to the mill. Take two or three bushels at a time, pour in water and stir it, and then pour off the water. Repeat this till the water is clear. Do not let the grain stand in the water, as it will swell and be injured; spread it on a large cloth in the sun, or where it will have warmth and fresh air, and stir it often, and in a day or two it will be dry. The flour is much improved by this process.

Newly ground flour which has never been packed, is very superior to barrel flour, so that the people in Western New York, that land of finest wheat, say that New England people do not know what good flour is.

Indian meal, also, is much the best when freshly ground. The meal made of Southern corn is often injured by salt water, or *dampness* acquired in the hold of a ship.

Rye flour is very apt to be *musty* or *grown.* There is no way to detect this but by trial. It is well to engage a farmer to supply you with the same he provides for his own family.

On Yeast.

Good yeast is indispensable to good bread. Many of the compounds sold for yeast are unfit for use.

The best kinds are *dry yeast, soft hop yeast,* and *potato yeast.* The hard yeast should be made in the month of May, or *early* in June, for summer use, and in September or October, for the winter. This kind sometimes loses its vitality during the damp weather of August, but it is not invariably the case. Soft hop, or potato yeast, should be made once a week in the summer, and once in two weeks in the winter. No soft yeast can be fit for use, if kept week after week; it may be rectified with saleratus, but the bread will not be very good.

Every housekeeper should make sure, by her own personal attention, that the yeast is properly made, and the jar well scalded. A jar having a close cover is best. Bottles will burst, and you cannot be perfectly sure that a jug is cleansed from every particle of old yeast. To scald the jar, put it into a kettle of boiling water. This must be done every time you make yeast. Stone ware is liable to be cracked by the pouring of boiling water into it.

Soft Hop Yeast.

To three pints of water put a small handful of hops, or if they are in compact pound papers, as put up by the Shakers, half a handful; boil them about half an hour. If the water wastes, add more. Put into the jar six or seven table-spoonfuls of flour, and a teaspoonful of salt. Set it near the kettle, and dip the hop tea, as it boils, into the jar through a small colander or sieve. When you have strained enough of the tea to wet all the flour, stir it, and let none remain dry at the bottom or sides of the jar; then strain upon it the remainder of the hop-water, and stir it well. This mixture should be about the consistency of batter for griddle-cakes. The reason for straining the hop-water while boiling is, that if the flour is not scalded, the yeast will soon become sour.

After it becomes cool (but not cold), stir in a gill of good yeast; set it in a slightly warm place, and not closely covered. Do not leave an iron spoon in it, as it will turn it a dark color, and make it unfit for use. When the yeast is fermented, put it in a cool place, covered close.

Yeast which is made in part of Graham flour rises light sooner than that which is made of white flour alone, and does not affect the color of the bread.

When yeast has a strong tart smell, and a watery appearance on the surface, it is too old for use.

Dry Yeast.

Put four ounces of hops to six quarts of water; boil it away to three quarts. Strain, boiling hot (as directed for the Soft yeast) upon three pints of flour, a large spoonful of ginger, and another of salt. When it is cool, add a pint of sweet yeast. When it is foaming light, knead in sifted Indian meal enough to make it very stiff. Mould it into loaves, and cut in thin slices, and lay it upon clean boards. Set it where there is a free circulation of air, in the sun. After one side has dried so as to be a little crisped, turn the slices over; and when both sides are dry, break them up into small pieces. It thus dries sooner than if not broken. Set it in the sun two or three days in succession. Stir it often with your hand, so that all parts will be equally exposed to the air. When perfectly dry, put it into a coarse bag, and hang it in a dry and cool place. The greatest inconvenience in making this yeast is the danger of cloudy or wet weather. If the day after it is made should not be fair, it will do to set the jar in a cool place, and wait a day or two before putting in the Indian meal. But the best yeast is made when the weather continues clear and dry; and if a little windy, so much the better.

To use it, take, for five loaves of bread, one handful; soak it in a very little water till soft, which will be in a few minutes; stir it into the sponge prepared for the bread. This yeast makes less delicate bread than the soft kind, but it is very convenient.

Potato Yeast.

Pare, and boil very soft, six potatoes; mash them fine, add one cup each of flour and white sugar, and a teaspoonful of salt. Boil a small handful of hops twenty minutes in two quarts of water; strain it as it boils upon the mixture. When it has become milk warm, add a cup of good yeast. It will rise quickly, and if set in a cool place will keep sweet two weeks in winter, and ten days in summer.

A sponge set early in the morning with this yeast, will be light enough to knead and mould in two or three hours, and the bread ready to bake before noon. In winter make the sponge over night. Make half the quantity for a small family.

Good Family Bread.

For five common-sized loaves, make a pint and a half of thin water gruel. Use half a teacupful of fine Indian meal. Salt it a little more than if it were to be eaten as gruel, and boil ten or fifteen minutes. This is of importance, as, if the meal is only scalded, the bread will be coarse. Add enough milk to make two quarts of the whole. If the milk is new, the gruel may be poured into it in the pan; if not, it should be scalded in the kettle with the gruel. This is particularly important in the summer, as at that season milk which is but a few hours old, and is sweet when put into the bread, will sour in the dough in a short time. When the mixture is cool, so that you are *sure* it will not scald, add a teacupful of yeast, and then stir in sifted flour * enough to make a thick batter. This is called a sponge. This being done in the evening, let it stand, if in summer, in a cool place, if in winter, in a moderately warm place, till morning. Then add flour enough to make it easy to mould, and knead it very thoroughly.

This process of kneading is very important in making bread, and there are but few domestics whom it is not necessary to instruct how to do it. They generally work over the dough without expending any strength upon it. The hands should be closely shut, and the fists pressed hard and quickly upon the dough, dipping them into flour whenever the dough sticks to them. A half an hour is the least time to be given to kneading a baking of bread, unless you prefer, after having done this till

* All kinds of flour and meal should be sifted for use, except buckwheat and Graham flour.

it ceases to stick to your hands, to chop it with a chopping-knife four or five hundred strokes. An hour's kneading is not too much.

All this looks on paper like a long and troublesome process; but I venture to say that no lady, after having learned the benefit of it, will be willing to diminish any portion of the labor and attention necessary to secure such bread as these directions, observed, will make. Practice will make it easy, and no woman of sense will hesitate in choosing between sour, tough, ill-baked bread, with heaps of wasted pieces, a dyspeptic husband, and sickly children on the one hand, and comfort, economy, and health on the other.

But to return to the bread. After it is thoroughly kneaded, divide it into four or five equal pieces, and mould according to the form of the pans in which you bake it. These being greased with clean drippings, put in the dough and set it in the sun or near the fire (according to the season) to rise. Loaves of this size will bake in an hour; if the oven be rather hot, in a few minutes short of an hour. Practice and good judgment must direct these things. If the bread rises rather slowly, take a dish of warm water and wet the top with your hand.

When the loaves are baked, do not lay them flat upon the table; good housewives think it makes them heavy. Set them on the side, one against another, and put a coarse cloth closely over them; this makes the crust tender by keeping in the steam. If bread is baked too hard, wring a towel in cold water and wrap around it while it is yet hot. Care is necessary that bread does not rise too much, and thus become sour, especially in warm weather; and even if it does not, the freshness is lost, and an insipid taste is produced, and it becomes dry sooner by long rising. No exact rule can be given; experience and observation must teach. When dough becomes so light as to run over after being moulded and put into pans, it is best to mould it again, kneading it hard two or three minutes, but using as little flour as possible; then lay it back into the pans, and put it immediately into the oven; this prevents its being tasteless and dry; it will be perfectly light, but of a different sort, and much preferred by some persons.

Some people invariably use saleratus in bread, and there are tables where the effluvia of this article, and the deep yellow color of the bread, offend the senses before it is tasted. If all the materials used are good, and the dough has not been permitted to sour, white bread except that which is made with water, is far better without saleratus. If dough has become sour, a teaspoonful of saleratus for every quart of the milk or water that was used for wetting the bread, will be sufficient to correct it. The tray or pan in which the bread is made, should be scalded after being washed, every time it is used, except in cold weather. It is not good economy to buy skimmed milk, as some persons do, for making bread. It renders it tough and indigestible, if used in the ordinary way. In case it is used for this purpose, it should be boiled, and thickened with a little Indian meal in the same way, and the same proportions as directed for making gruel, in the receipt for Good Family Bread. Use no water with it.

Bread made without a Sponge.

In cool weather the milk should be warmed. A little more yeast is necessary than for sponge-bread, and it should be made up over night. When it is light, knead and mould it, and raise it again in the pans in which it is to be baked.

If brewer's yeast is used, a table-spoonful is enough for every quart of wetting, and it should not stand over night, as it rises very quickly.

Water Bread.

Take a quart of warm water, a teaspoonful of salt, and a small gill of yeast. Add flour enough to make a sponge, as before directed. In the morning add half a teaspoonful of saleratus. The design of this is to make it tender. It should be kneaded longer than bread made with milk — an hour at least. None but the best of flour will make good bread with water alone.

Rice Bread.

Allow half a pint of ground rice to a quart of milk, or milk and water; put the milk and water over the fire to boil, reserving enough to wet the rice. Stir out the lumps, add a large teaspoonful of salt, and when the milk and water boil, stir in the rice, exactly as when you make gruel. Boil it up two or three minutes, stirring it repeatedly; then pour it out into your bread-pan, and *immediately* stir in as much flour as you can with a spoon. After it is cool enough (and of this be very sure, as scalding the yeast will make heavy, sour bread, full of great holes), add a gill of yeast, and let it stand until morning. Then knead in more flour until the dough ceases to stick to the hands. It is necessary to make this kind of bread a little stiffer than that in which no rice is used, else there will be a heavy streak through the loaf. It is elegant bread, keeps moist several days, and is particularly good toasted.

Bread made with Milk.

To make the sponge, simply warm the milk if the weather is cold; if warm weather, boil it; when cool enough, stir in the gill of yeast, and a little salt; make it with the same care as that which is made with Indian meal gruel.

All these various *sponges* are very nice baked on a griddle like buckwheat-cakes, or poured into a buttered, shallow pan and baked in the cooking-stove; and better still, baked in muffin rings.

Third Bread.

Take equal parts of white flour, rye flour, and Indian meal. It is good made with water, but made with milk is much better. Add salt and a gill of yeast to a quart of water or milk. It should not be made so stiff as to mould, but as thick as you can stir it with your hand, or a large spoon. Like all other bread it should be thoroughly worked together. Bake in deep pans.

Graham Bread.

Take a pint of warm water, one teacup of white flour, a spoonful of scalded Indian meal, a small teacup of yeast, a spoonful or two of molasses, a teaspoonful of salt, a small one of saleratus, and stir them together; then add as much unbolted, or Graham flour (*not* sifted) as can be stirred in with a spoon. Do this over night, and in the morning stir it again a few minutes, and pour it into two deep tin pans. Let it rise up again, and bake an hour. This is very excellent bread — a different thing from the hard, unpalatable article which many a dyspeptic eats as a penance.

Like the wheat sponge, it is good baked in rings on a griddle for breakfast; it will, however, take several minutes longer, and will more easily burn, owing to the molasses which is in it.

Another (one loaf).

Take one coffee-cup of white flour, two of Graham flour, one of warm water, half a cup of yeast, and a little molasses, a small teaspoonful of salt, and half a teaspoonful of saleratus dissolved in the water. It should be made as stiff as can be stirred with a spoon. If you prefer to add a spoonful of Indian meal it is very well, but it should be scalded. Let it rise over night, and when it is very light, bake it about an hour in a moderate heat.

Boston Brown Bread, to be baked in a Brick Oven.

Take a quart of rye meal, and the same of fine Indian meal. (If this is bitter, scald it before mixing it with the rye. If it is sweet and fresh, almost every thing in which it is used is lighter without its being scalded.) Mix with warm water, a gill of molasses, a teaspoonful of saleratus, a large teaspoonful of salt, and half a gill of yeast. Such bread is improved by the addition of a gill of boiled pumpkin or winter squash. Make it stiff as can easily be stirred. Grease a deep, brown pan, thickly, and put the bread in it, and dip your hand in water and smooth over the top. This will rise faster than other bread, and should not be made over night in the summer. If put into the oven in the forenoon, it will be ready for the tea-table. If in the afternoon, let it stand in the oven till morning. This may be steamed, as directed in the next receipt.

Steamed Brown Bread.

For a very small family, take half a pint of rye meal, not sifted, and a pint of sifted Indian meal, a pint of sour milk, a half a gill of molasses, a teaspoonful of salt, and a large teaspoonful of saleratus. Mix all the ingredients except the saleratus, dissolve that (as it should always be) in a little boiling water, and add it, stirring the mixture well. Grease a tin pudding pan, or a pail having a close lid, and having put the bread in it, set it into a kettle of boiling water. The bread should not quite fill the pail, as it must have room to swell. See that the water does not boil up to the top of the pail, and also take care it does not boil entirely away. The bread should be cooked at least four hours. To serve it, remove the lid, and set it a few minutes into the stove oven, without the lid, to dry the top; then it will turn out in perfect shape.

If used as a pudding, those who have cream, can make an excellent sauce for it of thick *sour* cream, by stirring into it plenty of sugar, and adding nutmeg. This bread is improved by being made, and put into the pan or pail in which it is to be boiled, two or three hours before it is set into the kettle. It is good toasted the next day.

Indian Loaf.

To one quart of sweet milk, put a gill of molasses, a teaspoonful of saleratus, a heaping pint of Indian meal, a gill of flour, and a teaspoonful of salt. Stir it well together, put it into a deep brown pan, and bake in a brick oven. It should be stirred the last thing before being set into the oven. It must be in the oven many hours, at least eight or nine, if it is a brick oven, and if set in towards night should stand till morning. If it is baked in a range, it will require five or six hours of moderate heat.

Rye Bread.

Take a pint of water, and a large spoonful of fine Indian meal, and make it into gruel. Add a pint of milk, and when cool enough, a small gill of yeast, and then the flour. Fine, bolted rye flour is necessary to make this bread good. Knead it about as stiff as white bread. Let it rise over night, and then mould and put into three pans to rise again. When light, bake it about an hour. Rye is very adhesive, and a young cook will be troubled with its sticking to her fingers, but practice will make it easy to manage it.

To make Stale Bread, or Cake, Fresh.

Plunge the loaf one instant in cold water, and lay it upon a tin in the stove ten or fifteen minutes. It will be like new bread without its deleterious qualities. Stale cake is thus made nice as new cake. But bread or cake heated over thus, should be used immediately.

Various convenient Uses of Bread Dough.

In the winter, dough may be kept sweet many days in a place where it will be cold, without freezing, and it will grow better till the last. It should be raised light, then kneaded a little, and then covered with a damp cloth, so that a dry crust will not form on the top. Fresh bread can thus be furnished for the table every day, without extra work. Doughnuts, bread, cake, or rusks can be made of it by adding butter, sugar, and spice; tea biscuit also, fried biscuit, crust for apple dumpling, and for pan pie. See the receipts for these articles.

The dough should be made, at least in part, with milk, when it is to be used for these purposes.

These directions are particularly recommended to persons who do their own house-work, and of course wish to save time and labor, as much as possible.

BISCUITS, TEA CAKES, GRIDDLE CAKES, &c.

Raised Biscuit.

Take a pint bowl full of light dough; break into it a fresh egg, and add a piece of butter the size of an egg. Knead in these until perfectly incorporated with the dough. It will require about ten minutes. Roll it out about an inch thick, cut it into biscuit. Lay them upon a tin sheet, or shallow baking-pan, and let them rise in a moderately warm place. They will become very light and should be baked in a quick stove, baker, or oven. They will bake in twelve or fifteen minutes, and are injured by being baked very slowly. Very nice eaten fresh, but not hot. This measure will make about two dozen. They are not so good the next day as biscuit made without an egg.

Butter-milk Biscuit.

Take a half pint of butter-milk, or sour milk, and a pint of flour. Rub into the flour a piece of butter half the size of an egg. Add a little salt and stir the milk into the flour. Dissolve a teaspoonful of saleratus in a very little hot water, and stir into it.

Add flour enough barely to mould it smooth; roll it out upon the board, and cut out and bake exactly like the tea biscuit. The advantage of putting in the saleratus after the dough is partly mixed, is, that the foaming process occasioned by combining the sour milk and alkali, raises the whole mass; whereas if it is stirred first into the milk, much of the effervescence is lost, before it is added to the flour.

Cream Biscuit.

These are to be made in the same manner as the butter-milk biscuit, except that no butter is required; the cream will make them sufficiently short.

Cream of Tartar Biscuit.

Stir into one quart of flour, two teaspoonfuls of cream of tartar, and a little salt. Add two table-spoonfuls of thick cream, or rub in one spoonful of lard or butter. Put in a teaspoonful of soda or saleratus, dissolved in a very little hot water. Mix the whole rather soft with milk. Bake like the tea biscuit.

It is a convenient way to make the mixture soft enough with milk to enable you to stir it well with a spoon, and then drop it into the baking pan. It should spread a little, but not run. To vary these drop-cakes add an egg, and two spoonfuls of sugar. For a family of three or four, make half the measure.

Cream of Tartar Biscuit without Milk.

Rub a piece of butter the size of an egg into a quart of flour till there are no little lumps. Then add a teaspoonful of salt, and scatter in two heaping teaspoonfuls of cream of tartar. Have ready a pint of cold water, in which a heaping teaspoonful of saleratus or soda has been dissolved; pour it into the flour, stirring it quickly with your hand. Do this several minutes that the ingredients may become well mixed; then add flour enough to enable you to mould it smooth. Roll it out the same thickness as tea biscuit. If these are made right, they are as light as foam. They may be made of unbolted flour, if preferred. Make half the measure for a small family.

Litchfield Crackers.

To one pint of cold milk, put a piece of butter the size of an egg, a small teaspoonful of salt, and one egg. Rub the butter into a quart of flour, then add the egg and milk. Knead in more flour until it is as stiff as it can possibly be made, and pound it with an iron pestle, or the broad end of a flat-iron, for at least one hour; then roll it very thin, cut it into rounds, prick, and bake in a quick oven, twelve or fifteen minutes.

Jenny Lind.

Take one egg, one teacup of sugar, one of sweet milk, two and a half of flour, a dessert-spoonful of butter, two teaspoonfuls of cream of tartar, one of saleratus, and a very little salt. To mix it, stir the cream of tartar, sugar, and salt into the flour, then the milk, add the egg without beating, dissolve the saleratus, and melt the butter in a spoonful of hot water, then stir all together a few minutes. Bake in fifteen minutes in two pans about the size of a breakfast plate. If you prefer, make it with sour milk, and omit the cream of tartar.

With the addition of one more egg, a teaspoonful more of butter, and half a cup of sugar, and some spice, this is a nice cake for the basket, and may sometimes be very convenient, because so quickly made.

Sally Lunn.

A quart of flour, a piece of butter the size of an egg, three table-spoonfuls of sugar, two eggs, two teacups of milk, two teaspoonfuls of cream of tartar, one of saleratus, and a little salt.

To mix it, scatter the cream of tartar, the salt, and the sugar into the flour; add the eggs without having beaten them, the butter melted, and one cup of the milk; dissolve the saleratus in the remaining cup, and then stir all together steadily a few minutes. Bake in three pans the size of a breakfast plate, fifteen or twenty minutes. For a family of four or five, make half the measure. Add spice, and twice the measure of sugar, and you have a good plain cake for the cake-basket.

Rusk.

To a pint bowl of light dough add a gill of sugar, half as much butter, and either a little cinnamon, allspice, or lemon. Work these ingredients together, and then add flour enough to enable you to mould it smooth and roll it out. Let it be about an inch thick; cut it into biscuit, and lay them into a baking-pan to rise. They should become very light before being baked; and, therefore, in cold weather it is well to let the dough stand, after the ingredients are added, until the next day, then roll out the biscuit, and raise them in the bake-pan. Their appearance is improved by wetting the top with a mixture of sugar and milk, when they are nearly baked; then return them to the oven for a short time. They require fifteen or twenty minutes to bake.

A double measure may be made in cold weather, and when light be set in a cool place, but where it will not freeze, and a pan be baked whenever needed. Each day it will be better than the previous one.

Another.

To one tumbler of milk, put half a gill of yeast, three eggs, one coffee-cup of sugar, two ounces of butter, and one small nutmeg. Beat the sugar and eggs together, rub the butter into the flour, of which use enough to enable you just to mould it. Let it rise over night; and when very light, roll out and put it on tins to rise again, after which, bake as above.

Whigs.

Half a pound of butter, the same of sugar, six eggs, two pounds of flour, a pint of milk, a gill of yeast, and a little salt. Melt the butter in the milk, and pour into the flour; beat the sugar and eggs together and stir in. Add the yeast last, and be careful to mix the whole very thoroughly. Bake in tin hearts and rounds, in the stove, or baker.

Waffles.

To a quart of milk, put six eggs, a quarter of a pound of butter, a large gill of yeast, a little salt, and flour enough to make a batter the thickness of griddle cakes. The iron must be heated on hot coals, and then buttered or greased with lard, and one side filled with batter, then be shut and laid on the fire. After a few minutes turn it upon the other side. It takes about twice the time that it would to bake them on a griddle, and they are really no better, but look more inviting.

Sour Milk Muffins.

To a pint of sour milk put one egg, without first beating it; a little salt, a teaspoonful of saleratus, and one of butter, melted with the saleratus in a spoonful of hot water. Make rather a thick batter. To bake well in rings, have the griddle of a moderate heat, grease it, and also the rings, lay them on, and fill them only half full of the batter; increase the heat a little. In about eight minutes, turn them and let them lie two or three minutes more.

To turn them without spilling requires some dexterity.

Cream of Tartar Muffins.

A quart of flour, a small pint of rich milk, two eggs, a table-spoonful of sugar, a teaspoonful of saleratus, two of cream of tartar, half a teaspoonful of salt.

Mix the salt, the cream of tartar and the sugar, dry, in the flour, add the eggs without beating, then the milk with the saleratus dissolved in it, and beat these ingredients very thoroughly. Half fill the rings, and bake in a quick oven.

Raised Muffins.

Melt a table-spoonful of butter in a pint of milk, add a little salt, two eggs, and a large half gill of yeast, then stir in flour enough to made a thick batter. In cold weather this may stand two or three days without becoming sour.

Top-Overs.

Two cups of sweet milk, two of flour a little heaped, a bit of butter large as a walnut, two eggs, one large spoonful of sugar, a little nutmeg and salt. Melt the butter; add the milk slowly to the flour, to avoid lumps. Bake in cups, or iron drop-cake pans. Twenty minutes in a quick oven will be sufficient.

Drop-Cakes.

Break four eggs into a pint of sweet milk, melt a piece of butter the size of an egg and add it, with a little salt, and flour enough to make a batter about as thick as cup-cake. Beat all together several minutes. If the cakes are to be eaten cold, add two spoonfuls of brown sugar. Bake in very small scalloped tins, or in cups.

Rye Drop Cakes.*

To a pint of sour-milk, or butter-milk, put two or three eggs, not quite a teaspoonful of saleratus, a little salt, and sifted rye meal (this is much better than rye flour), enough to make a batter that will spread a little, but not run. Drop them in muffin-rings with a spoon. They will require about twice as much time to bake as common griddle cakes. They will bake very nicely in a stove in fifteen minutes. Graham flour may be substituted for rye if preferred.

GRIDDLE CAKES.

White Flour.

To a quart of milk, put four eggs, a little salt, a large spoonful of butter, melted into the milk, a small gill of yeast, and flour enough to make a batter about as thick as for buckwheat cakes. Some persons eat them with a sauce made of butter, sugar, water, and nutmeg. Made in the morning they will be light for tea.

Butter-milk, or Sour milk.

Make a thin batter with a quart of sour, or butter-milk, white flour, a spoonful of fine Indian meal, a teaspoonful of salt, another of saleratus, and an egg. Try a spoonful on the griddle before you proceed to bake them, so that you may add more flour, if it is too thin to turn easily, or more milk if too thick.

---

* See directions for Cream of Tartar Drop Cakes in the recipe for Cream of Tartar Biscuit, page 34.

Another (without an egg).

Make a batter just like the last receipt, only without the egg. Omit the Indian meal if you choose.

Indian Meal.

These are made like the sour milk cakes, only that the milk is chiefly thickened with Indian meal. A spoonful or two of flour should be added, and it is well to use two eggs instead of one, but not necessary.

NOTE.—In all these various kinds of cakes in which sour milk is used, it is an improvement to substitute buttermilk. But that which is sold in cities as buttermilk, is often adulterated.

Rice.

Put a teacupful of rice into two teacupsful of water, and boil it till the water is nearly absorbed, and then add a pint and a half of milk. Boil it slowly until the rice is very soft. When cool, add a small gill of yeast, three eggs, a little salt, and flour enough to make a batter of suitable thickness to bake on a griddle. Let it rise very light. To bake in muffin rings, make it a little thicker.

Ground Rice.

Boil a quart of milk. Rub smooth a teacupful of ground rice, in a gill or two of cold milk, and stir it into the boiling milk. Add salt, and when cool, add a teacup of yeast, four eggs, and flour to make it the right thickness for baking. Let it rise light.

Buckwheat.

For a family of four or five, take a quart of warm water, a spoonful of scalded Indian meal, a heaping teaspoonful of salt, and a gill of yeast. Stir in buckwheat flour enough to make a thin batter. Let it rise over night. In the morning add a quarter of a teaspoonful of saleratus or soda. Do this whether the cakes are sour or not. Buckwheat cakes cannot be made in perfection without this addition; but it should never be put in till just before they are baked. Such cakes are often made too thick, and fried with too much fat. They should be as thin as they can be, and be easily turned with a griddle shovel, and no more fat should be used than is necessary to keep them from sticking. To prevent the use of too much, tie a soft white rag, tight, round the tines of a large fork, and keep it for this purpose. If a gill of the batter is left, it will raise the next parcel.

Buckwheat cakes are as much better made with milk as other cakes are; but no others are so good made with water. They are very nice made of sour milk, with nothing added but salt and saleratus. These should be made only a short time before being baked. All kinds of griddle cakes should be well beaten.

Fritters or Pan-Cakes.

Make a batter of a pint of milk, three eggs, salt, and flour to make a rather thick batter. Beat it well, then drop it with a spoon into hot fat, and fry like doughnuts. These, and the snow fritters are usually eaten with sugar and cider, or lemon juice.

Snow Fritters.

Stir together milk, flour, and a little salt, to make rather a thick batter. Add new-fallen snow in the proportion of a teacupful to a pint of milk. Have the fat ready hot, at the time you stir in the snow, and drop the batter into it with a spoon. These pancakes are even preferred by some, to those made with eggs.

Corn Cake.

To a pint of sour milk, two cups of Indian meal, one of flour, one egg, two table-spoonfuls of molasses, a teaspoonful of salt, and one of saleratus. Mix it thoroughly, and bake twenty-five minutes in two shallow pans, or thirty-five in a deep one.

Another.

Take a pint of sweet milk, half a gill of yeast, one gill of flour, a teaspoonful of salt, and half a teaspoonful of saleratus; stir in Indian meal enough to make it rather stiffer than griddle cakes; let it rise over night, and in the morning bake as directed above.

This kind of cake has the advantage over those made without yeast, that if a piece of it is left, it is not heavy when cold, but is as palatable a lunch as a slice of good bread.

Another.

Take a pint of sour milk, or butter-milk, break an egg into it, stir in a spoonful or two of flour, and add Indian meal enough to make a thick batter; put in a teaspoonful of salt, stir it five or six minutes, and then add a heaping teaspoonful of saleratus dissolved in hot water. If it is the season for berries of any kind, put in a gill or two; bake in a pan or on the griddle.

Another.

A pint of sweet milk, two eggs, a pint of Indian meal or corn flour, half a pint of white flour, one teaspoonful of tartaric acid, or cream of tartar, and one of soda, mixed dry in the flour. Bake in a pan, about an inch thick, or in drop-cake tins.

DIRECTIONS FOR MAKING CAKE.

When cake or pastry is to be made, take care not to make trouble for others by scattering materials, and soiling the table or floor, or by the needless use of many dishes. Put on a large and clean apron, roll your sleeves above the elbows, tie something over your head lest hair may fall; take care that your hands are clean, and have a basin of water and a clean towel at hand. Place every thing you will need on the table; butter the pans, grate the nutmegs, and squeeze the lemons. Then break the eggs, each in a cup by itself, lest adding a bad one to the others should spoil the whole. Then weigh or measure flour and sugar, and, if not already done, *sift* them. Make your cake in an earthen, and not in a tin pan.

In warm weather put your eggs into cold water some time before you are ready to break them. They cut into a much finer froth for being cold. For some kinds of cake the whites should be cut to a stiff froth, and the yolks beaten and strained, and then put to the butter and sugar after these have been stirred till they look like cream. Then mix the flour gradually.

When cream or sour milk is to be put in, half of it should be added when half the flour is mixed in; then the remainder of the flour, and then the saleratus dissolved in the other half of the cream or milk. Lastly, add the spice, wine, lemon-juice, or fruit.

In summer do not stir cake with the hand; the warmth of it makes it less light. A wooden spoon, kept on purpose, is the best thing. In winter, soften, but do not melt the butter, before using it. Cake not raised with yeast, should be baked *as soon as it is made*, except such as is hard enough to be rolled. Cookies and sugar gingerbread roll out more smoothly the next day.

Firkin butter must be cut in small pieces, and washed, to remove some of the salt. Drain it well, or it will make heavy cake. Never put strong butter into cake; it renders it disagreeable and unhealthy.*

Fresh eggs are needed for nice white cake. Those kept in lime-water will do for raised cake and cookies.

New Orleans, or other good brown sugar, is best for raised,

---

* See directions for keeping butter in rose-leaves. Page 216.

fruit, and wedding cake, but it should be coarse-grained and clean. It will answer also for cup cake, especially if fruit is used. White sugar must be used for sponge and other white cake.

The fruit should be added to raised cake when it is ready for the oven. Spread it equally over the top, and press it only a little below the surface, else it will sink to the bottom.

Cask raisins should be washed before being stoned, and box raisins also, unless fresh. In stoning them, cut them in two or three pieces, or chop them.

Keep currants ready prepared for use. To do this, wash them in warm water, rubbing them between the hands, and then pour off the water. Repeat this till the water is clear, then drain them in a sieve, spread them on a cloth on a table, and rub them dry with the ends of the cloth. Then brush the good ones into a dish in your lap, putting aside the bad ones on the table. Dry them in a gentle warmth, and set them away for use.

Buttered white paper in the bottom and sides of pans for cake requiring long baking, is needful; and paper not buttered is good for other kinds of cake, as it prevents burning. It will readily peel off when the cake is taken from the pans.

Attention and practice will teach when cake is well baked. When it is done enough, it settles a little away from the pan. Even well made cake becomes heavy by being taken out of the oven before it is perfectly baked. Moving it carelessly while it is baking will also make light cake fall. If you have occasion to change the position of the pans, do it gently.

A tin chest or a stone jar is good to keep cake in, and it is a good way to let that which is not to be kept long, remain in the tins in which it was baked.

Directions for beating the Whites of Eggs.

On breaking eggs, take care that none of the yolk becomes mingled with the whites. A single particle will sometimes prevent their frothing well. Put the whites into a large, flat dish, and beat them with an egg-beater made of doubled wire, with a tin handle; or with a cork stuck crosswise upon the prongs of a fork. Strike a sharp, quick stroke through the whole length of the dish. Beat them in a cool place till they look like snow, and you can turn the dish over without their slipping off. Never suspend the process nor let them stand, even for one minute, as they will begin to return to a liquid state, and cannot be restored, and thus will make heavy cake. After they are beaten to a stiff froth they will not return to a liquid state.

The above directions are designed to prevent the necessity of repetition and minuteness in each receipt. The young cook is advised to refer to them in making cake, that she may know at once how to proceed.

Frosting.

A pound of the best of fine white sugar, the whites of three fresh eggs, a teaspoonful of nice starch, pounded, and sifted through a piece of muslin or a very fine sieve, the juice of half a lemon, and a few drops of the essence.

Beat the whites to a stiff froth, then add them to the sugar, and stir it steadily until it will stay where you put it. It will take nearly two hours, perhaps more. Dredge a little flour over the cake, and brush it off with a feather. This is to prevent the frosting from being discolored by the butter contained in the cake. Lay it on smoothly with a knife, and return the cake to the oven twelve or fifteen minutes.

Another (measured).

To a coffee cup of sifted sugar, the white of one egg, half a teaspoonful of powdered starch, and a teaspoonful of lemon juice. Observe the directions for making it, in the previous receipt. This will frost two small pans or one large one.

Another way.

A pound of the best crushed or loaf sugar, the whites of three eggs, the juice of a lemon, and a teaspoonful of finely powdered starch. To mix it, put the sugar into a deep bowl, and pour upon it just cold water enough to soften the lumps, then beat the whites of eggs about half as much as for nice cake — not to a stiff froth; add them to the melted sugar, and set the bowl into a kettle of boiling water, and stir the mixture steadily. It will soon become thin and clear, and afterwards thicken. When it has become quite thick, take it from the fire and stir it till it is cold, and thick enough to spread with a knife. This is enough for a large loaf.

FRUIT CAKES.

Wedding.

Five pounds each of flour, butter, and sugar, six of raisins, twelve of currants, two of citron, fifty eggs, half a pint of good Malaga wine, three ounces of nutmegs, three of cinnamon, one and a half of mace. Bake in three large pans four hours.

Another.

Three pounds each of flour, butter, and sugar, six of currants, six of raisins, an ounce each of nutmegs and cinnamon, half an ounce of clove, a pound of citron, the grated peel of two lemons, half a gill each of brandy and rose-water, or a small teaspoonful of the essence of rose, and thirty eggs.

To mix either of these two receipts, stir the sugar and butter to a cream, beat the yolks and whites of the eggs separately, and add them to the butter and sugar, then by degrees put in two thirds of the flour, then the spice and brandy or wine, and last the fruit, mixed with the remaining third of the flour. Have the citron ready cut up, and when you have put a little of the cake into the pan, put in a layer of citron, then more cake, and again citron and cake alternately. This quantity will bake in one cake in five hours, in two cakes, three hours. Each of these two kinds will keep years, if frosted.

Maine Plum.

A pound each of butter, sugar, and flour, ten eggs, a pound of raisins, two of currants, half a pound of citron, a teaspoonful of powdered clove, half as much mace, a nutmeg, the juice of a lemon and the grated peel, and a half a teacup of good molasses. Before you proceed to mix it, scatter one teaspoonful of cream of tartar into the flour; and the last thing, before you put in the fruit, dissolve a half a teaspoonful of saleratus in a spoonful of boiling water, and add it, stirring the cake fast two or three minutes. Mix this in the same way as directed in the two previous receipts. If baked in a brick oven, bake it three hours in one pan; if in a stove, an hour and a half, in two.

Although this cake has no wine or brandy, it will keep fresh (if frosted) almost any length of time.

One Loaf (plainer).

A pound each of flour and sugar, ten ounces of butter, five eggs, a pint of milk, two pounds and a half of raisins and currants, a gill of wine, a nutmeg, a large spoonful of cinnamon, half a teaspoonful of clove. Add the same measure of cream of tartar and saleratus as in the last receipt, and in the same way, and bake the same length of time.

To make just frosting enough for either of these two last cakes, take the whites of four eggs, if the weather is cold, three, if it is warm, cut them to a stiff froth, add a pound of finest sugar, and beat it two hours. Add lemon, rose, or any essence you prefer, and a teaspoonful of sifted starch. When the loaf is baked, lay on the icing with a knife, and return it to the oven fifteen minutes.

Washington.

To one pound of flour, put one pound of sugar, three quarters of a pound of butter, eight eggs, two nutmegs, one pound of raisins, and one of currants.

RAISED CAKES.

Commencement.

Four pounds of flour, two and a half of sugar, two of butter, a small quart of milk, half a pint of wine, eight eggs, two gills of yeast, two nutmegs, two teaspoonfuls of cinnamon, one of clove, or a little mace. Make up the flour, yeast, and milk, exactly like bread, and when fully light, add the other ingredients, and put it into deep pans. If the weather is cool, let it stand till the next day. When it is again very light, add one pound of currants and two of raisins; and bake two hours.

This is excellent cake, and will keep good many weeks.

Loaf.

Three pounds of flour, two of sugar, one and a half of butter, two of fruit, six eggs, half a pint of yeast, a gill of wine, two nutmegs, a teaspoonful each of cinnamon and clove, and a little mace. Make up the flour and yeast with milk, just like bread; when it is very light add all the other ingredients, except the fruit. Put in the eggs without beating, warm the wine, and mix the whole very thoroughly. Then put it in pans and set it to rise till the next day, and when light enough to bake, put in the fruit as directed in the general observations at the beginning of this chapter.

Another.

A pound and a half of flour, one of sugar, three quarters of a pound of butter, a pound of raisins and currants, four eggs, a nutmeg, a glass of wine, a teaspoonful of cinnamon, half a one of clove. Make up the flour like bread, with a gill of yeast and new milk warmed. When it is perfectly light, add the eggs without beating, and stir all the ingredients together thoroughly. Put it into pans, and when it has risen again, add the fruit, and bake it.

Bread Cake.

Five teacups of very light bread dough, that is wet with milk; three of sugar, two of butter, three or four eggs; or if they are scarce, two. Mix it thoroughly, using both hands. Flavor it with such spice, or essence as you prefer, and then put it into three pans such as you use for cup cake, and let it stand till perfectly light before you bake it. In winter let it stand in a warm closet, or some place where it will not become very cold, and remain till the next day.

By the addition of spice, fruit, more sugar, &c., you can make it as rich as you please.

Another.

Take two cups of light dough, a small cup of butter, a cup and a half of sugar, one of sour milk, two and a half of flour, two eggs, and a teaspoonful of saleratus. Flavor it with nutmeg and cinnamon, or lemon. Let it rise in the pans.

Another (plainer).

To three cups of light dough, one of butter, one and a half of sugar, one of sour milk, a heaping cup of flour, a teaspoonful of saleratus, and some spice. Put the materials together as directed in the last receipt.

CUP CAKES.

[The *cup* used as a measure for the receipts in this book is not the tea-table china cup, but the common large earthen teacup, except where a small one is specified; and the teaspoon used is neither the largest or smallest, but the medium sized.]

Howard.

To ten cups of flour, put six of sugar, three of butter, three of sour milk (a little warm), eight eggs, a glass of wine, a large teaspoonful of saleratus, a nutmeg, a pound of currants, a pound of raisins.

Tunbridge.

Four cups and a half of flour, three of sugar, one of butter, one of cream, one teaspoonful of saleratus, six eggs, spice, currants, citron, and a little wine.

Bridgeport.

To one teacup of butter, put two of sugar, three and a half of flour, four eggs, one cup of sour milk, the juice and part of the rind of a lemon, a small teaspoonful of saleratus and two cups of currants. Bake in small pans.

Superior.

One very heaping cup of butter, two and a half of sugar, four eggs, four cups of flour, and one and a half of ground rice, one and a half of sweet milk, a nutmeg, a little grated lemon-rind, the juice of a lemon squeezed into the milk, and a teaspoonful of saleratus.

Barnard.

One cup of butter, three of sugar, four and a half of flour, four eggs, a cup of sour milk, the juice, and a little of the rind of a lemon, a teaspoonful of saleratus.

It is a good way to use butter that has been kept a few days in a jar of rose leaves, for these cup cakes, and then very little spice is necessary.

All delicate soft cake is improved in appearance by sifting a little fine sugar over the top, just as it goes into the oven.

Mount Pleasant.

Five teacups of flour, one heaping cup of butter, two cups and a half of sugar, one cup of sour milk, four eggs, a teaspoonful of saleratus, one nutmeg.

Provence.

Four cups of flour, one of sugar, one of butter, one of sour milk, one of molasses, four eggs, one nutmeg, one small tea spoonful of saleratus, and a pound and a half of raisins.

Composition.

A coffee cup of butter (small measure), two of sugar, three of flour, one and a half of good ground rice, one of sour milk, half a nutmeg, a little essence of lemon, a large teaspoonful of saleratus, and three eggs. If you have sour cream, instead of the milk, use half a cup of butter.

Diet Bread.

Two cups of sugar, three and a half of flour, one of milk, four eggs, half a teaspoonful of soda, a teaspoonful of cream of tartar in the juice of half a lemon. Beat the eggs and sugar together, then add half the milk and flour; when these are mixed, the rest of the milk with the half teaspoonful of soda dissolved in it, the remainder of the flour, the lemon-juice and cream of tartar; and last, a little essence of rose.

SPONGE CAKES.

The goodness of all delicate cake, but specially of sponge, depends very much upon its being made with fresh eggs. There are several ways of making this cake which all result well. For those who choose not to be cheated of eggs by the use of cream of tartar, two excellent receipts, and two different methods of mixing, are given.

Two receipts for making it by measure are added, each of them perfect, if made right, and the last one requiring the least possible time and labor.

For the old-fashioned sponge cake, beat the yolks thoroughly, and the whites to a very stiff froth, and mix the ingredients thus: Stir the sugar and whites together, then add the yolks, next the flour, and last, the lemon or spice, or,

Mix the yolks and whites after they are beaten, and having

stirred the flour and sugar together, add them, and the spice. It should then be stirred fast two minutes, and baked in rather a quick oven. It is made *sticky*, and less light by being stirred long. There is no other cake, the goodness of which depends so much upon care, and good judgment in baking.

Lyman.

To one pound of flour, put one and a half of sugar, fifteen eggs, the rind of two lemons, and juice of one, and a little salt.

Brooklyn.

To three quarters of a pound of flour, put one and a quarter of sugar, twelve eggs, and one lemon, juice and rind. A little salt.

Measure.

Twelve fresh eggs, three cups of flour, three of sugar, a little salt, and spice or lemon as you prefer. Break the eggs together, and put them without beating into the sugar, then beat steadily with a smart stroke half an hour, then stir in the flour, and bake in rather thick loaves three quarters of an hour.

No one but a person having a very strong arm can make this kind of sponge cake well. It is elegant when well made.

Berwick.

Beat six eggs, yolks and whites together, two minutes; add three cups of sugar, and beat five minutes; two cups of flour with two teaspoonfuls of cream of tartar, and beat two minutes; one cup of cold water, with one teaspoonful of saleratus dissolved in it, and beat one minute; the grated rind, and half the juice of a lemon, a little salt and two more cups of flour, and beat another minute. Observe the time exactly, and bake in rather deep cup cake pans.

VARIOUS KINDS OF CAKE.

Queen's.

One pound of flour, one of sugar, half a pound of butter (that which has lain in a jar of rose-leaves is best), five eggs, a gill of wine, a gill of cream, a nutmeg, half a teaspoonful of saleratus, two pounds of currants, or chopped raisins.

Stir the butter and sugar to a cream, beat the whites and yolks of the eggs separately, and after they and the flour are also mixed with it, warm the cream and wine together, and add them, then the saleratus, and last the fruit. Frost it, or sift fine sugar over the top just before it is put into the oven.

Snow, or Bride's.

A pound each of flour and sugar, half a pound of butter, and the whites of sixteen eggs beaten to a stiff froth. Flavor it with rose.

Federal.

A pound each of butter and sugar, a pound and two ounces of flour, a pound of raisins, five eggs, a cup of sour cream (or, if milk is used instead of cream, add a quarter of a pound more of butter), half a nutmeg, a wineglass of brandy, and a teaspoonful of saleratus. Stir the butter, sugar, and nutmeg to a cream, then add the eggs, then the cream and saleratus mixed, next the flour (a little at a time), except a handful in which to mix the raisins, and last, the brandy and fruit.

Very delicious for persons who like rich cake.

Gold.

A pound each of flour and sugar, three quarters of a pound of butter, the yolks of fourteen eggs, and the juice and grated rind of two lemons. Stir the sugar and butter to a cream, and add the yolks well beaten, and strained. Then put in the lemon peel, and the flour (dried), and a teaspoonful of saleratus dissolved in a spoonful of hot water. Beat it fifteen minutes, and just before it goes into the oven, stir in the lemon juice very thoroughly. Bake it in a square, flat pan, ice it thickly, and cut it into square pieces.

Silver.

One pound of sugar, three quarters of a pound of dried flour, six ounces of butter, the whites of fourteen eggs. Add mace and citron. Beat the sugar and butter to a cream, and add the whites, cut to a stiff froth, next the flour, and then the mace and citron. Bake in a pan of the same size as for the golden cake. They are not difficult to make, and are very beautiful together.

Jelly-Cake, or Washington Pie.

Make cup cake, and when the ingredients are well mixed, spread it upon round shallow tins, three table-spoonfuls to each tin. It will bake in ten or fifteen minutes; then turn it upon a hair sieve, the under surface uppermost. While it is warm spread upon it raspberry jam, currant, or other jelly; then lay the second sheet of cake upon it, the under side next to the jelly. If you wish to make several alternate layers of cake and jelly make the sheets of cake very thin; one large spoonful of the batter will be enough for each tin.

White-Mountain.

Six eggs, six cups of flour, three of sugar, two of butter, one of milk, one nutmeg, one teaspoon of saleratus. To mix it, stir the butter and sugar to a cream, beat the whites and yolks of the eggs separately; add the yolks to the butter and sugar, next part of the milk and half of the flour, and the whites, then the rest of the milk with the saleratus dissolved in it, and then the remainder of the flour, and last the grated nutmeg.

Lemon.

A pound each of flour and sugar, half a pound of butter, eight eggs, the rind of one lemon, and the juice of half of one.

Rice.

Weigh nine eggs, and their weight in sugar, and the weight of six in ground rice. Add a lemon, and a little salt. A very delicate cake.

Another.

One pound of sugar, three quarters of a pound of ground rice, thirteen eggs with the whites of four taken out, a small teaspoonful of salt. Flavor as above, or with the essence of lemon.

Pound.

A pound each of flour, sugar, and butter, ten eggs, half a nutmeg, the juice and part of the rind of a lemon. Some persons use only fourteen ounces of butter, and add a quarter of a teaspoonful of saleratus.

Cream.

Stir one teacup of cream, and two of sugar till well mixed, add two eggs beaten to a froth, and a little salt. Dissolve a teaspoonful of saleratus in a spoonful or two of milk, and add it. Then, immediately put in a cup or two of flour, and some essence of lemon, or other spice, and stir it a little. Then add flour enough to make it as thick as cup cake; stir it well eight or ten minutes, and bake in common cup-cake pans.

Harrison.

To two cups of molasses, put one of brown sugar, one of butter, one of sour cream, or milk, a cup of raisins, and one of currants, a teaspoonful of powdered clove, and two (rather small) of saleratus.

To mix it, cut the butter in little pieces, and put into a saucepan with the molasses, to melt. When the molasses boils up, pour it immediately upon three or four cups of flour, and add the sugar, and half the cream. Stir it well, then add the saleratus, the rest of the cream, the spice, and flour enough to make it of the consistence of cup cake, and last, the fruit. Bake in cup-cake pans, rather slowly. All cake containing molasses is more liable to burn than that which has none.

CREAM CAKES, COOKIES, WAFERS, KISSES, JUMBLES, GINGERBREAD, ETC.

The eggs for these articles, except for the wafers, need not be broken separately, but yolks and whites may be added without beating, after the sugar and butter have been stirred. When all has been well beaten together eight or ten minutes, add part of the flour, then the saleratus and spice or ginger; and then place the pan upon a table, and work in flour enough to enable you to handle it without its sticking.

Dough for cookies or gingerbread, is much more easily and neatly rolled out and stamped the day after it is made, than on the same day. In cold weather, set it when made where it will not become hard, or else bring it into a warm room an hour or two before it is to be rolled out. Cookies should be about as thick as the end of your little finger; gingerbread half as thick. These things bake very quickly, and should be carefully attended to. Sugar gingerbread should be cut up as it lies in the pan, before it has time to cool, and laid upon a sieve. It cannot be cut after it is cold without being very much broken.

Cream Cakes.

A pint of water, half a pound of butter, three quarters of a pound of flour, and ten eggs. Boil the water, melt the butter in it, stir in the flour dry while it boils ; when it is cool, add a teaspoonful of saleratus, and the eggs well beaten. Drop the mixture on buttered tins with a table-spoon, and bake twenty minutes.

To make the inside, take one cup of flour, two cups of sugar, one quart of milk, and four eggs. Beat the flour, sugar, and eggs together, and stir into the boiling milk. When the mixture is sufficiently scalded, season it with lemon.

When the cakes are cool, cut them open and add the cream.

Cookies.

One tea-cup of butter, three of sugar, half a cup of milk or cream, three eggs, one small teaspoonful of saleratus, and flour to make it rather stiff. Flavor with nutmeg and cinnamon.

Another.

Two cups of butter, three of sugar, one of sour milk or cream, one nutmeg, three eggs, one large teaspoonful of saleratus, and flour enough to roll out. These cookies should not be rolled thin.

Wafers.

One cup of butter, two of sugar, half a cup of new milk, three eggs, half a nutmeg, the juice of a lemon, one teaspoonful of saleratus, and flour enough to roll out. If you prefer, flavor with a few drops of essence of rose and ground cinnamon. Roll the dough very thin, sprinkle granulated white sugar over it, and slightly press it into the dough with the rolling-pin. Then cut in large rounds, and bake quickly.

Kisses.

Beat the whites of nine fresh eggs to a stiff froth, then mix with it fifteen spoonfuls of finest white sugar, and five or six drops of essence of lemon. Drop them on paper with a teaspoon, sift sugar over them, and bake them in a slow oven.

Cocoanut Drops.

Grate a cocoanut, and weigh it, then add half the weight of powdered sugar, and the white of one egg cut to a stiff froth. Stir the ingredients together, then drop the mixture with a dessert spoon upon buttered white paper, or tin sheets, and sift sugar over them. Bake in a slow oven fifteen minutes.

Fruit Jumbles.

A pound and a quarter of flour, a pound of sugar, three quarters of a pound of butter, five eggs, a quarter of a pound of currants, a gill or small teacup of milk, half a teaspoonful of saleratus, half a wine-glass of wine. Drop them on tins with a spoon, and bake in rather a quick oven.

Hard Sugar Gingerbread.

Two cups of butter, four of sugar, two eggs, a cup and a half of milk, two teaspoonfuls of ginger, and one of saleratus. Flour to make rather a stiff dough.

Another (very plain).

Ten ounces of butter, twenty ounces of sugar, a cup and a half of milk, four teaspoonfuls of ginger, one large teaspoonful of saleratus, a few drops of essence of rose, or half a cup of rose-water; in which case omit the half cup of milk.

Soft Sugar Gingerbread.

Two pounds of flour, one of butter, one and a half of sugar, seven eggs, half a gill of rose-water or wine. To be baked in such pans as are used for cup cake. This keeps good a long time, and is very nice.

Another (without eggs).

One pound of butter, two of sugar, three of flour, a pint of milk, a large spoonful of ginger, two teaspoonfuls of cream of tartar mixed in the flour, and one teaspoonful of saleratus. Stir the butter and sugar to a cream, then add half of the milk, and a large part of the flour; then the remainder of the milk having the saleratus dissolved in it, and the rest of the flour. Make half the quantity for a small family. Bake it in cup-cake pans.

Ginger Crackers.

A pint of molasses, two cups of butter, one and a half of sugar, one teaspoonful of saleratus, and two of ginger; add flour enough to make it easy to roll out. Stir the butter and sugar together, boil the molasses and pour it into the pan, and stir steadily until the butter and sugar are melted, then put in a few handfuls of flour, and add the saleratus. Stir it a few minutes, and then work in all the flour. To be rolled very thin, and baked but a few minutes.

New York Ginger Snaps.

Half a pound each of butter and sugar, two and a half pounds of flour, a pint of molasses, a teaspoonful of saleratus, caraway seeds, or ginger. Mix it just like the ginger crackers, and bake them thin.

Soft Molasses Gingerbread.

For three pints of flour, allow a pint of molasses, a pint of sour milk, or butter-milk, a gill of butter, half a gill of nice drippings, three teaspoonfuls of ginger, two of saleratus, and a very little salt.

To mix it, boil the molasses with the butter and shortening cut up in it, and pour it hot upon the flour. Stir it a little, and then add the sour milk with the saleratus and ginger. Stir it well. Gingerbread is as much better for being thoroughly beaten, as any other cake. You can make it rather more delicate by using butter only, adding a gill of brown sugar, and substituting cinnamon and clove instead of ginger. On the other hand, very good gingerbread is made by omitting the butter, and using shortening instead, and cold water or cider in place of the sour milk. A teaspoonful of salt is necessary where the butter is omitted.

Hard Molasses Gingerbread.

A half a pint of molasses, a gill of butter, half a gill of nice drippings, half a gill of sour milk, two teaspoonfuls of saleratus, and the same of ginger. Melt the butter, drippings, and molasses together, and pour hot upon a quart of flour; add the ginger and saleratus, and when well mixed add more flour until it can be handled without sticking. Then roll it out about as thick as the little finger, stamp or mark it, and bake it in shallow iron or tin pans. Bake it in a moderate heat. When done, cut it up before you take it out of the pans, as it cannot be done after it is cold without crumbling the edges.

If you prefer to have it thin, and cut into rounds like cookies, it is a very good way.

By omitting the sour milk and adding a cup of sugar, a rather nicer gingerbread is made.

Another.

Melt one cup of butter in two of molasses, pour it hot upon a quart of flour; dissolve one teaspoonful of saleratus in a little hot water and add it. Put in flour enough to roll it out neatly. Make it very thin, cut it in rounds, and bake it quick. These cakes are very crisp, and keep so in a tin chest.

FRIED CAKES.

On Frying Cakes.

To have fried cakes good, it is necessary that the fat should be of the right heat. When it is hot enough, it will cease to bubble, and be perfectly still. It is best to try it with a little bit of the cake to be fried. If the heat is right, the dough will rise in a few seconds to the top, and occasion a bubbling in the fat; it will swell, and the under-side quickly become brown. It should then be turned over. Cakes should be turned two or three times. The time necessary to fry them, depends on their thickness; if about as thick as the little finger, they will be done in seven or eight minutes. It is best to break open one, in order to judge. When done, drain them well with a skimmer. If the fat is too hot, the outside will be burned before the centre is cooked at all; if too cool, they will become fat-soaked, which makes them very unhealthy and disagreeable. The fire must be carefully regulated. A person who fries cakes must attend to nothing else; the cakes, the fat, and the fire will occupy every minute. The use of many eggs prevents cakes from absorbing much fat. But they can be so made without eggs, as not to take up much fat.

Crullers.

To two pounds of flour, put three quarters of a pound of sugar, half a pound of butter, nine eggs, mace, and rose-water unless the butter has been kept in rose leaves.

Another.

To six teacups of flour, put two of sugar, half a one of butter, half a one of cream, eight eggs, one nutmeg; or if more convenient, nine eggs, no cream, and a full cup of butter.

Another (plainer, but very good).

To a pint of warm milk, put two spoonfuls of lard, and three of butter cut into little bits. Beat four eggs and five heaping spoonfuls of sugar together, and stir into the milk. Grate in a nutmeg, put in a very heaping teaspoonful of saleratus, and knead in flour enough to roll out.

Cream of Tartar.

Make them precisely like the cream of tartar biscuit (see page

34), with the addition of five spoonfuls of sugar, half a nutmeg, one egg, and a small piece more of butter.

Raised Doughnuts.

Boil a quart of milk, and rub smooth in a little cold milk a large gill of ground rice; when the milk boils up, stir in the rice and a little salt. Let it boil till it thickens, stirring it two or three times. Pour it, hot, upon a quart of flour; when cool enough, add a gill of yeast, and flour enough to make it stiff as bread. Knead it a great deal. Let it rise over night, and when very light, work in three quarters of a pound of butter, a pound and a half of sugar beaten in five eggs, and add nutmeg and lemon, juice and rind. Let it rise again, and then roll out and fry it.

Light bread dough, which is wet with milk, may be made into plain, or rich dough-nuts, as preferred, with very little trouble. Prepare the dough as directed in the receipt for rusk, and add two or three eggs, if convenient. It is not necessary.

Fried Biscuit.

Work a piece of butter the size of an egg into a large pint of light bread dough. When it has risen again, roll it very thin, cut it into circles or squares, and fry them for breakfast. Eat them with salt, or with cider and sugar. All crullers and dough-nuts are much more healthful fried in clarified drippings of roast meat, than in lard; and it is, besides, good economy.

ON MAKING PASTRY.

The flour, as in making bread or cake, should be sifted. The best looking pastry is made with lard, but it is not so healthy or good, as that which is made with half or two thirds butter. Whichever you use, rub a third of it into the flour, but do not try to rub out every lump; the less the hands are used, the better. Add cold water; in summer, ice water. If your crust is shortened wholly with lard, allow a teaspoonful of salt to a pound (or quart) of flour, and a small teaspoonful of saleratus to every three pounds. Sprinkle the salt into the flour, and dissolve the saleratus in the water. If butter only or chiefly is used, omit the saleratus. When you have put in the water, stir it quickly, rather stiff, with a knife. Do not mould it; it will make it tough; but when it is barely stirred together, put it on the board, roll it out, lay thin shavings of butter on every part, sprinkle a little flour over it, and roll it out again then lay on butter as before. To avoid much handling of the crust, roll it so thin that all the butter will be taken up by two or three times rolling in. When it is all rolled in, fold up the crust in a long roll, and double it, laying the ends together; then lay it aside, and cut from it for each pie. In rolling out for the plates press the pin equally, so as to make all parts of the same thickness, and as nearly circular as possible. Have the plates ready buttered, or greased with lard, lay in the crust, and see that all parts touch the plate. Take the dish up on the palm of the left hand, and with the right trim the edges, holding the knife under and *aslant*, and so cut the crust that the edge of the dish will be perfectly covered. People differ in regard to the proper thickness of pie-crust. A pie in which the fruit constitutes one third of the thickness, and the two crusts the other two thirds, although it may look more elegant, is neither so healthful or good as one made with thinner crust and plenty of fruit. Some fruit requires thicker crust than others; for apple, peach, and pumpkin it should be thin as a common earthen plate; for juicy fruits, such as berries, cherries, currants, plums, and for mince, it should be a little thicker. Lay some of the trimmings round the rim of the plate to make the edge of the pie handsome, and put the rest by themselves, and when there are enough, roll them out for an under-crust.

In making cherries, currants, &c., into pies, use deep dishes, and be careful not to fill them even full, as the syrup will boil over, and thus, much of the richness of the pie be lost. There is one way effectually to prevent the loss of syrup. After you have laid in the fruit, or mince, and rolled out the upper-crust, wet the rim of the under-crust all around with cold water not omitting a single spot, (if you do the syrup will escape at that spot), and sprinkle a very little flour upon it, lay the trimming upon the rim, wet and flour that in the same manner, then lay the upper-crust immediately over, and press it down gently upon the rim. The flour and water act as a paste to fasten the crusts together. Trim the edge as before, and prick the top eight or ten times with a fork. This is necessary for the escape of the steam, and without it, the closing of the edge will not avail to keep in the syrup. It is a good way to invert a teacup in the centre of a juicy fruit-pie, as in making an oyster-pie.

A clammy lower crust is neither good or digestible. Therefore never fill pies made of moist materials until just before putting them into the oven. Squash pies, cocoanut, and Marlborough puddings, &c., should not be filled until the last minute, and mince and stewed apple should only stand long enough for the upper crust to be laid on. Pie-crust becomes yellow from standing long before being baked; therefore, delay rolling out the upper crust for any kind of pies until the oven is nearly ready. Pastry should be baked in a quick oven, to be light, and be slightly browned to be healthy. When you bake pumpkin and similar kinds of pies, if you have the least doubt whether the crust is well done, set the dishes a few minutes on embers, or the top of a cooking stove. This sort of pies requires nearly an hour to bake; more, if the dishes are very deep. When done enough, the top will be gently swelled all over, and in moving, tremble like jelly; if not done, the middle will look like a thick liquid. Most pies require an hour to bake; those made of stewed apple or cranberry, three quarters of an hour. Much depends on the kind of oven used.

It is difficult to make flaky crust in warm weather. But cooling the butter and water with ice, and having the pastry-table in the cellar, will insure tolerable success.

There is hardly another article of food in which so much is

sacrificed to appearance as in pastry. Everybody likes a light crust, a little brown, and not excessively rich, better than one that is half butter or lard, and baked white.

Cherries should not be stewed or stoned for pies. Apples, after they are pared, cut, and cored, should be washed. Steam pumpkin and squash, or stew it with very little water. Meat for pies must not be chopped till after it is cold.

After a little practice and observation, it will be just as well to omit weighing the materials for pastry. One very heaping handful of flour will make a common-sized pie; not, however, allowing for the flour to be used in rolling the paste.

When all the pies but the last one are made, scrape the remains of crust from the moulding-board and the rolling-pin, and add any parings of edges that you have, work them together, and use for the under-crust.

For almost all kinds of pies, good brown sugar is nice enough. The Havana is seldom clean. The Porto-Rico and Santa Cruz are considered the best. The New Orleans is very sweet.

The very early apples, when used for pies or sauce, should not be pared, as the greatest part of the richness of the fruit, at that season, is in the skin. Some kinds are so delicate, that when stewed, the skin is entirely absorbed in the pulp, so as not to be visible, and the cólor, if it is red, is beautifully diffused through the whole mass.

Rich Puff Paste.

For a pound and a half of flour, take one pound of butter; divide it into three parts, and reserve a third of the flour for use in rolling in two parts. Rub one third of the butter into the flour, add water enough just to make it a stiff dough, then roll it out, and put in the rest of the butter as directed above.

A plainer Paste.

Three pounds (or quarts) of flour, half a pound of lard, and a pound of butter.

Good common Pie-crust.

Allow one heaping handful of flour for a pie, and a table-spoonful of lard or butter for each handful.

Bread-dough Pie-crust.

Take very light dough and roll in shavings of butter three times, using as little flour as you can.

Potato-crust.

Boil six good-sized mealy potatoes, and mash them fine; add salt, a spoonful of butter and two of water while they are hot. Then work in flour enough for making a paste to roll out, or put in two or three spoonfuls of cream, and no butter or water. This is a good crust for pot-pies or dumplings.

PIES.

Of Stewed Apple.

Stew the apple with water enough to prevent its burning; sweeten and flavor it to your taste, and, while it is hot, add butter in the proportion of a dessert spoonful to a quart of apple. The spices most appropriate are nutmeg and lemon, cinnamon and orange. Two kinds are enough; one does very well. When you have laid the under crust in the plate, roll out the upper one, so that it may be laid on the moment the apple is put in, as the under crust will be clammy if the pie is not put immediately into the oven.

Another (without an upper crust).

Pare and quarter fourteen or eighteen fair sour apples; weigh them, and make a syrup of the same weight of sugar and a little water. Grate off the outside of a lemon and set it aside; take out the seeds, cut up the inside, and put it into the syrup. When the syrup is boiled clear, lay in half of the apples and boil them, but not till they are very soft. Take them out carefully, and lay them separately on a dish, so as not to break them. Stew the rest of the apples, and when they are taken out, boil the syrup a little while longer. Have ready three or four medium sized deep plates, with a nice paste in them. If any of the apple is broken or stewed soft, lay that into the middle of the plate, then put the quarters around in regular tiers, one above another, so as to form a sort of half sphere or pyramid, then sprinkle the grated lemon over the top, and pour on some of the syrup. Bake in a quick oven half an hour. When they are taken out, sift fine sugar over the top.

Of uncooked Apples.

To eat immediately, the following is excellent. Lay the slices into the plate upon an under crust; fill it quite full; sprinkle the rim with a little flour, to prevent the upper crust from adhering to the under one. Bake forty minutes, or till the apple is tender, and then slide off the upper crust and add a small bit of butter, some nutmeg or lemon, and sugar to your taste. Mix them well with the apple with a silver spoon, and return the upper crust to its place.

Another.

The other method is to lay the apples into a deep dish with an under crust, and for a large family, no matter how large a dish is used; grate a whole or half nutmeg over, according to the size of the pie, or if you have a fresh orange, cut small the peel of half a one, and sprinkle in with the apple; add a few sticks of cinnamon, a few little bits of butter, and lastly, put on as much sugar as your judgment directs. Cover it, and close the edge, so that the syrup will not escape. Bake from an hour and a half to two hours.

Another (sweetened with molasses).

Make a plain crust, and line a deep dish; fill it with sliced apples, grate a good deal of nutmeg over them, and lay on two or three thin shavings of butter. Then pour over a teacupful or two of good molasses, according to the size of the pie; lay on the upper crust, and close it so that the syrup cannot escape. Bake it two hours and a half.

For directions how to make a pie of Dried Apples, see the receipt for stewing them.

Whortleberry.

Fill the dish not quite even full, and to each pie of the size of a large soup plate, add four large spoonfuls of sugar (for blackberries and blueberries, five). Dredge a very little flour over the fruit before you lay on the upper crust. Close the edge with special care.

Cherry.

The common red cherry makes the best pie. Bake it in a deep dish. Use sugar in the proportion directed for blackberries. All cherries, except the very sweet ones, are good for pies.

Cranberry.

Take the sauce as prepared to eat with meat; grate a little nutmeg over it, put three or four thin shavings of butter on it, and then lay on the upper crust. If not sweet enough, add more sugar. Make it without an upper crust, if you prefer, and lay very narrow strips across diagonally.

Green Currants and Gooseberries.

These require a great deal of sugar, at least two thirds as much in measure as of fruit. Currant pies should be made in a deep plate or a pudding dish, and with an upper crust.

Gooseberries should be stewed like cranberries, sweetened to suit the taste, and laid upon the under crust, with strips placed diagonally across the top, as directed for the cranberry tarts. Currants that are almost ripe make a nice pie, and require the same measure of sugar as blackberries.

Lemon.

Make a nice paste, and lay into two medium-sized plates; then prepare the following mixture. To the juice, and grated rind of one lemon, made very sweet with white sugar, add three well-beaten eggs, and a piece of butter half the size of an egg, melted. Stir these ingredients together, then add a pint of rich milk, or thin cream, stirring very fast. Fill the plates and bake immediately.

Another.

An egg, a lemon, and a cup of sugar prepared as directed in the last receipt; then add half a cup of water, and two small crackers, pounded and sifted. Bake in a plate, with a paste.

Rich Mince.

To one beef's tongue, allow a pound of suet, a pound of currants, another of raisins, a pound and a quarter of sugar, half a pound of citron, eight large apples, a quart of wine or boiled cider, salt, a nutmeg, cinnamon, cloves, the juice and pulp of a lemon, and the rind chopped fine. Let the meat be chopped very fine, then add the apples and chop them fine also. Put the sugar into the cider or wine, and just boil it up so as to skim off the top; let it stand a few minutes, and then pour it off into a pan containing all the other ingredients. Be careful, in pouring it, not to disturb any sediment there may be from the sugar. Use loaf sugar if you choose.

Another (not as rich).

Chop the meat, apples, and suet separately, and then measure the ingredients thus: three bowls of meat, three of apple, one of suet, one of citron cut small, two of raisins, four of sugar, one of molasses, one of vinegar, one of some kind of syrup (quince or peach), or wine instead, if you prefer. Add powdered clove, nutmeg and cinnamon to suit the taste.

Temperance.

Boil five pounds of meat in water enough to have one quart when it is done ; chop the meat very fine when it is cold, and add a quarter of a pound of suet, or salt pork, three pounds and a half of sugar, three of chopped apple, two and a half of box raisins and one of Sultana raisins, one of citron, and a pint of syrup of preserved peach, quince, or both ; or any other syrup you may have ; add salt, nutmeg, and powdered clove. To mix the ingredients, remove the fat from the juice of the meat and put it into a kettle with the apple, sugar, raisins, and citron, and let them boil a few minutes; if froth rises, take it off; have the meat ready in a pan mixed with the spices, pour the mixture boiling hot upon it, and stir it together; add, if you choose, the juice and pulp of three lemons. This process cooks the ingredients so thoroughly that, if you prefer, you can bake the paste first and then fill the dishes ; and if you choose to reserve part of it, it will keep in a cool place several weeks.

Very Plain.

These may be made of almost any cheap pieces of meat, boiled till tender; add suet or salt pork chopped very fine, half or two thirds as much apple as meat; sugar and spices to your taste. If mince pies are eaten cold it is better to use salt pork than suet. A lemon, and a little syrup of sweetmeats will greatly improve them. Clove is the most important spice.

Without Suet.

Boil up a quart of good brown sugar in three pints of cider ; set it off, and after a few minutes take off the scum ; then put in a pint of chopped meat, a quart of chopped apple, and four large crackers pounded and sifted. Add a grated nutmeg, a large teaspoonful of powdered clove, and any other spice you prefer. Make the mixture more sweet if you choose. Boil it again four or five minutes. This will not keep so long as mince which contains no cracker.

Without Meat.

To twelve apples chopped fine, add six beaten eggs, and a half pint of cream. Put in spice, sugar, raisins or currants just as you would for meat mince pies.

Another.

A cup of molasses, a cup of sugar, half a cup of vinegar, and half a cup of butter, boiled up together for a minute. Then add three crackers pounded and sifted, a half a pint of chopped raisins, two beaten eggs, and spice to suit the taste.

Peach.

If the peaches are dried, stew them first in a little water; if fresh, pare them, but do not take out the stones. Make the pie in a large deep dish, and close the edge well, to prevent the escape of the syrup. The free-stones are best, because most tender; the cling-stones require long cooking.

Rhubarb.

Peel the stalks, and cut them into pieces about an inch long; lay them in a soft cloth in order to absorb some of the juice, as the quantity is very great. Put them in a sauce-pan and stew gently; add sugar enough to make it sweet as you wish, but no water; cover close. Be careful not to stew it so long as to break the pieces. Lay it into dishes for the table, and having baked your paste of the right size, lay it over. Some persons prefer the rhubarb without spice. If any is used, it should be the rind of a lemon.

Rhubarb tarts are good made, like the gooseberry, with a lower crust, and strips laid across the top.

Squash or Pumpkin.

To a quart of boiled milk, put a large pint of strained squash, two cups of sugar, three eggs, two crackers pounded and sifted (or four eggs without the crackers), a teaspoonful of salt, a few drops of lemon or rose, half a teaspoonful of ginger or powdered cinnamon, and a dessert-spoonful of butter, melted in the hot milk. To mix it, stir the spice and salt into the strained squash first, then add the cracker, and sugar, and when these are mixed, pour in half the milk, and when this is well stirred, add the remainder, and lastly the eggs, which should be thoroughly beaten. If you make up two quarts of milk, use four eggs, and five pounded crackers, and double the other ingredients. Bake with a crust, in rather deep plates, or in dishes made for such pies.

Another.

Six eggs, eight table-spoonfuls of strained squash, one quart of boiled milk, a little salt, two table-spoonfuls of rose-water, a lemon (juice and rind), sugar to your taste, a spoonful of butter melted. Grate nutmeg over the top. Mix the ingredients as directed in the last receipt. The mode of making pumpkin puddings or pies, may be almost endlessly varied. They are very good without eggs, substituting a little more pumpkin and three crackers pounded and sifted, to a quart of milk; omitting rose-water, use cinnamon and a very little ginger. When you have only one or two eggs to a quart, use two crackers.

Puffs.

Make a rich paste of a quart of flour; after you have rubbed in part of the butter, cut the white of an egg to a stiff froth; reserve half a spoonful of it, and stir the rest, and the water into the flour with a knife; then proceed to roll in the remainder of the butter in the usual way. Cut rounds in the paste of the size you wish to have them, and twice as many as you intend to have of puffs. Then cut out of half of them, a small round in the centre, so as to leave a circular rim of crust. Take up these rims with a wide-bladed knife, and lay them upon the large rounds so as to form a raised edge, and with the knife lay them, thus prepared, on tin sheets, or a nice sheet-iron pan. Take a feather, and lightly brush the edges with a little of the reserved white of egg. This will make them brown handsomely. Bake them in a quick oven. Bake also the small rounds which were cut out from the rims. When all are baked, put raspberry jam, quince, currant, or lemon jelly in the puffs and lay the small rounds over it. Some people like them best, without covering the jelly.

To make lemon jelly for the purpose, beat one egg and a cup of sugar together; when well mixed, add the juice of a lemon, and then two table-spoonfuls of cold water. Put the mixture in a shallow dish, set it on the stove, and stir it steadily, until it thickens, then take it off immediately. Be careful it does not boil. When it is cool, put it into the puffs.

DIRECTIONS ABOUT PUDDINGS.

THE eggs for all sorts of puddings in which they are used, should be well beaten, and then strained. If hot milk is used, the eggs should be added after all the other ingredients. Milk for pumpkin, squash, cocoanut, tapioca, ground rice, sago, arrowroot, and sweet potato puddings, should be boiled; for bread and plum puddings also, unless the bread is soaked in milk over night. When suet is used in puddings, it should be chopped fine as possible.

In making batter puddings, but a small portion of the milk should be put to the flour at first, as it will be difficult to stir out the little lumps, if the whole quantity is mixed together at once. After the flour is stirred smooth, in a part of the milk, add the eggs not beaten, and beat the mixture well; then add the remainder of the milk, and stir all together till equally mixed. A flour pudding is much lighter, when the materials are all beaten together, than if the eggs are done separately. When berries or cherries are to be used, put them in last. A batter pudding, with berries, requires at least a third more flour than one without. For cherry pudding but a small addition of flour is needed.

A buttered earthen bowl, with a cloth tied up close over it, is a very good thing in which to boil a pudding or dumpling; but some persons think they are lighter boiled in a cloth. A large square of thick tow or hemp cloth does very well; but if a bag is preferred, it should be so cut that the bottom will be several inches narrower than the top, and the corners rounded. The seam should be stitched close with a coarse thread on one side, and then turned and stitched again on the other, in order to secure the pudding from the water. When used, let the seam be outside. A strong twine, a yard long, should be sewed at the middle to the seam, about three inches from the top of the bag. When the bag is to be used, wring it in cold water, and sprinkle the inside thick with flour,* and lay it in a dish; pour in the batter and tie up the bag quickly, drawing the string as tight as possible. Allow a little room for the pudding to swell. (An Indian pudding made with cold milk, swells more than any other.) Lay it immediately into the boiling pot, and after ten minutes, turn it over to prevent the flour from settling on one side. If there is fruit in the pudding, it should be turned three or four times during the first half hour. Keep it covered by adding water from the tea-kettle if necessary, and be careful that it boils steadily. If it does not, the pudding will be watery. When you take it up, plunge it for a moment in a pan of cold water; then pour off the water, untie the twine, and gently lay back the top of the bag. Have a dish ready, and turn the pudding out upon it. A batter pudding without berries cooks very nicely in a tin pudding pan, set upright in a kettle of boiling water.

To cut a boiled pudding without making it heavy, lay the knife, first one side and then the other, upon it, long enough to warm the blade.

---

* Some persons prefer to spread the inside with butter and then flour it. Perhaps this method excludes the water most effectually. Either way does well. Always butter the dish in which a pudding is to be baked.

If these directions seem needlessly minute, it should be remembered that those things which seem perfectly obvious to the experienced, are often very perplexing to the uninitiated.

Elegant Pudding Sauce.

To four large spoonfuls of fine white sugar, put two of butter, one of flour, and stir them together to a cream in an earthen dish. Cut the white of an egg to a stiff froth, and add it; then pour into the dish a gill of boiling water, stirring the mixture very fast. Put it into the sauce tureen and add essence of lemon, or rose, or grate nutmeg over the top as you prefer.

A Plainer Sauce.

To three large spoonfuls of clean brown sugar, put rather more than one spoonful of butter, and half a one of flour; stir all together in an earthen dish until white, then add a gill of boiling water, and stir it steadily till it is all melted, then set it upon the coals long enough just to boil up. Add rose-water, a few drops of lemon juice, or a spoonful of boiled cider.

Cold Sauce.

Take the same measure of butter and sugar as given in either of the above receipts, and stir them to a cream. Omit the flour; but add the white of egg.

Sour Cream Sauce.

Put together a cup of sugar and a cup and a half of thick sour cream. Beat the mixture five or six minutes, then put it into a sauce tureen and grate nutmeg over it.

This sauce is specially appropriate for Indian puddings, baked or boiled, and for the boiled suet puddings.

Apple Pudding.

To a quart of stewed sour apple, put while it is hot, a piece of butter the size of an egg, and sugar enough to make it quite sweet. Beat it several minutes in order to mix it thoroughly.

Beat four eggs and stir into it, add lemon or any essence you choose. Butter a cold dish thick, with cold* butter, and strew the bottom and sides with cracker crumbs, or very fine bread crumbs; then pour in the mixture, sift plenty of the cracker crumbs on the top, grate a little nutmeg upon it, and sprinkle it with sifted sugar. Bake forty or fifty minutes in one dish, or half an hour in two. It is an improvement to line the dish with a plain paste, rolled thin.

Another (Marlborough).

Make a nice paste and lay into your dishes. Take one quart of strained apple, one quart of sugar, eight eggs, three nutmegs, a pint of cream, a quarter of a pound of butter, a fresh lemon, pulp and juice, and the rind grated. If you have no cream, milk will do, but it should be boiled, and half a pound of butter, instead of one quarter, melted into it. The apples should be very sour. This will fill six deep dishes or soup plates. Bake three quarters of an hour.

Another (Pemberton).

To six large, sour apples, put a pint of cream, an ounce of butter, six eggs, one lemon, sugar to the taste.

To be prepared exactly in the same way as the Marlborough pudding.

Almond.

Blanch (that is, peel off the brown skin) of five bitter, and ten sweet almonds; to do this, easily, pour boiling water on them, then pound them fine in a mortar. Set a pail with a quart of rich milk into a kettle of hot water; when it boils, put in the almonds. Mix two and a half table-spoonfuls of ground rice smooth, with a large tumbler of milk, and stir it in. Boil it

* In all cases, where the sides of a dish are to be strewed with crumbs, both the dish and the butter should be cold.

half an hour, stirring it often; then add the yolks of three eggs beaten with half a coffee cup of fine sugar, and in about a minute take the pail from the kettle, and stir in another half cup of sugar. Pour it into a dish and set it away to cool. Cut the whites of the eggs, and a large spoonful of fine sugar to a stiff froth, drop them on the top with a large spoon, and set the pudding into the oven till the top is brown. To be eaten cold.

Baked Batter.

Allow a pint of cold milk, four table-spoonfuls of flour, two eggs, and a little salt.

Stir the flour smooth in a part of the milk, then put in the eggs without first beating, and beat them well with the mixed flour. Then add the remainder of the milk, and the salt, and when well stirred together, pour it into a buttered dish, and bake it half an hour. When it is done, the whole top will have risen up. So long as there is a little sunken spot in the centre, it is not baked enough. Make a cold or melted sauce as you prefer. This makes an ample pudding for a family of four. A flour pudding will not be light unless it is put into the oven immediately on being made.

Boiled Batter.

Use the very same proportions; butter a tin pudding-pan having a close cover, and put in the mixture; set it immediately into a kettle of boiling water. See that the water comes up high enough around it to cook the pudding, but so that it will not boil quite up to the top. If it boils away, add more hot water.

Another.

To a quart of milk put six eggs, eight spoonfuls of flour, and a teaspoonful of salt. To be boiled two hours.

If you wish to make a nice addition to your dinner on short notice, prepare this batter, and butter little cups that hold about a gill, fill them three quarters full, and bake in the stove.

They will bake in fifteen minutes. They should be turned out upon a dish, and be eaten with sauce. Such a pudding requires forty minutes to bake in one dish.

Rye Batter.

To a pint of cold milk, put three heaping spoonfuls of sifted rye meal, a little salt, and three eggs. Boil it an hour and a half in a buttered bowl with the cloth tied very tight over it. The bowl should be of a size to allow a very little for swelling.

Bird's Nest.

For a pint of cold milk allow three eggs, five spoonfuls of flour, six medium sized, fair apples, and a small teaspoonful of salt.

Pare the apples, and take out the cores; arrange them in a buttered dish that will just receive them (one in the centre and five around it). Wet the flour smooth in part of the milk, then add the eggs and beat all together a few minutes; then put in the salt, and the rest of the milk. Stir it well and pour it into the dish of apples. Bake it an hour, and make a melted sauce. For a large family make double measure, but bake it in two dishes, as the centre apples of a large dish will not cook as quickly, as those around the edge.

Bread.

Take nice pieces of light bread, break them up, and put a small pint bowl full into a quart of milk; set it in a tin pail or brown dish on the back part of the stove or range, where it will heat very gradually, and let it stand an hour or more. When the bread is soft enough to be made fine with a spoon, just boil it up; set it off, and stir in a large teaspoonful of butter, a little salt, and from two to four beaten eggs. Bake it an hour. Make a sauce for it. To be eaten without sauce, put in twice the measure of butter, beat the eggs with a cup of nice brown sugar, a teaspoonful of cinnamon, and half as much powdered clove.

Bread and Butter.

Cut five slices of light bread across the loaf, very thin; spread them thick with butter; cut the slices in two or four parts; butter a dish and lay them in with a few dried currants between each slice. Lay them so that the top will be even, and not quite as high as the dish; pour over them a quart of custard made with boiled milk, and five or six eggs, and flavored with peach and nutmeg. It will bake in less than an hour. Some persons prefer to toast the bread.

Cottage.

One teacup of sweet milk, three of flour, one coffee-cup of brown sugar, one egg, one table-spoonful of butter, half a teaspoonful of saleratus. Melt the butter. Dissolve the saleratus in a little of the milk, and stir it in after the other ingredients are mixed. Bake half an hour. To be eaten with sweet sauce.

Another (more rich).

One teacup of sugar, three table-spoonfuls of melted butter, one egg, one teacup of milk, two heaping cups of flour, a teaspoonful of saleratus or soda, and two of cream of tartar. If it is made with sour milk, the cream of tartar is to be left out.

Cocoanut.

Grate a cocoanut, and save the milk. Boil a quart of milk and pour upon it; add five eggs, with a coffee-cup of sugar beaten in them, an ounce of butter, two table-spoonfuls of rose-water, a little salt. If you have cream and plenty of eggs, make it of cream instead of milk, and add three more eggs, and any essence or spice you choose, and bake in one dish nearly an hour; or make a nice paste, and bake it in three deep plates like squash pies, forty minutes.

Cracker.

To a pint of boiled milk, put four crackers, pounded and sifted, three eggs, and a small teaspoonful of salt. Add whortleberries if convenient, and in that case, half of another cracker. Make a sweet sauce. Bake half an hour, or forty minutes. The same mixture made with cold milk is a nice pudding boiled an hour and a half.

Another.

Take the same proportions as in the previous receipt, of crackers, milk, and eggs; and add a cup of sugar, a table-spoonful of butter, cinnamon, a very little clove, and a cup of chopped raisins, and eat it with a sauce, or without. It is good cold.

Farina.

Two table-spoonfuls of farina, a pint of milk, two eggs, a small cup of sugar, and a half teaspoonful of salt; flavor with lemon or nutmeg. To mix it, set the milk in a pail into a kettle of hot water. When the top of the milk foams up, stir in the farina gradually, and add the salt. Let it remain in the kettle ten or fifteen minutes, and stir it repeatedly. Take the pail from the kettle, beat the eggs and sugar together, and stir them in; add the essence, and pour the mixture into a buttered dish. Bake half an hour or forty minutes. No sauce is necessary.

Potato.

Weigh two pounds of good potatoes, after they are pared; boil them, and when done, dry them; then pound them well in the kettle with a pestle. While they are still hot, add half a pound of sugar and half a pound of butter, which have been previously stirred together to a cream; and last, and a little at a time, seven eggs, a glass of wine, and spice to your taste. Bake with or without a paste. Omit the wine if you prefer, both in this, and the next receipt, and use lemon-juice.

Another.

To half a pound of boiled potato, rolled or pounded, put two ounces of butter, two eggs, half a gill of cream, one table-spoonful of white wine, sugar to your taste, and a very little salt. Beat it to a froth, and bake with or without a paste. If it is wanted more rich, add almonds and another egg.

Sweet Potato.

Boil the potatoes and rub them through a sieve; add eggs, milk, sugar, and spice precisely as for squash pies, only making the mixture a very little thicker with the potato. Bake in a deep dish with a paste, or without if preferred.

Sweet Potato Pone.

Pare and grate several sweet potatoes, and to three pounds of grated potato add two of sugar, twelve eggs, a little more than three pints of milk, the juice and grated rind of a lemon, a quarter of a pound of butter (melted), a table-spoonful of rose-water, a nutmeg, a little cinnamon and mace, a teaspoonful of salt. Mix thoroughly together and bake in deep pans two hours. It is usually eaten cold, as cake.

Plum.

A pound of bread or six pounded crackers, one quart of milk, six eggs, a large spoonful of flour, a teacup of sugar, one nutmeg, a teaspoonful of cinnamon, half a one of powdered clove, a piece of butter the size of an egg, the same quantity of chopped suet, and a pound of raisins. Boil the milk. It is very well to soak the bread in the milk over night; then the entire crust becomes soft, and mixes well with the other ingredients.

These puddings are served with a rich sauce, if eaten warm, but are excellent cold, cut up like cake. People that are subject to a great deal of uninvited company, find it convenient in cold weather to bake half a dozen at once. They will keep several weeks, and when one is to be used, it may be loosened from the dish by a knife passed around it, and a little hot water be poured in round the edge. It should then be covered close, and set for half an hour into the stove or oven.

Another.

Soak a pound of soft bread in a quart of boiled milk till it can easily be strained through a coarse hair sieve; then add seven eggs, two gills of cream, a quarter of a pound of butter (melted), a gill of rose-water, or some extract of rose, a little cinnamon or nutmeg, and a pound of raisins. For a small family, bake it in two dishes, an hour; and reserve one for another day. To warm it, see the directions in the last receipt.

Rice.

Boil a teacupful of rice in two teacups of water. When it has swelled so as to absorb the water, add a quart of milk and five or six peach leaves, and boil it until the rice is perfectly soft. Take it from the fire, remove the peach leaves, add a small piece of butter, a little salt, and three or four eggs, beaten with a teacup of sugar. Put it into a buttered dish, grate nutmeg over the top, and bake three quarters of an hour. Most people prefer this pudding cold.

Another (Crested.)

Prepare the same measures of rice and milk, and in the same way as in the last receipt. Boil the rice very slowly after the milk is added, so that it may become very soft, and not get burned. Break six eggs, the yolks and whites separate; beat the yolks with a large cup of white sugar; and stir them, with salt, and a small bit of butter into the rice and milk. Then return the kettle to the fire two or three minutes, and see that it does not burn. Then put the mixture into a buttered dish, and cut the six whites and two large spoonfuls of fine sugar to a stiff froth. Flavor the froth with lemon, lay it over the pudding in folds like a turban, and set it into the oven long enough to brown the top. Ten minutes will be sufficient.

Ground Rice.

To a teacup of ground rice, allow a quart and a gill of milk, six eggs, a heaping teacup of sugar, a piece of butter the size of a small nut, one teaspoonful of salt, and any spice you prefer. Rose-water and nutmeg are generally considered best. Bake it from three quarters to one hour. The milk should be boiled, and the ground rice wet with a part of it reserved for the purpose. When the milk boils up, stir in the rice; mix it thoroughly with the milk, then let it boil up one or two minutes. When it has become a little thick, take it off, put in the butter and salt, add the eggs and sugar, and last of all, the spice. Bake it in one dish, in a moderately hot oven, an hour. If your family is small, bake it in two dishes, forty minutes. It is quite as good the second day as the first.

Sago.

A pint of milk, a table-spoonful and a half of *pearl* sago, two eggs, two large spoonfuls of sugar, and half a teaspoon of salt. Wash the sago in warm, but not hot water, twice; then put it with the milk into a pail and set it into a kettle of hot water. Stir it very often, as it swells fast, and will else lie in a compact mass at the bottom. When it has boiled two or three minutes, take the pail from the kettle, add the salt, and the eggs beaten with the sugar. Flavor it with vanilla or a few drops of essence of lemon, put it into a dish, and grate nutmeg over it. Set it immediately into the oven, and bake it about three quarters of an hour. If you make a quart of milk, three eggs answer very well. It should then bake an hour. With this number of eggs, the sago settles a little. To have it equally diffused take five eggs.

Squash, or Pumpkin.

A pint of milk, a large coffee-cup of strained pumpkin or squash, two eggs, three large spoonfuls of sugar, a teaspoonful of butter, a little salt, a small teaspoonful of cinnamon, half as much ginger, and some nutmeg.

To prepare it — first, stir the cinnamon and ginger into the squash, as, if they are added after the milk, they will float dry on the top; add salt, then the eggs beaten with the sugar; boil the milk and melt the butter in it, and add it slowly to the other ingredients, stirring fast meantime. Butter a cold dish with cold butter, and sprinkle the bottom and sides with sifted cracker, pour in the mixture, grate nutmeg over the top and then sprinkle it with pounded cracker, sift white sugar over, and bake it forty minutes.

To make a more economical pudding, use the same measure of milk, squash, sugar, ginger, and cinnamon, with but one egg. Stir a pounded and sifted cracker into the squash, before the boiled milk is added; simply butter a dish in the usual way; omit the nutmeg and also the sugar and cracker on the top.

The receipt for squash pies (see page 71) is a very nice rule for a pudding; omit the paste, and substitute the cracker crumbs in the dish. Such puddings, when made with a quart of milk, should be baked in two dishes, because if baked in one, the edges become too dry, before the centre is cooked.

Tapioca.

To a quart of milk, put two thirds of a cup of tapioca, five or six eggs, a dessert spoonful of butter, a cup of sugar, a teaspoonful of salt, and flavor with lemon, nutmeg, or extract of rose. Do not wash the tapioca, as the fine powder is the nicest part; but pick it over carefully, and soak it over night in half of the milk. If you have not done this, and need the pudding for dinner, it will soak in cold water (twice as much water as tapioca) in two or three hours. Boil it in the milk, set into a kettle of hot water; stir it often, beat the eggs and sugar thoroughly, together; stir them and all the other ingredients into the milk while it is yet hot. If the pudding is put immediately in the oven, it will bake in three quarters of an hour, or a little less. Three eggs to a quart of milk will make a very good tapioca pudding.

PUDDINGS WITHOUT EGGS.

Berry.

To a quart of washed whortleberries, put a pint of flour in which you have put a small teaspoonful of salt. Add a very little water. That which is upon the berries will be nearly enough. Boil it two hours in a cloth tied close, allowing no room to swell. To be eaten with melted sauce.

Another.

A pint of berries, a pint of flour, a pint of sour milk, a teaspoonful of salt, and one of saleratus. Boil it two hours. All boiled fruit puddings should be turned often in the pot, to prevent the fruit from settling on one side. Make a sweet sauce.

Baked Indian.

Two quarts of milk, a large teacup of meal, half a teacup of white flour, two eggs, half a cup of molasses, a large teaspoonful of salt, half a teaspoonful of ginger, and the same of cinnamon.

To mix it, boil three pints of the milk and set it off from the fire. Have ready, beaten together, all the other ingredients in part of the remaining pint of milk. Stir them into the hot milk. Grease a stone pan, shaped like a common gallon pan of potter's ware. Let the mixture cool a little before putting it into the pan. Bake it in a moderate heat. When the top begins to brown, pour a little of the cold milk over it, and cover it with a plate. Bake from four to five hours. Put cold milk on the top two or three times while it is baking. If most convenient, a little finely-chopped suet can be substituted for the eggs.

Another (with Sweet Apples).

Pare twelve sweet apples and slice them, or take out the cores with a tap-borer. Stir up a pudding of a quart of milk, and almost a quart of Indian meal; the measure may be filled quite full by using a spoonful or two of wheat flour. Add some salt, a teacup of molasses, and a little chopped suet. The milk should be boiled, and after it is taken from the fire, the meal and other ingredients stirred in. Then pour the whole over the apples. Bake three hours.

Boiled Plum.

Put to a quart of boiled milk twelve pounded crackers, a quarter of a pound of suet, a pound of currants, half a pound of raisins, a little salt, and a teacup of molasses. Steam in a pudding-pan, or boil it three hours and a half in a cloth or buttered bowl. To be eaten with sauce.

Railroad.

One cup of molasses, one of sweet milk, one of suet or of salt pork chopped fine; four cups of flour, one teaspoonful of saleratus, and if suet is used, one of salt, one cup of chopped raisins, one of currants. Warm the molasses and stir the saleratus into it; mix the suet or pork with the flour, then stir all together, and steam it four hours, according to the directions for Steamed Brown Bread (see page 31). Make a melted sauce, or the sour cream sauce.

Rice.

Wash a small coffee-cup of rice and put it into three pints of milk over night. In the morning add a piece of butter half as large as an egg, a teacup of sugar, a little salt, cinnamon, or nutmeg. Bake very slowly two hours and a half in a stove or brick oven. After it has become hot enough to melt the butter, but not to brown the top, stir it (without moving the dish, if you can) from the bottom. If raisins are to be used, put them in now. They add much to the richness of the pudding. It is a very good pudding for so plain a kind, and is very little trouble. For a Sunday dinner, where a cooking stove is used, it is very convenient, as it employs but a few minutes to prepare it in the morning.

Sago.

Wash six table-spoonfuls of pearl sago and put it to soak in a large pint of warm water. Pare six good-sized, mellow, sour apples, and remove the cores with a tap-borer. Wash them, butter a deep pudding dish, and lay them in, with the open end up. Measure a teacup of sugar, fill the holes with it, and then grate half a nutmeg over the apples. Dissolve a little salt and the rest of the sugar, in the water with the sago; pour two thirds of the mixture over the apples, and set the dish in the oven or stove. After one hour take it out, pour the remainder of the sago and water into the dish, and press the apples down gently without breaking them. See that none of the sago lies above the water. Return the dish to the oven and bake it another hour. It is to be eaten with sugar and milk, or cream, and is a very delicate and healthful pudding.

Salem.

Three coffee-cups of flour, one of milk, one of chopped raisins, one of suet or salt pork chopped very fine, two thirds of a cup of molasses, a small teaspoonful of powdered cloves, half a nutmeg, a teaspoonful of saleratus, and if suet is used instead of pork, a little salt. Warm the molasses and dissolve the saleratus in it, mix the suet, flour, and raisins, then put all the ingredients together. Boil or steam it four hours. Make a melted sauce.

Suet.

A pint of suet chopped very fine, a pint of chopped apples, two gills of milk, a gill of molasses, a large teaspoonful of salt, and flour enough to make it rather stiff. Boil it four hours. This, and the last before it, should be boiled in a close tin pail or pudding pan, in a kettle of water.

Such a pudding as this is too hearty to be eaten after meat, and is substantial enough to constitute a dinner.

DUMPLINGS, FLUMMERIES, AND OTHER INEXPENSIVE ARTICLES FOR DESSERT.

Apple Dumplings (boiled).

The best and most healthful crust for them is made like cream tartar biscuit, or with potatoes, according to the directions under the head of *Pastry*. It is better to make one or two large dumplings, than many small ones; because in drawing up the crust, there must necessarily be folds which, when boiled, are thick; and thus, in small dumplings, the proportion of crust to apple, is too great. Make a large crust and let the middle be nearly a third of an inch thick; but roll the edges thin, for the reason above mentioned. Wring a thick, square cloth in water, sprinkle it with flour, and lay it into a deep dish; lay the crust into it, and fill it with sliced apples; put the crust together and draw up the cloth around it. Tie it tight with a strong twine or tape, allowing no room for it to swell, and be sure to draw the string so close that the water cannot soak in. Boil a dumpling holding three pints of cut apple, two hours. When taken out of the pot, plunge it for a moment into cold water, then untie it and turn it out into a dish. Eat with cold sauce, or butter and sugar. Molasses and butter boiled together make a very good sauce for apple dumplings. The process of boiling molasses takes away, in some degree, its strong taste; and improves it for this purpose, and for making gingerbread. All boiled dumplings and puddings should be put into boiling water. Some persons prefer to boil dumplings in a buttered bowl, with a cloth tied close over it. This is a very good way.

Steamed.

Butter a tin pudding pan or pail that will hold two quarts, and lay a thin crust in the bottom, then half fill it with sliced apples, and lay in another thin crust. Nearly fill the pail with apples, and lay a crust on the top. Use light bread dough with a little butter rolled in, or cream tartar biscuit. Half the measure of this last makes crust enough. Shut the lid close, and set the pail into a kettle of boiling water. Boil two hours.

Baked.

Pare large, fair apples, and take out the cores, lay each one into a piece of plain pie crust, just large enough to cover it. Fill the centre of the apple with brown sugar, and add a little cinnamon, or small strips of fresh orange peel. Close the crust over the apple, and lay them, with the smooth side up, into a deep, buttered dish, in which they can be set on the table. Bake them in a stove an hour and a half. If, after an hour, you find that the syrup begins to harden in the bottom of the dish, put in half a gill of hot water. Make a cold, or melted sauce as you choose.

Blackberry (baked or steamed).

Put a small cup of berries and two teaspoonfuls of sugar into a crust large enough to contain them. To close the crust well, dip your fingers in water and then in flour, and thus paste the folds together. Lay as many dumplings as you wish to have into a deep patty-pan, because blackberries are a very juicy fruit. Bake them an hour and a quarter in a moderate heat. Make a cold sauce for them.

To steam them, put the fruit and crust into a tin pudding pan, exactly like steamed apple dumpling.

Roley Poley.

Make a potato crust, or a paste of light bread, with butter rolled in, or one of cream tartar biscuit, as you prefer; roll it narrow and long, about a third of an inch thick; spread it with raspberry jam or apple sauce; take care that this does not come too near the edge of the crust; roll it up and close the ends and side as tight as possible, to keep the sauce from coming out and the water from soaking it. Sew it up in a cloth, and boil it an hour and a half or two hours, according to its size. Make a sauce.

[The quart measure used in the following articles, and throughout this book, is the beer quart, except where a *small* quart is specified. In cooking such dishes as those which immediately follow, the milk should always, as in making custards, be boiled in a pail set into a kettle of hot water. They are much more delicate than when it is boiled in a saucepan; and then there is no danger of its being burned.]

Potato Starch Flummery.

To one quart of boiled milk, put four beaten eggs and four spoonfuls of potato starch, wet in a little milk. Add the starch and a little salt first; then the eggs, and boil the whole a minute more. Take it up in a mould and eat it with sauce. Boil a few peach leaves in the milk if you like the flavor.

Ground Rice.

Measure a quart of milk, and then take out two cupfuls. Set the remainder into a kettle of hot water; then wet a teacupful of ground rice, and a teaspoonful of salt, with the reserved cold milk. When that which is in the kettle boils, add the ground rice mixture gradually, and continue to stir it, until it is well scalded, else it will be lumpy, or lie compactly at the bottom. Let it remain in the kettle eight or ten minutes, and stir it now and then. Just before you take it up, stir in a large tablespoonful of dry ground rice, and as soon as that is well mixed take the pail from the water-kettle, and put the mixture into a bowl, or blanc-mange mould, wet in cold water. If it is of the right consistency, it will turn out in good shape in fifteen or twenty minutes. To be eaten like blanc-mange with sugar and milk or cream. It is nice cold, and if it is made for the next day, a half a spoonful less of dry rice will be enough. It should be only stiff enough to retain the shape. For this and all similar milk preparations, peach leaves are better than any spice. Boil in the milk three or four fresh leaves from the tree. Remember to take them out before you stir in the rice. If you put in too many, they will give a strong flavor to the article. Experience will teach how many to use.

Farina.

Set a pail containing a quart of milk into a kettle of boiling water. Put in a few pieces of stick-cinnamon. When the milk boils, take out the cinnamon and add a teaspoonful of salt, and stir in, very gradually, four table-spoonfuls of dry farina; beat out the lumps, and stir it often during the first ten minutes, then leave it to boil half an hour or more, remembering to stir it repeatedly during that time. Put it in a mould till the next day. Serve it as blanc-mange.

Made thin, like gruel, it is excellent food for young children.

Tapioca.

Soak a cup of tapioca in a pint of cold water over night; then boil it in a pint of milk with a little salt. Add any essence you choose. It is very good without. Serve it warm, and use sugar and cream.

Sago Apple.

Wash a table-spoonful and a half of pearl sago, and put it into a teacup of cold water to soak. Pare and slice very thin two fair sour apples, and boil them very soft in a teacup of water; then add the sago and water with half a teaspoonful of salt, and stir it every minute or two. Boil it till the sago and apple are perfectly mixed, then add a large spoonful of white sugar, and boil it a minute more. Set it off and add lemon (the essence or juice as you prefer). Put it in a mould, and serve it like blanc-mange.

This is a very good article for an invalid, leaving out the essence.

The same preparation of sago, and two or three table-spoonfuls of currant jelly dissolved in it instead of the apple, is very pretty, and good.

SWEET DISHES.

In making blanc-mange, custards, ice-creams, &c., do not boil the milk in a sauce-pan, but set it, in a tin pail, into a kettle of boiling water. The milk does not rise, when boiled thus, as it does in a sauce-pan, but when the top is covered with foam, it boils enough.

In making ice cream, it is an improvement to churn the cream until it becomes frothy, before adding the other ingredients.

Apple Island.

Stew apple enough to make a quart, strain it through a sieve, sweeten it with fine white sugar, and flavor it with lemon or rose. Beat the whites of six eggs to a hard froth, and stir into the apple slowly; but do not do this till just before it is to be served. The apples should be stewed with as little water as possible. Put it into a glass dish. Serve a nice boiled custard, made of the yolks of the eggs, to eat with it.

Apple Snow.

Put twelve large apples, without paring, into cold water enough to stew them. Boil them slowly; when they are very soft strain them through a sieve; beat the whites of twelve eggs to a stiff froth, then add to them half a pound of fine white sugar, and when these are well mixed, add the apple, and beat all together, until white as snow. Then lay it in the centre of a deep dish, heap it high as you can, and pour around it a nice boiled custard made of a quart of milk, and eight of the yolks of the eggs.

Floating Island.

Put the juice of two lemons, the whites of two eggs, three spoonfuls of currant jelly, and a gill and a half of fine sugar together and beat to a stiff froth; then put it into the middle of the dish, dress it with sweetmeats, and just before it is served, pour into the dish cream enough to float it.

Arrow-root Blanc-mange.

To three large spoonfuls of pure Jamaica arrow-root, a quart of milk, a large spoonful of fine sugar, a spoonful of rose-water, and a little salt. Reserve a gill of milk to wet the arrow-root, and boil the rest. When it boils up, stir in the arrow-root, and boil it up again a minute or two; add the sugar, salt, and rose-water, and put it into the mould.

Isinglass Blanc-mange.

Wash an ounce and a half of calf's-foot isinglass, and put it into a quart of milk over night. In the morning add three peach leaves, and boil it, slowly, twenty minutes or half an hour. Strain it into a dish upon a small teacupful of fine sugar. If it is to be served soon, add two or three beaten eggs while it is hot. Put it into the mould and set in a cool place. In hot weather this should be made over night, if wanted at dinner the next day, as it hardens slowly.

Calf's Foot Blanc-mange.

Put four calf's feet into four quarts of water; boil it away to one quart, strain it, and set it aside. When cool, remove all the fat, and in cutting the jelly out of the pan, take care to avoid the sediment. Put to it a quart of new milk, and sweeten it with fine sugar. If you season it with cinnamon or lemon peel, put it in before boiling; if with rose or peach-water, afterwards; or, if you choose, boil peach leaves in it. Boil it ten minutes, strain it through a fine sieve into a pitcher, and stir it till nearly cold. Then put it into moulds.

Gelatine Blanc-mange.

Allow a quart of milk. Take a quarter of a paper of English gelatine, and put it into a gill of the milk to soften. In a quarter of an hour, set the remainder of the milk in a tin pail into a kettle of hot water, with a few sticks of cinnamon in it. When the milk boils (or foams up) add a small teaspoon of salt, and stir in the cold milk and gelatine. Stir it steadily a few minutes, till the particles of gelatine are dissolved, then put it into moulds. If lemon or some other essence is preferred to the cinnamon, add it after the pail is taken out of the hot water. A beaten egg is an improvement.

Moss Blanc-mange.

In making this blanc-mange as little moss should be used as will suffice to harden the milk. If the moss is old, more is necessary than if it is fresh. Allow half a teacupful for a quart of milk. Wash it, and put it in soak over night; in the morning, tie it up in a piece of muslin, and boil it in the milk, with sticks of cinnamon, the rind of a lemon, or peach leaves. Boil it gently twenty minutes or half an hour. Then put in half a salt-spoonful of salt, strain it upon a large spoonful of crushed sugar, and put it into a mould immediately, as it soon begins to harden. Eat it with sugar and milk or cream.

Charlotte Russe.

Make a boiled custard of a pint of milk and four eggs; season it with vanilla, or any essence you prefer; make it very sweet, and set it away to cool. Put a half an ounce of isinglass or English gelatine into a gill of milk where it will become warm. When the gelatine is dissolved, pour it into a pint of rich cream, and whip it to complete froth. When the custard is cold, stir it gently into the whip. Line a mould that holds a quart with thin slices of sponge cake, or with sponge fingers, pour the mixture into it, and set it in a cold place.

Calf's-foot Jelly.

Scald four calf's feet only enough to take off the hair, (more will extract the juices). Clean them nicely. When this is done, put them into five quarts of water and boil them until the water is half wasted; strain and set it away till the next day, then take off the fat and remove the jelly, being careful not to disturb the sediment; put the jelly into a sauce-pan with sugar, wine, and lemon juice and rind to your taste. Beat the whites and shells of five eggs, stir them in, and set it on the coals, but do not stir it after it begins to warm. Boil it twenty minutes, then add one teacupful of cold water and boil five minutes longer; set off the saucepan, and let it stand covered close half an hour. It will thus become so clear that it will need to run through the jelly bag but once.

Another (made of English Gelatine).

To one of the papers of gelatine containing an ounce and a half, put a pint of cold water; after fifteen minutes, add a quart of boiling water, and stir till the gelatine is dissolved. Then add a coffee-cup of sugar, the juice of a lemon, and the grated rind, or any other spice or essence you prefer, and just boil it up a minute. If the jelly is for an invalid, and wine is a part of the appropriate regimen, omit the lemon and spices, and add two gills of wine, after it is boiled. The gelatine is so pure, that the jelly need not be passed through a jelly-bag. This will keep several weeks in winter, and is convenient for persons who are in the habit of providing little delicacies for the sick.

Almond Custards.

Blanch and beat in a marble mortar, with two spoonfuls of rose-water, a quarter of a pound of almonds; beat the yolks of four eggs with two table-spoonfuls of sugar, mix the almonds with the eggs and sugar, and then add the whole to a pint of cream, set into a kettle of hot water in a pail. Stir it steadily till it boils. Serve in little cups.

Boiled Custards.

Put a quart of milk into a tin pail or a pitcher that holds two quarts; set it into a kettle of hot water. Tin is better than earthen, because it heats so much quicker. Put in a few sticks of cinnamon, or three peach leaves. When the milk foams up as if nearly boiling, stir in six eggs which have been beaten, with two spoonfuls of white sugar; stir it every instant, until it appears to thicken a little. Then take out the pail, and pour the custard immediately into a cold pitcher, because the heat of the pail will cook the part of the custard that touches it, too much, so that it will curdle. This is a very easy way of making custards, and none can be better. But in order to have them good, you must attend to nothing else until they are finished. You may make them as rich as you choose. A pint of milk, a pint of cream, and eight eggs will make them rich enough for any epicure. So, on the other hand, they are very good with three or four eggs only to a quart of milk, and no cream.

Another (good, and very simple).

Boil a quart of milk in the way directed in the preceding receipt, excepting one gill; beat two or three eggs with three spoonfuls of fine sugar; wet three teaspoonfuls of corn-starch in the reserved gill of milk, then mix the beaten eggs and corn starch together, and add a little salt. When the milk in the pail boils, stir them in, and continue to stir a minute or two, till the custard thickens. Then take the pail to the table and pour the custard into china cups (as glass will crack), or else into a cold pitcher. Use what seasoning you please. The old fashion of using cinnamon is economical and very good. Boil some pieces of cinnamon a few minutes only, in two or three spoonfuls of water. Put some of this into the custard, and put what is left into a vial for another time.

Another (still more economical).

Put a quart of milk, excepting two gills, to boil in a kettle of water; with the reserved milk mix three large spoonfuls of flour till it is entirely smooth; add a little salt, and when the milk boils stir it in. Let the mixture remain in the boiling kettle half an hour, or if most convenient, still longer, while you attend to other things; but remember to stir it often. Beat one or two eggs with two or three spoonfuls of sugar, and stir in. Then take the pail to the table, and when the custard has stood a few minutes to cool, add any essence you prefer.

Baked Custards.

Boil the milk with a stick of cinnamon in it, then set it off from the fire, and while it cools a very little, beat (for a quart of milk) five or six eggs, with three large spoonfuls of fine sugar; then stir the milk and eggs together, and pour into custard-cups, or into a single dish that is large enough. If you bake in a brick oven, it is a good way to set custard, in cups, into it, after the bread and other things have been baked. They will become hard in a few hours, and be very delicate. If you bake in a stove, or range oven, it is best to use a dish, and bake it in a very moderate heat, else it will turn, in part, to whey.

DIRECTIONS FOR MAKING ICES.*

Mix equal quantities of coarse salt and ice chopped small; set the freezer containing the cream into a firkin, and put in the ice and salt; let it come up well around the freezer. Turn and shake the freezer steadily at first, and nearly all the time until the cream is entirely frozen. Scrape the cream down often from the sides with a knife. When the ice and salt melt, do not pour off any of it, unless there is danger of its getting into the freezer; it takes half an hour to freeze a quart of cream; and sometimes longer. A tin pail which will hold twice

* The process of freezing is very much simplified by the patent freezers, which have recently come in use.

the measure of the cream, answers a good purpose, if you do not own a freezer. In winter, use snow instead of ice.

Several nice receipts for ice-creams will be given under this head, but a custard made of one quart of rich milk, one or two eggs, two teaspoonfuls of corn-starch, a teacup of sugar, a very little salt, and seasoned with vanilla, makes a delicious ice-cream.

A rich Ice-cream.

Squeeze a dozen lemons, and strain the juice upon as much fine sugar as it will absorb; pour three quarts of cream into it very slowly, stirring very fast all the time.

Another.

A quart of new milk, a quart of cream, a pint of sugar, three eggs, a large spoonful of arrow-root or ground rice, a piece of cinnamon. Boil the milk with the cinnamon in it; when it boils up, stir in the arrow-root or ground rice, wet with a little milk; set it off the fire, stir in the cream, the sugar and eggs. The eggs should be beaten a good deal, and then beaten several minutes in the cream before being put into the boiled milk; add vanilla or lemon as you prefer.

Another (simple, but very good).

Heat a quart of milk quite hot, but do not let it boil; add the yolks of four eggs, beaten, with a large coffee-cup of fine sugar, and flavor with lemon or vanilla.

FRUIT ICES.

Apricot.

Pare, stone, and scald twelve ripe apricots; then bruise them in a marble mortar. Then stir half a pound of fine sugar into a pint of cream; add the apricots and strain through a hair sieve. Freeze and put it into moulds.

Peaches would be a good substitute for the apricots, using, if they are large, nine, instead of twelve.

Strawberry or Raspberry.

Bruise a pint of raspberries, or strawberries, with two large spoonfuls of fine sugar; add a quart of cream, and strain through a sieve, and freeze it. If you have no cream, boil a spoonful of arrow-root in a quart of milk, and, if you like, beat up one egg and stir into it.

Currant.

Take a gill of fresh currant juice, make it very sweet, and stir in half a pint of cream and freeze it. In the winter, or when fresh currants are not to be had, beat a teaspoonful and a half of currant jelly with the juice of one lemon, sweetened, and put to it half a pint of cream.

Lemon.

Having squeezed your lemons, add sugar enough to the juice to make it quite sweet, and about a third as much water as to make lemonade; strain it, and then freeze it.

Imperial Cream.

Boil a quart of cream with the thin rind of a lemon; then stir it till nearly cold; have ready, in the dish in which it is to be served, the juice of three lemons, strained, with as much sugar as will sweeten the cream; pour the cream into the dish, from a teapot or pitcher, holding it high and moving it about so as to mix thoroughly with the juice. It should be made six hours before being served. Eat with sweetmeats, apple island, or apple-pie.

Snow Cream.

To a quart of cream add the whites of three eggs, cut to a stiff froth, four spoonfuls of sweet wine, sugar to your taste, and a little essence of lemon, or the grated rind; whip it to a froth, and serve in a glass dish.

If you have not a whisk such as is made expressly to whip cream. it can be easily, though not as quickly done, with a spoon.

After the materials are mixed, beat them, not over and over like the yolks of eggs, but back and forth, keeping the spoon below the surface; and as fast as the froth forms, take it off and lay it into the dish, or glasses, for the table. It will not return to the liquid state. If it were to stand several days it would become crisped in the form in which it was left.

Wine Custard.

Beat the yolks of three eggs with two spoonfuls of crushed sugar, and cut the whites to a stiff froth; put them into the dish which is to go to the table, and add a quart of milk, and a few drops of peach or rose-water, and when these are well mixed, stir in a spoonful and a half of rennet wine.* In cold weather, the milk should be warmed a little; in warm weather it is not necessary. It should be immediately set where it will not be disturbed. It will harden soon, perhaps in five minutes. This depends somewhat on the strength of the rennet, and the measure of wine necessary to harden a quart of milk will depend on this. Sometimes a spoonful will prove enough. There is no way to judge but by trying, as in using rennet for making cheese. The strength of this article varies exceedingly.

It is a very good, and more economical way to warm the milk a little, sweeten it, and add nothing but the rennet wine, and grate nutmeg over the top. Soda biscuit or butter crackers are good with wine custard.

Stained Froth.

Take the whites of three or four eggs, and cut them to a stiff froth, then beat into them the syrup of damsons, blood-peaches, or any highly colored preserve. This makes an elegant addition to a dish of soft custard. Some persons, when making custards, lay the white of eggs, cut in this way, upon the top of the boiling milk for a minute or two. This hardens it, and it is taken off upon a dish, and when the custard glasses are filled, a piece of it is laid upon the top of each.

* The Liquid Rennet prepared, with directions for use, by Wyeth & Brother Philadelphia, and sold by many of the grocers, is very convenient

TO PRESERVE FRUIT AND MAKE JELLIES.

A KETTLE should be kept on purpose. Brass, if very bright, will do. If acid fruit is preserved in a brass kettle which is not bright, it becomes poisonous. Bell-metal is better than brass, and the iron ware lined with porcelain, best of all.

The chief art in making nice preserves, and such as will keep, consists in the proper preparation of the syrup, and in boiling them *just long enough*. English housekeepers think it necessary to do them very slowly, and they boil their sweetmeats almost all day, in a jar set into a kettle of water. Brown sugar should be clarified. The crushed and granulated sugars are usually so pure as not to require being clarified. Loaf sugar is the best of any. Clean brown sugar makes very good sweatmeats for family use; but the best of sugar is, for most fruits, necessary, to make such as will be elegant, and keep long.

Sweetmeats should be boiled very gently lest the syrup should burn, and also that the fruit may become thoroughly penetrated with the sugar. Furious boiling breaks small and tender fruits. Too long boiling makes sweetmeats dark, and some kinds are rendered hard and tough.

Preserves keep best in glass jars, which have also this advantage, that you can see whether or not fermentation has commenced, without opening them. If stone jars are used, those with narrow mouths are best, as the air is most easily excluded from them; and small sized ones, containing only enough for once or twice, are best, as the frequent opening of a large jar, injures its entire contents, by the repeated admission of the air. When sweetmeats are cold, cover them close, and if not to be used soon, paste a paper over the top, and with a feather, brush over the paper with white of egg. When you have occasion to open them, if a thick, leather-looking mould covers them, they are in a good state, as nothing so effectually shuts out the air; but if they are specked here and there with mould, taste them, and if they are injured, it should be carefully removed, and the jar set into a kettle of water (not hot at first, lest the it should crack) and boiled. If the taste shows them to be uninjured, this mould may be the beginning of a leather-mould; therefore wait a few days, and look at them again, and scald them if necessary. A very good way of scalding them, and perhaps the easiest, is to put the jar (if it is of stone ware) into a brick oven as soon as the bread is drawn, and let it stand three or four hours. If the oven is quite warm a shorter time will do. This, or setting the jar into a kettle of water, as mentioned above, is much better than to scald them in the ordinary way, as they are exposed to the air when poured into the preserving kettle, and also when returned to the jar.

In making jellies, the sugar should be heated and should not be added, until the fruit-juice boils; and for this reason, — that the process is completed in much less time than if they are put together cold. Thus the diminution of the quantity, which long boiling occasions, is avoided, and the color of the jelly is much finer. Sometimes ladies complain that, for some inexplicable reason, they cannot make their currant jelly harden. The true reason was doubtless this, — that while making it, it was suffered to stop boiling for a few minutes. Let it boil gently but steadily, until by taking a little of it into a cold silver spoon, you perceive that it quickly hardens around the edges. A practised eye will readily judge by the movement of the liquid as it boils. Put jelly in little jars, cups, or tumblers; when it is cold, paste paper over the top and brush it over with white of egg. When *this* is used, the old method of putting brandy papers upon jelly is unnecessary. *Particular attention is requested to these suggestions in regard to making jellies.*

To make Syrup for Preserves.

Put a large teacup of water for every pound of sugar. As it begins to heat, stir it often. When it rises towards the top of the kettle, put in a cup of water; repeat this process two or three times, then set the kettle aside. If the sugar is perfectly pure, there will be no scum on the top. If there is scum, after it has stood a few minutes, take it off carefully. If the syrup then looks clear, it is not necessary to strain it.

To clarify sugar, put into every two pounds a beaten white of an egg. Five whites will do for a dozen pounds. Proportion the sugar and water as directed above, and after it has boiled enough take it from the fire, and let it stand ten minutes, then take the scum very carefully from the top, and pour off the syrup so gently as not to disturb the sediment. Have the kettle washed, return the syrup, and add the fruit. Some persons always strain the syrup through a flannel bag, but if the above directions are observed, it is not necessary. To use a flannel bag, always wring it very dry in hot water. This prevents a waste of the article strained. The bag should be soft, and not fulled up.

To preserve Apples.

Weigh equal quantities of Newtown pippins, and the best of sugar; allow one sliced lemon for every pound. Make a syrup, and then put in the apples. Boil them until they are tender; then lay them into the jars and boil the syrup until it will become a jelly. No other apple can be preserved without breaking. This keeps its shape, and is very beautiful. Quarter the apples, or take out the core and leave them whole, as you prefer. Other sour hard apples are very good preserved, but none keep as well, or are as handsome as the Newtown pippins.

Crab Apples.

Weigh them, and put them into water enough to almost, but not quite, cover them. Take them out when they have boiled three or four minutes, and put into the water as many pounds of sugar as you have of fruit, and boil it till clear, then set it aside till it is cold; skim it, and return the fruit to the kettle, and put it again on the fire. The moment it actually boils take it off; lay the fruit into the jar with care, so as not to break it.

Pine-apples.

Take equal quantities of pine-apple and the best of loaf sugar. Slice the pine-apple, put nearly or all the sugar over it. Put it in a deep pan, and let it stand all night. In the morning take the apple out and boil the syrup. When it begins to simmer, put the apple in and boil fifteen or twenty minutes. Tie a piece of white ginger in a bit of muslin, and boil it in the syrup before adding the apple. After boiling the whole ten or fifteen minutes, take out the apple and boil the syrup ten minutes longer; then pour it over the pine-apple. The apples should be ripe, and yet perfectly sound. If the syrup does not taste enough of ginger, boil it with the ginger till it suits the taste.

Pine-apples (without boiling).

Select large, fresh pine-apples. Pare them with a very sharp knife, having a thin blade. Carefully remove the little prickly eyes. Slice the fruit round and round about half an inch thick. Weigh a pound and a quarter of best granulated sugar, to a pound of fruit; and put into a glass jar a layer of sugar, and then a layer of fruit till it is filled. Make the layers of sugar very thick, else you will have a quantity left when the fruit is all laid in. Cover the jar close, and set it in a very cold place. This will keep perfectly, and have the taste of freshly sugared pine-apples a year afterward.

Blackberries.

To a pound of the low, running blackberries, allow a pound of fine sugar. Put them together in the preserving kettle, the fruit first, and the sugar on the top. These berries are so juicy that no water will be necessary; but they must begin very slowly to stew, and boil gently an hour. If blackberries are well done at first, they will not need scalding afterwards.

The high blackberries are not good preserved, but make an excellent syrup for medicinal purposes.

Currants.

Weigh equal quantities of sugar, and fruit stripped from the stems. Boil the fruit ten minutes, stirring it often, and crushing it. Add the sugar, and boil another ten minutes. Measure the time from the minute boiling commences. This keeps till currants come again. Clean brown sugar does very well. If it is to be used up in the course of the autumn, ten or twelve ounces of sugar to a pound of fruit is enough.

Cranberries.

Pour scalding water upon them, as this will make it much more easy to separate the defective ones from the good, than if they are washed in cold water. Measure the fruit, and allow two quarts of sugar for five of fruit. Boil the cranberries till they are soft in half as much water as fruit. Stir them very often. When they are soft add the sugar, and boil gently as possible half an hour more. They are very liable to burn, and therefore should be carefully attended to. If you like cranberry sauce very sweet, allow a pound of sugar for a pound of fruit.

Cranberries keep very well in a firkin of water in the cellar, and if so kept, can be stewed fresh at any time during the winter.

Damsons.

Wash, drain, and weigh them, put them into the kettle, and add the same weight of sugar and (to six or eight pounds) a pint of water. Boil them gently but steadily an hour; press the top ones down carefully, several times. They will break some, and the pricking each one with a needle before stewing them, makes little, if any difference. But they break less than other small plums, and are more solid. The syrup gives an elegant color to a beaten white of egg, for ornamenting custards or delicate puddings.

Other small sized blue plums are preserved in the same way.

Egg Plums.

To make the most elegant of all plum sweetmeats, take the Duane, or the Egg plums, ripe, but not very ripe. The skin can usually be pulled off. If you cannot remove it without tearing the fruit, pour on boiling water, and instantly pour it off, or lay them into a cullender, and dip boiling water over them once. Allow equal quantities of fruit and sugar, and make the syrup in the usual way. Then lay in a few plums at a time, and boil gently five minutes; lay them into a jar as you take them from the kettle, and when all are done, pour the boiling syrup over them. After two days, drain off the syrup, boil it, and pour it upon them again. Do this every two or three days till they look clear. Then, if you wish the syrup to be very thick, boil it half an hour, and when cold, pour it upon the plums.

Peaches.

Select peaches that are ripe, but not soft. Pour boiling water upon them, and let it stand five or six minutes; then pour it off, and pull off the skins. This is the easiest way, and the most economical, as none of the peach is wasted with the skin. In a lot of peaches for preserving, there may be a few that you will have to pare; but most of them will part with the skin when scalded, except the cling-stones.

Weigh equal quantities of fruit (with the stones in), and fine sugar, and put them together in an earthen pan over night. The next day pour off the syrup, and boil it a few minutes; then set off the kettle and remove the scum. Return the kettle to the fire, and when it boils lay the peaches into it. Boil them very slowly three quarters of an hour, then lay them into the jars; boil the syrup fifteen minutes more, and pour over them.

The blood peaches are a beautiful fruit when preserved. The yellow cling-stone is handsome, but very inconvenient as the fruit adheres so closely to the stone. Almost any kind of peach is good, stewed in half a pound of clean brown sugar to a pound of stoned fruit, and will keep several weeks in the autumn.

Pears.

Weigh three quarters of a pound of sugar for a pound of pears. Boil the fruit whole, with the stems on, in barely water enough to cover them, till they are tender, but not very soft. Then take them from the kettle, and put in the sugar, boil it ten or fifteen minutes, then set it off, and after removing the scum, put in the pears, and boil them till they begin to have a clear look. The difference in the size, and in the solidity of this fruit is so great that exact directions as to time cannot be given. When you have laid the pears into jars, boil the syrup another half hour, skim it if necessary, and then pour it upon the fruit. If you wish to give a more decided flavor to preserved pears, add peach water, or sliced lemons, when the syrup is boiling. Clean brown sugar does very well for preserving this fruit.

In selecting pears to preserve, choose such as are rather acid. The sweet ones are best baked. The *Iron pears*, if you will have patience to boil them long enough, make an excellent preserve. Divide them into halves or quarters if you choose. But they are often done whole. Boil them in just water enough, covered close, two or three hours. Make a syrup as directed above, and boil them in it an hour and a half.

Quinces.

Procure the apple, or orange quince. It is much less apt to be hard, when preserved, than the pear quince. Pare and core the fruit, and allow equal weights of fruit and fine sugar. Boil quinces in water enough to cover them, till they are tender; then take them out one by one with a silver spoon and lay them separately on a flat dish. Make a syrup and save all the water not used for it. When it is ready, return the fruit to the kettle, and boil it slowly three quarters of an hour, then lay it in jars, and pour the syrup over it. It is a good way to cut part of the quinces in halves, and preserve a part of them whole. Remove the cores with a fruit-corer, or if you have not this, use a common tap-borer; it answers the purpose very well.

Quinces with Sweet Apples.

To increase the quantity, without an addition of sugar, have as many large fair sweet apples pared, quartered, and cored, as will weigh one third as much as the quince. When the quince is boiled enough take it out, and put the sweet apples into the syrup, and boil them till they begin to look red and clear; an hour and a half will not be too long. Then put the quince and apple into the jars in alternate layers. The flavor of the quince will so entirely penetrate the apple, that the one cannot be distinguished from the other, and the sugar necessary to preserve the quince, will be sufficient for the apple.

Quinces (without boiling the Syrup).

Weigh twelve ounces of sugar for every pound of fruit. Boil the quinces in water enough to cover them, until they are so soft that care is necessary not to break them, in taking them out. Drain the pieces a little as you take them from the water, and put them into a jar in alternate layers with the sugar. Cover the jar close *as soon as it is filled*, and paste a paper over the top. Quinces done in this way are very elegant, about the color of oranges, and probably will not need scalding to keep them as long as you wish. If any tendency to fermentation appears, as may be the case by the following April or May, set the jar (if it is stone) into a brick oven after bread has been baked, and the quince will become a beautiful light red, and will keep almost any length of time, *and never become hard.*

It may be well to mention that in damp houses, none of the fruits preserved without boiling keep as well as those which are boiled. I have known a very few instances in which persons who were skilful in all these things did not succeed in preserving fruits in this way.

The water in which quinces are boiled should be saved. Boil the parings in it for a short time, if you intend to make a jelly, as long boiling them will make the water less clear. If you do not make jelly, boil the parings a good while, then strain off the water, and when it is cold bottle it. It will keep without the addition of sugar two or three weeks, and will give a fine flavor to apple-pies or sauce. There is so much richness in the parings of quinces that they should never be thrown away without being boiled. The fruit should therefore be washed and wiped before it is pared, and all defective parts removed.

[The pear quince, though it becomes hard when preserved, and therefore is not as good for that purpose as the orange quince, is very rich, and makes fine marmalade.]

Marmalade.

Wash and wipe the quinces, and take out any dark spots there may be on the skins. Cut them up without paring, cores and all; cover them with water in the preserving kettle, and boil them until they are soft enough to be rubbed through a coarse hair sieve. Then weigh equal quantities of pulp and refined sugar, and boil the mixture an hour, stirring it steadily.

Made with nice brown sugar, it is very good, though not quite as handsome. When brown sugar is used it should be stirred an hour and a half.

Put it into moulds or deep plates, and when it is cold put a paper over it, pasted at the edges, and brushed with white of egg. Marmalade can be kept for almost any length of time.

Strawberries.

Take large strawberries not extremely ripe; weigh equal quantities of fruit and best sugar; lay the fruit in a dish, and sprinkle half the sugar over it; shake the dish a little, that the sugar may touch all the fruit. Next day make a syrup of the remainder of the sugar and the juice which you can pour off from the fruit in the pan, and as it boils lay in the strawberries, and boil them gently twenty minutes or half an hour.

Another.

Weigh equal quantities of fruit and sugar, and put them together over night. The next day boil the strawberries long enough to scald without shrinking them, — six or eight minutes after they commence boiling. Then skim them out, and boil away the syrup half an hour; then pour it, hot, upon the strawberries.

Apple Jam (which will keep for years).

Weigh equal quantities of brown sugar and good sour apples. Pare and core them, and chop them fine. Make a syrup of the sugar, and clarify it very thoroughly; then add the apples, the grated peel of two or three lemons, and a few pieces of white ginger. Boil it till the apple looks clear and yellow. This resembles foreign sweetmeats. The ginger is essential to its peculiar excellence.

Pine-Apple Jam.

Grate sound but ripe pine-apples, and to a pound put three quarters of a pound of loaf sugar. Make a syrup and boil the grated pine-apple in it fifteen minutes.

Grape Jam.

Boil grapes very soft, and strain them through a sieve. Weigh the pulp thus obtained, and put a pound of crushed sugar to a pound of pulp. Boil it twenty minutes, stirring it often. The common wild grape is much the best for this use.

Quince Jam.

Weigh twelve ounces of brown sugar to one pound of quince. Boil the fruit in as little water as will do, until it is sufficiently soft to break easily; then pour off all the water and mash it with a spoon until entirely broken; put in the sugar, and boil twenty minutes, stirring it very often.

Another.

Chop a pound of quince (not boiled) in a pound of best sugar. When chopped fine, boil it twenty minutes. If you have some of the water in which quinces have been boiled, put in a gill;

if you have not this, use pure water. This is very good, but not as easily digested as the other.

Raspberry Jam.

Pick the fruit over very carefully, as it is more apt than any other to be infested with worms. Weigh equal quantities of fruit and sugar; put the fruit into the kettle, or preserving pan, break it with a ladle, and stir continually. Let it boil quickly four or five minutes, then add the sugar, and simmer slowly a little while. The fruit, preserved in this way, retains its fresh taste much better than if the sugar is added at first. It is scarcely inferior to raspberries gathered from the vines. Some persons prefer to add currants or currant juice. A quart of currant juice to four quarts of raspberries is a good proportion. Boil it up, and put the fruit into it. If you wish to add currants, take fresh, ripe ones, a quart to three quarts of raspberries.

Strawberry Jam.

Put three pounds of sugar to two quarts of strawberries. Sprinkle the sugar upon the fruit, and let it stand an hour or two; then boil it twenty minutes, and meantime bruise the fruit with a spoon or ladle.

Apple Jelly.

Take any juicy, sour apples; wash and wipe them very clean, and cut them up without paring or taking out the cores. Put them into an earthen jar or baking pan with a very little water, and cover it with a paste of bread dough, rolled thin; (this keeps in the steam more effectually than a plate or lid). Put it in the oven after the bread is baked, and let it remain several hours. Then pour the whole into a linen bag, suspended in such a manner that it can be left to drip for some time. Put a pound of sugar to a pint of syrup; add any thing which is preferred, to flavor it. Boil ten minutes.

Another.

Take good sour apples, wash and wipe them, cut out any black spots upon the skin, and cut them up without paring or coring. Much of the richness of the apple is in the skin and core. Boil them in water enough to cover them, and when they become very soft, put the whole into a coarse linen bag, and suspend it between two chairs, with a pan under it, and leave it until it ceases to drip. Then press it a very little. Allow a pound of fine sugar to a pint of apple-syrup. If you choose, add the juice of a lemon to every quart of syrup. Boil up the apple-syrup, and skim it; heat the sugar in a dish in the stove oven, and add it as the syrup boils up, after being skimmed. Boil it gently twenty minutes or half an hour. Put it up in cups, tumblers, or moulds.

Crab-Apple Jelly.

Boil the fruit in water enough to cover it, until it is perfectly soft; then proceed just as directed in the last receipt.

Barberry Jelly.

This is made by boiling the fruit until the water is very strongly flavored with it; then put a pound of best sugar to a pint of juice. It should boil a little longer than currant or quince jelly.

Cranberry Jelly.

Wash and pick over the fruit carefully, and boil it till very soft in water enough to cover it. Then strain it through a hair sieve, and weigh equal quantities of the pulp and fine sugar. Boil it gently, and with care that it does not burn, fifteen or twenty minutes.

Currant Jelly.

Pick over the fruit, but leave it on the stems. Put it into the preserving kettle, and break it with a ladle or spoon, and when it is hot, squeeze it in a coarse linen bag until you can press out no more juice. Then weigh a pound of sugar to a pint of juice. Sift the sugar, and heat it as hot as possible without dissolving or burning; boil the juice five minutes very fast, and while boiling add the hot sugar, stir it well, and when it has boiled again five minutes, set it off. The time must be strictly observed. Jelly to eat with meat does very well made with brown sugar, but must boil longer.

Another (without boiling).

Squeeze the currants in a coarse linen cloth, without taking off the stems. Weigh the juice, and allow a pound for a pound. The sugar should be sifted, and stirred in with the hand until it feels smooth and well dissolved. Put it into glasses, and set them in the sun near a window for two or three days. Then cover as directed for preserves and jellies. This will taste like newly made currant jelly at the end of a year, if kept in a cool and dry place. It will not keep well in a damp house.

Quince Jelly.

Take the water in which quinces have been boiled for preserving and for marmalade, and boil the clean parings until they are soft. (See directions in the receipt for preserving quinces without boiling the syrup). Then strain the water while very hot through a flannel bag, and allow a pound of best sugar for every pint. Put the sugar on a dish into the stove oven to heat; boil up the quince water; if any scum rises, take it off, and then stir in the hot sugar, and boil it slowly, but steadily, twenty minutes, or half an hour. The time necessary will depend somewhat on the water being more or less strongly flavored with the fruit.

To Can Fruit.

Prepare peaches just as for preserving in the old way, except that it is best to take out the stones. Put part of the kernels in with the fruit. Add a third of a pound of white sugar for a pound of fruit, several hours before stewing it. Boil it gently until cooked. Allow the same proportion of sugar for strawberries, blackberries, raspberries, cherries, plums, quinces, and pears. These last two to be stewed longer than other fruits.

If you use tin cans, procure those which are made of the best tin. Gilmore's, patented in 1858, are most easily closed, the air being effectually excluded without soldering or the use of rosin.

Put the cans into hot water, take out and drain quickly one at a time, set it on the stove by the side of the preserving kettle, fill it full, and instantly put on the cover and turn down the screw. Put the cans in a cool, dry place.

If you use cans which are closed with rosin, proceed in the same way. Have the rosin ready hot, and dip it into the groove with a small tin ladle made for the purpose. Avoid getting any of the rosin into the fruit, as a single drop will make the whole contents of the can bitter. Besides, it is poisonous. To open a can closed in this way, set it where the rosin will become a little warm, so that the lid can be easily removed. If it is melted, it will be difficult to prevent some of it from falling into the open mouth of the can.

Glass cans are good, but their liability to be broken in the heating process of preparing and filling them is an objection to their use. The essentials to success are, *to have the can hot, to fill it full, and to close it immediately.*

BAKED AND STEWED FRUITS.

THESE are economical, excellent, and healthy; and it is well worth while for every family possessing only a plot of ground large enough for two trees, to set out a pear and sweet apple tree.

Steamed Sweet Apples.

Wash and wipe a pailful of sweet apples; put them into a porcelain kettle, with cold water enough to come half-way toward the top, cover them and boil them slowly as possible an

10 *

hour. Then try them with a fork, and turn down the upper side of those which lie on the top. If they are considerably softened, scatter a coffee-cup of brown sugar over them, cover them close, and let them remain boiling another hour. Very large apples need half an hour more.

Baked Sweet Apples.

If they are of a good kind, they are very nice baked in an earthen dish, which is better than tin. If you cook them in a stove, there should be a little water in the pan, else the juice will burn and be lost. They are best done in a brick oven. Put them into a jar with no water or sugar, but cover them close, and bake five or six hours. A rich syrup will be found in the bottom of the jar, and the appearance and flavor of the apples will be very fine.

Baked Sour Apples.

These are best baked in a stove. They require only an hour. There should be a little water in the dish. Just before they are done, sprinkle a little brown sugar upon them, dip the syrup over them, and cover them close till wanted for the table. They are good done in this way to eat at breakfast or tea; and also at dinner, with any meat requiring apple sauce. Take out the cores before baking them if you choose.

Baked Pears.

The common early pears are very good put into a jar without paring, and with a teacup of molasses to every two quarts of pears. But little water is necessary. Bake them five or six hours in a brick oven; two in a range or stove. If you wish them more delicate, pare them, and put a teacup of sugar instead of molasses. The later and larger fall pears are very nice baked in a dish; but most kinds of heavy winter pears cannot be baked so as to be tender.

Boiled Cider Apple-Sauce.

Take apples, sweet and sour together, that will not keep

long, and pare a large quantity. When finished, wash and put them into a large brass kettle, in which you have turned down an old dish or large plate, that will nearly cover the bottom; this is to prevent the apple from burning. After you have put in all the apples, pour in a quart of cider (boiled as directed in the receipt for boiled cider) to every pailful of apples. After it has boiled an hour or two, add molasses in the proportion of two quarts to every four pails of apples. If you have refuse quinces, a peck of them gives a fine flavor to a large kettle of apple-sauce. The best way to boil apple-sauce is to put the kettle over the fire at night, and let the apple become partly done before bed-time. When you leave it for the night, see that the fire lies in such a way, that all parts of the apple boil equally, and that no brands can fall.* Burn charcoal or peat if you have it, as either of these will make a steady fire, and may be left without danger from snapping. The chief things to be observed, are, that there is not too much fire, that it lies safely, and that it will afford a moderate heat several hours. In the morning the apple-sauce will be of a fine red color, and must then be put away in firkins or stone jars. *Never use potter's ware* for this purpose.

Sweet Apple Marmalade.

This is made by boiling sweet apples alone, in cider made of sweet apples, and boiled down so as to be very rich. The sauce is in this case strained warm through a very coarse sieve or riddle, and boiled again a little while; or it may be put into deep dishes and set into the oven after the bread is drawn.

Coddled Apples.

Take fair early apples, wipe them, lay them in a preserving kettle, and put to half a peck a coffee-cup of brown sugar, and

---

* As the open fire-place is now seldom in use, these directions will not often be apropos. But where a range or coal stove is used, a large kettle of apple-sauce can, with care, be done well, on the top with the cover under it.

half a pint of water. Cover them and boil them gently, until they are tender and penetrated with the sugar.

They may be done quite as well in a jar in the oven, but care must be taken that they are not cooked too much. Early apples will bake with a very moderate heat.

Common Family Apple-Sauce.

Let your stock of apples be picked over several times in the course of the winter, and all the defective ones taken out. Let the good parts of these be pared, and if not used for pies, be made into apple-sauce. Boil it in a preserving kettle. After it is tender, add a pint bowl of brown sugar, and boil it gently fifteen minutes longer. Towards spring, when apples become tasteless, a teaspoonful of tartaric acid, dissolved in a little water, should be added to a gallon of apple.

Boiled Pears.

These are eaten with roast meat instead of apple or cranberry sauce. Choose fair, smooth ones; put them into cold water and boil them whole, without paring and without sugar. It will take an hour, or an hour and a half, according to the size of the fruit.

To Stew Dried Apples or Peaches.

Wash them in two or three waters, and put them to soak in rather more water than will cover them, as they absorb a great deal. After soaking two hours, put them into a preserving kettle in the same water, and with a lemon or orange cut up; boil them till very tender; when they rise up in the kettle press them down with a skimmer or spoon, but do not stir them. When they are tender, add clean brown sugar, and boil fifteen or twenty minutes longer.

Dried apples are rendered tasteless by being strained or stirred so as to break them up; and they are also injured by soaking over night.

If they are to be used for pies, there should be more sugar

added than for sauce, and a small piece of butter stirred in while they are hot. Nutmeg and clove are good spices for dried apple-pies.

Dried peaches are done in the same way, only the lemon and spice are omitted.

HOW TO SELECT AND TAKE CARE OF BEEF, MUTTON, LAMB, VEAL, AND PORK.

Ox beef is the best; next to this the flesh of an heifer; and both are in perfection during the first three months of the year. Choose that, the lean of which is red and of a fine grain, and the fat of which is white.* In cold weather, if you have a large family, it is good economy to buy a quarter. The hind quarter is considered best. Have the butcher cut it up. Pack the roasting pieces, which you do not want soon, in a barrel of snow, and set it where it will not melt. It is not necessary to freeze the meat first. The leg will furnish, besides a piece to cook alamode, two or three to smoke. The thin pieces at the end of the ribs are good corned, and the flank also; or it may be used for mince pies. The shank, although it has but little meat, is very good for some purposes. It should be cut up into several pieces and boiled four or five hours, no matter how long. There is a great deal of marrow and fat in it which, when cold, should be taken off and clarified for various uses. The meat is good used as is directed in the receipt for brawn, and the liquor makes excellent soup and gravies.

The best roasting pieces of beef are the sirloin, the second

---

* The flesh of diseased cattle is sometimes sold in city markets. Therefore never buy beef the fat of which is very yellow, nor mutton and lamb unless the fat is white. Yellow fat indicates that the meat is of an unhealthy kind.

cut in the fore quarter, and the rump. If you buy a sirloin for a family of six or eight, get eight or ten pounds. Cut off the thin end in which there is no bone. It is very good corned, and not very good roasted. The roasting piece will still be large enough for the family dinner, and the corned piece will do for another day, with a pudding or another small dish of meat. The back part of the rump is a convenient and economical piece, especially for a small family. It is a long and rather narrow piece, weighing about ten pounds, and contains less fat and bone than any other, equally good, in the ox. The thickest end affords nice steaks, and next to them is a good roasting piece, and the thinnest end which contains the bone, is very good corned, or for a soup. The whole is an excellent piece for roasting, in case so large a one is needed.

The spring is the best season for mutton. That which is not very large is to be preferred. It should be of a good red and white, and fine grained. There is a great difference between mutton and lamb killed from a pasture, and that which has been driven a distance to market.

Lamb is best in July and August.

Veal is best in the spring. It should look white and be fat. The breast is particularly nice stuffed; the loin should be roasted. The leg is an economical piece, as you can take off cutlets from the large end, make broth of the shank, and stuff and roast the centre.

Roasting pieces of all kinds of ribbed meat, except beef, should be jointed by the butcher, else the carving will be extremely difficult.

Always provide a sharp knife for carving. The juices of meat are extracted by its being *haggled.* An invalid, speaking of the kindness of a neighbor in sending him some slices of corned beef, said, "They were cut with a *sharp* knife." For the sake of economy, if for no other reason, carve smoothly, and only as much as is wanted at first. It is easy to cut more for replenishing plates; and meat is far better not to lie sliced in the dish. If no more is cut than is used, a handsome piece may often be reserved for the next day; whereas if all is cut up it cannot be so good, and some of it will certainly be wasted.

Ham and tongue should be sliced very thin.

Pork, to be the best, should not be more than a year old. The chine is the best roasting piece; the spare-ribs are very sweet food, but too rich to be healthy. The shoulder is good roasted, stuffed with bread and sage. If too large, half of it can be laid a week or two in brine, and will be good boiled, to eat cold. It is well for a small family, in November to buy half of a spring pig; this will furnish several nice pieces to roast, strips for salting, a ham and shoulder for smoking, and *leaf* enough for a pot or two of lard, besides remnants for sausage meat.

In winter, all meat may be kept a long time; and, with the exception of pork, is much better for it; therefore it is easier to furnish a table without waste in winter than in summer. Meat will keep in an ice-house or a good refrigerator several days in hot weather; if you have neither, take your meat the moment it is brought in, wipe it dry if at all damp, and hang it in the cellar, sprinkling first a little pepper and salt over it, especially over the parts which flies are most apt to visit. In mutton and lamb, these are the tenderloin and the large end of the leg. The pepper and salt will also tend to preserve the meat from taint.

If you wish to keep it longer than two days, wrap it in a piece of cloth (no matter if it is very thin), and lay it in a charcoal bin, and throw a shovel of coal over it. A leg of mutton will keep several days wrapped in a cloth which has been dipped in vinegar, laid upon the ground of a dry cellar.

Meat that is to be salted for immediate use, should, if the weather is cool, be hung up a day or two first.* Where a large quantity of beef is to be salted, a different method is pursued. In winter, unless you wish to keep meat several weeks, place it where it will be cold without freezing. Mutton never looks as nice after being frozen hard; it has a dark, uninviting appear-

---

* See directions for salting meat, page 162.

ance. To thaw frozen meat, bring it over night into a warm room. If this has been forgotten, lay it, early in the morning, into cold water. If meat is put to roast, boil, or broil, before being entirely thawed, it will be tough. It is best to preserve fowls without freezing. They will keep very well packed in snow; the liver, &c., being taken out and laid by themselves in the snow, and the body filled with it.

Meat that has been kept perfectly clean, or a beef steak just cut off, should not be washed; but, generally, it is necessary to wash a roasting piece. Pork having the rind on, needs great care in washing and scraping, to make it fit to cook.

Trim off the superfluous fat from beef, mutton, and fresh pork before cooking it.

Tough steak is made more tender by being pounded with a rolling-pin; but some of the juice of the meat is lost by the operation.

STOCK FOR GRAVIES AND SOUPS.

Wash a leg or shin of beef very clean, crack the bone in two or three places, put with it any trimmings you may have of meat or fowls, such as gizzards, necks, &c.; cover them with cold water in a stew-pan that shuts close. The moment it begins to simmer, skim it carefully till it boils up. Then add half a pint of cold water, which will make the remaining scum rise, and skim it again and again, till no more appears, and the broth looks perfectly clear. Then put in a moderate sized carrot, cut up small, two turnips, a head of celery, and one large or two small onions. Stir it several times that it may not burn, or stick at the bottom. Herbs and spices are not to be added until the broth is used for gravies for particular dishes. After these vegetables are added, set the pan where the broth will boil very slowly for four or five hours. Then strain it through a sieve into a stone pan or jar, and when cold, cover it, and set it in an ice-house or some other very cool place. The meat thus stewed may be used as directed for minced meat in the chapter on Common Dishes, &c., p. 187.

ON ROASTING MEAT.

If meat is to be roasted before the fire, allow a quarter of an hour for the cooking of every pound in warm weather, and in winter twenty minutes. Flour it well, and put two or three gills of water in the roaster. Put the bony side to the fire first, and do not place it very near. If meat is scorched in the beginning, it cannot be roasted through afterwards, without burning. Turn it often, and when all parts are slightly cooked, place it nearer the fire. When about half done, flour it again. Baste it very often. Salt it half an hour before serving it.

It is not well to salt meat at first, as salt extracts the juices. In roasting all meats, the art depends chiefly on flouring thoroughly, basting frequently, and turning so often as not to allow any part to burn.

To roast in a cooking stove, it is necessay to attend carefully to the fire, lest the meat should burn. Lay it into the pan with three or four gills of water in it. Turn the pan around often, that all the parts may roast equally. When it is about half done, flour it again, turn it over that the lower side may become brown. If the water wastes so that the pan becomes nearly dry, add a little hot water.

Among the *little* things which are worthy the attention of a housekeeper, is that of having a dinner served *hot.* It is often the case, that a well-cooked dinner loses much of its excellence, by a want of care in this particular. All the meat and vegetable dishes should be heated, and in winter the plates should also be warmed.

ON BOILING MEAT.

It is a common impression that boiled meat requires very little attention; and probably one reason why many persons dislike it, may be, that it is seldom so carefully cooked as roast meat.

If proper attention can be secured, meat should not be boiled in a cloth. But if the pot is not likely to be thoroughly skimmed, it is best to use one. All kinds of meat are best put over the fire in cold water, in the proportion of a quart to every pound of meat. The fibres are thus gradually dilated, and the meat is more tender. The fire should be moderate, and the water should heat gradually. If it boils in thirty or forty minutes it is soon enough.

All kinds of meat, poultry, and fish should boil very slowly. Fast boiling makes meat tough and hard. Allow twenty minutes to a pound of fresh meat; but a little more time is required to cook a hind than a fore quarter. Salt meat should boil longer than fresh; allow forty minutes for every pound.

A tongue that has been cured with saltpetre and smoked, should soak over night, and be boiled at least four hours; it is not easy to boil it too much, and nothing is more disagreeable or indigestible than a tongue not well boiled. A ham, if very salt, should also be soaked over night, and should be boiled from three to five hours, according to the size, unless you prefer to cook it the last half of the time in the oven, as is directed in the receipt for cooking a ham or shoulder. This is the better way. Calf's head should lie in a great deal of water several hours; and if large, will require two hours and a half to boil.

The two things most important in boiling meat, are, to boil it gently; and to skim it until no more froth rises. To do this, have a skimmer or a spoon and dish, and the moment the froth begins to rise, which will be when the water becomes very hot, skim it off. Put in a pint of cold water, which will cause it to rise more freely, and continue to skim it every minute or two, till all is taken off.* If the water boils fast before you begin to take off the froth, it will all return into the water, and will adhere to the meat, and make it look badly. Some nice housekeepers throw a handful of flour into the kettle to prevent scum from adhering to meat. Calf's head, and veal need more skimming than any other meat; but all kinds need to be skimmed several times. If the water boils away so that the meat is not covered, add more, as the part which lies above the water will have a dark appearance. Remember to put salt in the water for boiling fresh meat or fish.

DIRECTIONS FOR MAKING GRAVIES.

Many young housekeepers who succeed well in most kinds of cooking, are a long time in finding out how to make good gravy. To have it free from fat is the most important thing. For a small family it is not necessary to prepare stock. The water in which fresh meat, a tongue, or piece of beef slightly salted, has been boiled, should be saved for this purpose, and for use in various economical dishes. In cold weather it will keep a good while, and in warm weather, several days in a refrigerator.

The way to use meat liquor, or the stock for which a receipt is given, is this: In case you are roasting beef, mutton, lamb, or pork, pour off entirely, into a dish, half an hour before the dinner hour, all the contents of the dripping pan or roaster, and set it away in a cold place; then put into the roaster two or three gills of the meat liquor or stock; if you have cold gravy, or drippings of a previous day, remove all the fat from the top, and put the liquid that remains at the bottom into the pan.

---

* Froth from fat meat should be put into the soap-grease.

Wet some browned flour smooth, and when you take up the meat, set the pan on the top of the stove. The gravy will immediately boil, and the wet flour must then be stirred in. It will boil away fast, therefore see that it does not stand too long.

For veal and venison, gravy is made differently because there is but little fat on these meats, and what there is, is not gross. Put into the roaster, or dripping pan, some of the meat liquor or stock, when you first put the meat to roast, and if it is done in a stove or range, add a little more in case it boils away. When it is done, set the dripping pan on the stove, and having stirred in the wet flour, add a piece of butter half the size of an egg, and stir until it is all melted, else it will make the gravy oily.

Gravy for poultry is made by boiling the giblets (necks, gizzards, hearts, and livers) by themselves in five or six gills of water. Skim them carefully, as a great deal of scum will rise. After an hour, or hour and a half, take them out, and pour the water into the dripping-pan. Mash, or chop the liver fine, and when you make the gravy, add this, and a bit of butter, some pepper, the wet flour, and, if you choose, a little sweet marjoram.

The fat that roasts out of a turkey should be dipped off with a spoon before these ingredients are added. It is too gross to be palatable or healthy.

In making gravy for a goose, pour off all the drippings as in roasting beef or pork, and put in some of the stock or meat liquor.

It is best to brown a quart of flour at once. Put it into a spider, and set it in the stove oven, or on the top; stir it often lest it should burn. When it is a light brown, put it into a jar or wide-mouthed bottle.

Drawn Butter.

Take a small cupful of butter, and rub into it half a tablespoonful of flour, then pour upon it about a gill of boiling water, stirring it fast. Set it upon the coals, and let it boil up once. If it is suffered to remain boiling it will become oily. Some persons prefer to use boiling milk instead of water. Parsley is an improvement. Tie a few sprigs together with a thread and throw them for a minute into boiling water, then cut them fine, and add them to the butter.

STUFFING OR DRESSING OF VARIOUS KINDS.

For a fillet of veal, a turkey, chickens, partridges, and pigeons, take light bread enough to make three gills of fine crumbs. Cut off the crust and lay by itself in just enough boiling water to soften it. Rub the soft part into fine crumbs between your hands; put in a teaspoonful of salt, one or two of powdered sweet marjoram, a little pepper, and a piece of butter half as large as an egg; add the softened crusts, and mix the whole together very thoroughly. If it is not moist enough, add a spoonful or two of milk. Taste it, and if there is not seasoning enough, add more.

To put it into the fowl neatly, and without waste, use a teaspoon.

If stuffing is made of pounded crackers, the seasoning is the same, but crackers swell so much that two gills will be plenty for a turkey. Milk will be necessary to mix it, and also a beaten egg to make it cohere. Some people prefer dressing made of crackers, but it is hard and not as healthy as that which is made of good bread, without an egg.

Stuffing for ducks is usually made with a little finely chopped onion in it. For a goose, sage should be used instead of sweet-marjoram.

For a pig, or a shoulder of fresh pork, make a dressing without butter, moistened with milk, and seasoned with pepper, salt, and a good deal of powdered sage. This tends to prevent the deleterious effects of such rich meat upon the stomach.

For a dressing for alamode beef, and stewed lamb, salt pork, chopped fine, is substituted for butter, and for a fillet of veal it is very well to make it in the same way.

VEGETABLES AND SAUCES APPROPRIATE TO DIFFERENT MEATS.

POTATOES are good with all meats. With fowls they are nicest mashed. Sweet potatoes are most appropriate with roast meat, as also are onions, winter squash, cucumbers, and asparagus.

Carrots, parsnips, turnips, greens, and cabbage are eaten with boiled meat; and corn, beets, peas, and beans are appropriate to either boiled or roasted meat. Mashed turnip is good with roasted pork, and with boiled meats.

Tomatoes are good with every kind of meat, but specially so with roasts. Apple-sauce with roast pork; cranberry-sauce with beef, fowls, veal, and ham. Currant jelly is most appropriate with roast mutton. Pickles are good with all roast meats, and capers or nasturtiums with boiled lamb or mutton. Horseradish and lemons are excellent with veal.

DIRECTIONS FOR COOKING MEATS.

To Roast Beef.

SEE the directions for roasting meat.

Beef Steak.

The best slices are cut from the rump, or through the sirloin.

The round is seldom tender enough, and is very good cooked in other ways. Do not cut your slices very thick. Have the gridiron perfectly clean. Set it over moderately hot coals at first, and turn the steaks in less than a minute. Turn them repeatedly. If the fat makes a blaze under the gridiron, put it out by sprinkling fine salt on it. Steaks will broil in about seven minutes. Have ready a hot dish, and sprinkle each piece with salt, and a little pepper; lay on small pieces of butter, and cover close. This is a much better way than to melt the butter in the dish before taking up the meat. Some persons keep a small pair of tongs on purpose to turn beef-steaks, as using a fork wastes the juice. Steaks should be served hot as possible.

Stuffed Beef Steak.

Take a thick and tender slice of rump, of about two pounds weight; make two gills of stuffing, of crumbs of bread, pepper, salt, and powdered clove, or sweet marjoram, as you choose; roll the dressing up in the steak, wind a piece of twine around it, taking care to secure the ends. Have ready a kettle or deep stew-pan, with a slice or two of pork fried crisp. Take out the pork and lay in the steak, and turn it on every side, until it is brown. Then put in two gills of the stock, or of water in which meat has been boiled; sprinkle in a little salt, cover close, and stew slowly an hour and a half. Add more water after a while, if it becomes too dry. Some persons like the addition of chopped onion. There should, however, be very little; half of a small one is enough. When nearly done, add half a gill of catsup. When you take up the meat, unwind the string carefully, so as not to unroll it. Lay it in a fricassee dish, thicken the gravy, if not thick enough already, and pour it over the meat. Cut the meat in slices through the roll.

Tomato Steak.

Take two pounds of beef; cut it in small strips, and put it into the pot with seven medium-sized tomatoes. Stew it very slowly. Add a dessert spoonful of sugar, salt, a little clove, and, just before you take it up, a dessert spoonful of butter. If you have tomato catsup, add a little, and if you like chopped onion, that also. Very tender beef is, of course, to be preferred; but that which is tough becomes more palatable in this than in almost any other way. This dish is quite as good, if not better, heated over the next day.

Alamode Beef (in a plain way).

Take a thick piece of flank, or, if most convenient, the thickest part of the round, weighing six or eight pounds, for a small family of four or five persons. Cut off the strips of coarse fat upon the edge, make incisions in all parts, and fill them with a stuffing made of bread, salt pork chopped, pepper, and sweet marjoram. Push whole cloves here and there into the meat; roll it up, fasten it with skewers, and wind a strong twine or tape about it. Have ready a pot in which you have fried to a crisp three or four slices of salt pork; take out the pork, lay in the beef, and brown every side. When well browned, add hardly water enough to cover it, chop a large onion fine, add eighteen or twenty cloves, and boil it gently, but steadily, three or four hours, according to the size. The water should boil away so as to make a rich gravy, but be careful it does not burn. When you take up the beef, add browned flour to the gravy, if it needs to be thickened.

Another (more rich).

Take seven or eight pounds of the upper part of the round, cut off the coarse fat upon the side, and make deep incisions in every part. To a pint bowl of bread crumbs, put pepper, powdered clove, a small nutmeg, a teaspoonful of salt, some whole allspice, a large spoonful of butter, and, if you choose, a very little chopped salt pork, and two beaten eggs. Mix these ingredients well together, and fill the incisions, but reserve a part of the stuffing. Put in two or three skewers horizontally, near the edges, and tie twine across to keep in the stuffing. Push whole cloves into the meat here and there. Lay it, when thus prepared, into a bake-pan or stew-pan, having a lid which may be heated; put in water enough just to cover it, and set it where it will simmer, but not quite boil. Have the lid heated, and a few embers laid over it. After two hours, pour upon the top the stuffing which you reserved, heat the lid again, and cover the meat. Let it stew two hours more. If the gravy is too thin, add browned flour and boil it up again. Some persons use red wine, but it is very good without. Half the quantity of meat and stuffing for a small family.

Stewed Brisket of Beef.

Put three or four pounds of brisket into a kettle, and cover it with water. Take off the scum as it rises. Let it boil steadily two hours. Then take it from the pot and brown it with butter in a spider. When it is browned on every side, return it to the kettle, and stew it gently five hours more. Add more water if it boils away. Put in a carrot and a turnip or two, cut small, an onion also; a few cloves, and salt and pepper as you think necessary. Half an hour before dinner add tomato or mushroom catsup. To serve it, lay the beef upon a dish, and strew capers over it. The water in which it was stewed is a nice soup.

Stewed Beef (plain).

Take a square piece of beef from the best part of the round, weighing four or five pounds, and put it into water enough to cover it. When the water has been well skimmed, put in salt, two turnips, two carrots, and two onions, chopped small, and, if you choose, add half a dozen cloves. Boil very gently four or five hours. A short time before dinner, add a teaspoonful of sweet marjorum, half a cup of tomato ketchup, and a table-spoonful of flour wet smooth in cold water. Serve in a deep platter. This is a very economical dish. The beef is very good cold, and the soup excellent.

To Boil Corned Beef.

Wash it thoroughly, and put it into a pot that will hold plenty of water. The water should be cold; the same care is necessary in skimming it as for fresh meat. It is not too much to allow forty minutes for every pound, after it has begun to boil. The goodness of corned beef depends much on its being boiled gently and long. If it is to be eaten cold, lay it into a coarse earthen dish or pan, and over it a piece of board the size of the meat. Upon this put a clean stone or some other heavy weight. Salt meat is very much improved by being pressed.

To Roast Mutton.

Any part may be roasted, but the leg is the best. Allow fifteen minutes for a pound, and do according to the directions for roasting meat.

To Boil a Leg of Mutton or Lamb.

Cut off the shank bone. Have water enough to cover the meat. If the pot is well skimmed, the water will make excellent broth for another day.

A leg of lamb is a very nice dish if boiled well. It requires a little more time in proportion to the size than mutton, as mutton is good done rare, while lamb is neither good or healthy, unless well done.

Most people like capers, and drawn butter with mutton and lamb, and cut parsley added is an improvement.

Mutton or Lamb Steaks.

Have the leg cut into steaks at the market, or by the butcher. If this has not been done, you can do it yourself with a sharp knife. Cut through the largest part first; have the slices about the thickness of your finger; separate them from the bone neatly. Broil exactly like beef steak. The bone and fragments which are left will make a good broth.

Roast Lamb.

If it is a hind quarter, and very fat, take off the thickest from the kidneys; place it on the spit, or in the dripping-pan as it should lie on the dish, slightly drawn up. Do exactly as in roasting beef. An hour and a half will suffice to roast a quarter weighing five or six pounds.

The breast of lamb is very sweet and requires about as much roasting as the hind quarter.

Stewed or Alamode Lamb.

Pick off all the fat from a nice leg of lamb, or small leg of mutton. Cut off the shank, make deep incisions in various parts of the inside; fill them with stuffing made of crumbs of bread, salt pork, sweet marjoram, and pepper; stuff it very full. Fry two or three slices of pork crisp in the pot, then take them out, and lay in the leg; brown it on every side, then put hardly water enough into the pot to cover it. Throw in a dozen or two of cloves, half an onion sliced or chopped very fine, and a little salt. A half a teacup of catsup or a few tomatoes added half an hour before it is served, improve it very much. Let it simmer, steadily, three hours.

When you take up the leg, thicken the gravy, if it is not thick enough. Put a few spoonfuls over the meat, and the rest in a gravy tureen.

To Roast a Fillet of Veal.

Veal requires more time than any other meat except pork. It is scarcely ever done too much. A leg weighing eight or nine pounds should roast three hours. If your family is large, so that most of it will be eaten the first day, it is best to take out the bone, which is easily done with a sharp knife, the knuckle having been cut off by the butcher. Put this bone aside with the knuckle for a broth. If you design to use what is left cold for dinner the next day, let the bone remain in, as it keeps the leg in better shape. Prepare a stuffing of bread, pepper, salt pork, and sweet marjoram; make deep incisions in the meat and fill them with it. Fasten the fold of fat which is usually upon the fillet over the stuffed incisions with a skewer. Roast it slowly at first. Put into the dripping-pan some hot water with a little salt in it, or some of the stock. When the meat has roasted about an hour, flour it thickly, and skewer upon it four or five slices of salt pork. After the flour has become brown, baste the veal every fifteen minutes. If it is very good veal, the pork will flavor it without the addition of any butter; but if not, or if you wish it to be particularly nice, add a small piece of butter to the gravy in the roaster, before you begin to baste the meat. In cutting the incisions, endeavor to make them wider inside than at the surface, so that the stuffing may not fall out. See the directions (page 123) for making the gravy.

A Loin of Veal.

A breast or a loin of veal should be basted a great many times and roasted thoroughly. It is an improvement to put on slices of pork as in cooking the leg. Allow two hours for roasting; more, if it is large.

Veal Pot Pie.

Take the neck, the shank, and almost any pieces you have. Boil them long enough to skim off all the froth. Make a paste and roll it about half an inch thick. Butter the pot and lay in the crust, cutting out a piece on each side of the circle in such a way as to prevent its having thick folds. Put in a layer of meat, then flour, salt and pepper it, and add a little butter or a slice or two of salt pork, as you choose. Do this until you have laid in all your meat; pour in enough of the water in which the veal was boiled to half fill the kettle, then lay on the top-crust and make an incision in it to allow the escape of the steam. Watch that it does not burn, and pour in more of the water through the hole in the crust if necessary. Boil an hour and a half. The objection to this dish is, that boiled crust is apt to be heavy, and therefore unhealthy; but if it is made after the receipt for cream tartar biscuit, or of potato crust, it will be light.

Baked Veal Pie.

This is made in the same way as the boiled. The dish should be very deep, and when you are ready to lay on the upper crust, wet the edge of the under crust all around and flour it then lay on the upper crust and press your hand upon the edge, so that the flour and water will make it adhere, and thus prevent the gravy from escaping. Prick the top several times with a large fork. If you have pieces of crust left, cut them into leaves and ornament the pie. Bake it an hour and a half.

Stewed Breast of Veal.

Cut it into handsome pieces and fry it brown, either in drippings, or the fat fried out of salt pork. Brown all parts thoroughly; then pour in hot water enough barely to cover it. Add lemon peel cut fine and sweet marjoram Cover it close as possible, and stew it gently two hours; then pour off the liquor into a sauce-pan, and thicken it with browned flour. Take up the veal into a hot fricassee dish, and pour the gravy over it.

Always allow half an hour for frying veal brown. No other meat requires as much time.

Veal Cutlets.

Take slices from the broad end of the leg. Fry three or four slices of salt pork crisp, then take them out, lay in the veal half an hour at least before dinner time. When it has become brown, take it out and dip the slices, one by one, into a plate of fine bread crumbs, then fry them a few minutes longer. When done through, take them up on a hot dish, pour hot water into the spider or frying pan, and instantly when it boils up dredge in a little flour; pour it over the meat. Lay the slices of pork around the edge of the dish.

The best veal is to be had at the time when winter vegetables are not very good, and fresh ones have not come into market. Horseradish, spring cranberries, or fresh lemons are therefore the more acceptable with it.

Broiled Veal.

It must not be done too fast, and will take longer than beef. It is a great improvement to broil pork and lay between the slices of veal. Lay them upon the meat while it is broiling, and if they are not brown when the veal is done, put them a few minutes longer on the gridiron. If pork is not used, season with butter. In either case, add pepper and salt.

Calf's Head.

Let the head, feet, liver and lights, soak some hours in a plenty of cold water. Take out the brains. Boil the head, &c., till very tender, which will require from two hours to two and a half. Throw some salt into the water, and skim it thoroughly. Boil the brains ten or fifteen minutes, tied up in a piece of muslin; chop them, and put them with melted butter, and parsley cut fine. If you choose, boil an egg hard, cut it up and add it. Cold calf's head is good. It is also good hashed. To make it into soup the second day, see the receipt under the head of Soups.

Melton Veal, or Veal Cake.

Cut three or four pounds of raw veal, and half as much ham, into small pieces. If you have the remains of cooked veal or ham, add them. Boil six eggs hard, cut them in slices, and lay some of them in the bottom of a deep brown pan; shake in a little minced parsley; lay in some of the pieces of veal and ham, then add more egg, parsley, pepper, and salt; then more meat, and again parsley, pepper, and salt, till all the meat is laid in. Lastly add water enough just to cover it, and lay on about an ounce of butter shaved thin; tie over it a double paper, bake it an hour, then remove the paper, press it down with a spoon, and lay a small plate with a weight upon it, and let it remain another hour in the oven. When cold, it will cut in slices.

Venison.

Roast a haunch like a loin or leg of veal, and about as long. Flour it thickly. Put some of the stock for gravies, or water in which beef has been boiled, into the pan, and baste it often. Half an hour before serving it add a table-spoonful of butter to the gravy, and baste it again and again.

If you use *blazes* at the table, roast it but an hour. Most persons like venison cooked simply, without spices. But if you choose to have a dressing, make it as for veal, with the addition of powdered clove.

Venison steaks are cooked like beef steaks.

To Roast a Pig.

It should not be more than a month old. It is better a little less, and it should be killed on the morning of the day it is to be cooked. Sprinkle fine salt over it an hour before it is put to the fire. Cut off the feet at the first joint. Make stuffing enough to fill it very full, of bread crumbs moistened with a little milk, a small piece of butter, sweet marjoram, sage, pepper, and salt. When placed on the spit, confine the legs in such a manner as to give it a good shape. Rub it all over with butter or sweet oil, to keep it from blistering. Flour it at first a little. As soon as it begins to brown, dredge on a *very* thick covering of flour. Turn the spit every three or four minutes. If the flour falls off, instantly renew it. When it has all become of a dark brown color, scrape it off into a plate and set it aside. Put a piece of butter into the gravy in the roaster, and baste the pig very often, till it is done, which it is when the eyes fall out. The feet and liver should be boiled an hour or two, and the gravy from the roaster be poured into the water in which they were boiled. The liver should be cut or mashed fine, and the feet cut open and returned to the sauce-pan, the brains taken out and added, and the gravy thickened with the browned flour reserved in the plate. A pig of a month old will roast in two hours and a half.

A Shoulder of Pork.

One weighing ten pounds will require full three hours and a half to roast it. For a small family divide it, and roast one half and corn the other. With a sharp knife score the skin in diamonds, or in strips about an inch wide. Make a dressing, as directed under the head of Stuffing of Various Kinds. Put this into deep incisions made in the thick part of the meat. Rub a little fine powdered sage into the skin where it is scored; and then rub the whole surface with sweet oil, or drippings, to prevent its blistering. Observe the directions respecting the basting and frequent turning of meat. Pork burns very easily, and both the taste and appearance are much injured by its being burnt.

Spare-rib or Chine.

A spare-rib requires an hour and a half or two hours, according to the thickness. A very thin one will roast in an hour and a half. Flour it well, and take care it does not burn. Baste it often. The chine requires a longer time, being a thicker piece. It is more healthy, because less fat than the spare-rib, and having more meat in proportion to the bone, is a more economical piece. Before roasting either, trim off neatly, with a sharp knife, all the fat which can be removed without disfiguring the piece, and set it aside to be tried and used as lard.

Pork Steaks.

Cut slices from the loin or neck.

To fry pork steaks requires twenty-five or thirty minutes. Turn them often. If they are quite fat, pour off all that fries out when they are half done, and reserve it for some other use. Then dip the steaks in crumbs of bread with a little powdered sage, and lay them back into the frying-pan. When done through, take them up, dredge a little browned flour into the gravy, put in salt, pour in a gill of boiling water, and turn it instantly, as it boils up, upon the dish of steaks.

To Fry Sausages.

Sausages may be kept for some time, but fresh ones are considered best. Separate them, prick them to prevent their bursting, and lay them in a spider. If they are properly made, they will need no fat to fry them. Cook them slowly, at first, but brown every side of them before taking them up. They cook very well laid in a pan and set in a cooking-stove, but must be turned often, and care taken that they do not burn. Some persons fry bread in the fat which remains, in this way. Dip slices of bread, or crusts which have been cut and become dry, in salt and water, and lay them in the spider as soon as you take out the sausages. When brown one side, turn them. Serve them with the sausages. It takes twenty minutes to fry sausages in a spider, and half an hour to cook them in a stove. For those persons whose health is injured by eating them, it is best to lay them into a little water, and cook them thus, as long as they are usually fried, then pour off the water and brown them. This renders them comparatively harmless. The bread, fried as directed, does not absorb much fat.

To Boil a Ham or Shoulder.

A ham, weighing twelve pounds, should be cooked four or five hours. Boil it slowly in a plenty of water half the time it should be cooked; then take off the skin and any excrescences that were not removed by washing. Cover the fat side with pounded cracker, and lay it in a dripping pan, or iron basin, and put it into the stove. Let it remain the other half of the time.

The baking roasts out a great quantity of fat, and leaves the meat much more delicate. In warm weather it will keep in a dry, cool place, a long time. If after ten days you perceive a tendency to mould, set it a little while into the oven again. It is often a more agreeable dinner in hot weather than fresh meat.

If a ham is very salt, it should lie in water over night. In baking it, care should be taken that it is not done too much, and thus made dry. If the oven is a brick one and holds the heat a long time, it will do to put it in when the bread is taken out.

The fat which bakes out is good to fry eggs or potatoes, and if not strong, will do to use on the griddle.

To Fry Ham.

Cut thin slices, and take off the rind; if very salt, pour hot water upon them, but do not suffer them to lie long in it, as the juices of the meat will be lost. Wipe them in a cloth; have the spider ready hot, lay in the pieces and turn them in a minute or two. They will cook in a very short time. The secret of having good fried ham is in cooking it quick, and not too much. The practice of cutting thick slices, laying them into a cold spider and frying a long time, makes ham black and hard. It needs nothing added, but to be laid upon a hot covered dish.

To Broil Ham.

Cut the slices very thin, for which you must have a sharp knife; pare off the rind; lay them on the gridiron over hot coals. Do not leave them a moment, as they must be almost immediately turned, and will need attention to keep the edges from burning. Two minutes will broil them.

To Fry Salt Pork.

Cut slices and lay them in cold water in the spider; boil them up two or three minutes, then pour off the water and set the spider again on the coals and brown the slices on each side. Fried pork, with baked potatoes, and baked or fried sour apples, makes a very good dinner. It is an improvement to dip the pork, after being par-boiled, into Indian meal, before frying it.

Frizzled Smoked Beef.

Shave thin slices, and put them in a teacupful of milk into a small kettle or sauce-pan; boil it a few minutes, and then add a small bit of butter and an egg beaten with a teaspoonful of flour, and stir well. Put a little more milk to it if needed.

[Smoked beef is good in poached eggs, but in that case the beef should be boiled a few minutes in the milk before the eggs are added. The last remnants of a ham may be scraped from the bone, and put into poached eggs, but will not need the boiling which is necessary in the case of the smoked beef.]

To Shave Smoked Beef.

Use a very thin-bladed, sharp knife, and shave as thin as the thinnest paper. Do not attempt to cut it across the whole piece; no matter how small the shavings are, if they are but thin.

TO LAY MEAT AND POULTRY ON THE DISH FOR THE TABLE.

LAY a sirloin of beef with the tenderloin down, and the thick end towards the left hand of the person who carves.

A loin of veal or a quarter of lamb, with the thick edge toward the carver, and the inside uppermost. A leg of veal, with the inside up, and the thick end toward the right hand. A leg of mutton or lamb in the same way. A fore quarter of lamb or a breast of veal, with the outside up, and the thick edge toward the carver. A ham, with the outside up, and the thick end toward the right hand. A turkey or goose upon the back, with the neck toward the left hand. Fowls on the back, and if there is more than one, with the legs toward the carver.

The appearance of a fowl or turkey when on the table, depends much on its having been handsomely skewered.

TO SELECT POULTRY AND PREPARE IT FOR BEING COOKED.

A YOUNG turkey has a smooth leg, and a soft bill, and if fresh, the eyes will be bright, and the feet moist. Old turkeys have scaly, stiff feet.

Young fowls have a tender skin, smooth legs, and the breast bone readily yields to the pressure of the finger. The best are those that have yellow legs. The feet and legs of old fowls look as if they had seen hard service in the world.

Young ducks feel tender under the wing, and the web of the foot is transparent. The best are thick and hard on the breast.

Young geese have yellow bills, and the feet are yellow and supple; the skin may be easily broken by the head of a pin; the breast is plump, and the fat white. An old goose is unfit for the human stomach.

To keep fowls in warm weather, take out the heart and liver and parboil them, set them aside in a cool place, to be used in the gravy. Wash the fowls as clean as possible from the blood, and plunge one at a time into a kettle of boiling water for five minutes, moving it about, that the water may penetrate every part. Drain and wipe them dry and pepper the inside and the necks. This process will enable you to keep them two days in warm weather. In cold weather all sorts of poultry should be kept at least a week; but care should be taken that they do not freeze, as they are not quite so good for being frozen.

Pick out the pin feathers very carefully. A pair of tweezers is sometimes necessary to take out those which a knife will not remove. Cut out the oil bag above the tail. Singe off all the hair by turning it quickly over a blazing paper. Cut off the legs at the joint above the feet; trim the neck, and if too long cut off some of it; draw out the crop and be sure to take out every thing from the inside. The best way of removing the crop is to make an incision along the backbone, just below the neck. It can be removed in this way as easily as by the common method, and the appearance of the bird, when laid on the dish, is much better. Be careful, in removing the gall bag, not to break it, as it will make every spot it touches bitter, and the most careful washing will not remove it. If there is much fat, trim off some of it. Throw the liver, heart, and gizzard into water and wash them. Wash the fowl in several waters. It is then ready to be stuffed and skewered, as directed under the head, *To roast a Turkey.* Some persons think fowls much better not to be washed; but they cannot be clean without.

The sharpness of the breast bone, which is a defect in the appearance of a fowl on the table, may be remedied in the following way: When preparing it to be cooked, take a small sharp knife, and passing it up the body, cut off the little slender bones which join the *hug-me-close* * to the side. Then push down the breast bone by pressing heavily upon it. A little practice will make it easy to do this.

To Roast a Turkey.

Observe the directions under the head, *To prepare Poultry for being cooked.* Make a stuffing, and fill both the breast and body. Sew it up with a needle and coarse thread; tie the skin over the end of the neck with a thread or piece of twine. Push a short skewer through above the tail, and a long one through the body under the thighs; then tie the ends of the legs down with a twine, close upon the short skewer. Push another long skewer through the body, so as to confine the wings, and tie them round with a twine. Put the spit through the length of the body, and fasten it with two skewers; flour it, and put it to the fire with a little water in the roaster. It should be roasted rather slowly. A turkey weighing twelve pounds should roast

* This is the bone on each side the neck of a fowl, which answers to the collar bone in the human frame.

three hours; one weighing six or seven, an hour and a half. When half done, flour it again thickly; when this is browned, baste it often. If much fat roasts out, dip off most of it when the turkey is about half done, and put a small piece of butter into the gravy, and baste the turkey with it. Having washed the heart, liver, &c., boil them an hour and a half, in a saucepan in a pint of water; skim them when the water first boils up; if it boils away, add more.

To make the gravy, take out the heart and gizzard, mash the liver, and put it back into the water in which it was boiled, and pour the gravy also out of the roaster into it; set it on the coals, add browned flour, wet smooth, and a little butter and pepper, and boil it a minute or two, and then serve it. The liver should never be put under the wing, or laid upon the dish, but always be used in the gravy, as it is greatly improved by it.

More directions respecting gravies may be found under the head, *Directions for making various kinds of Gravies.*

To Boil a Turkey.

Stuff a young turkey, weighing six or seven pounds, with bread, butter, salt, pepper, and minced parsley; skewer up the legs and wings as if to roast; flour a cloth and pin around it. Boil it forty minutes, then set off the kettle and let it stand, close covered, half an hour more. The steam will cook it sufficiently. To be eaten with drawn butter and stewed oysters.

To Roast Chickens.

Observe the same directions in stuffing them as for a turkey. If you wish to roast several before an open fire, the spit may be put through side-ways, instead of length-ways, and four or five can thus be roasted at once, in a large roaster. Boil the inwards and make the gravy as for a turkey. Roast them an hour and a half.

To Boil Chickens.

Make the same dressing as directed for a boiled turkey, or boil them without stuffing if preferred. Skewer them up into a good shape, as when prepared to roast, and boil them an hour and a quarter. Serve them with drawn butter and cut parsley. It is an improvement to mash the livers and put into the butter. If chickens can be carefully skimmed, they need no cloth around them.

To Broil Chickens.

Cut them open through the back, take out the inwards, wash them and wipe them dry; place the inside down on the gridiron. They must broil slowly, and care be taken they do not burn. Turn them in ten minutes. To keep them flat, lay a tin sheet upon them, with a weight. Broil twenty-five minutes, and dress with butter, pepper, and salt. They can be broiled best over wood coals.

To Fricassee Chickens.

Boil them forty minutes in water enough barely to cover them. Take off the scum as fast as it rises. Take them up and carve them in the usual way. Put part of the water in which they were boiled into a spider or stew-pan. For two chickens rub a piece of butter as large as an egg, and a spoonful of flour together, and stir into the water as it boils up. Add some salt, and a gill of cream, or milk. Lay in the pieces of chicken, cover the pan close, and stew them gently eight or ten minutes. Parsley cut fine is a decided improvement.

Chicken Salad.

Boil or roast a nice fowl. When cold, cut off all the meat, and chop it a little, but not very small; cut up a large bunch of celery and mix with the chicken. Boil four eggs hard, mash, and mix them with sweet oil, pepper, salt, mustard, and a gill of vinegar. Beat this mixture very thoroughly together, and just before dinner pour it over the chicken.

Chicken Pie.

Boil chickens in water barely to cover them, forty minutes. Skim the water carefully. Take them out into a dish, and cut them up as they should be carved if placed upon the table. If the skin is very thick remove it. Have ready, lined with a thick paste, a deep dish, of a size proportioned to the number of chickens you wish to use; put in the pieces, with the hearts and livers, in layers; sprinkle each layer with flour, salt, and pepper, and put on each piece of chicken a thin shaving of butter; do this till you have laid in all the pieces; put rather more of the spice, flour, and butter over the top layer than on the previous ones, and pour in as much of the liquor in which the chickens were boiled as you can without danger of its boiling over. Lay on the upper crust, and close the edges very carefully with flour and water; prick the top with a knife. Cut leaves of crust and ornament it. Bake two hours. The crust for chicken pie should be twice as thick as for fruit pies. Use mace and nutmeg if you wish.

To Roast Ducks.

Flour them thick and baste them often. If they are roasted before the fire, an hour is long enough; if in a stove, an hour and a half. For making the stuffing and gravy, see the directions.

To Boil Ducks.

Scald and lay them in warm water a few minutes, then lay them in a dish, pour boiling milk over them, and let them lie in it two or three hours. Then take them out, dredge them with flour, and put them into a saucepan of cold water, cover close and boil them twenty minutes. Then take them out and set them, covered, where they will keep warm, and make the sauce as follows: —

Chop a large onion and a bunch of parsley fine, and put them into a gill of good gravy. [See receipt for Stock.] Add a table-spoonful of lemon juice, a little salt, pepper, and a small piece of butter. Stew these ingredients half an hour; then lay the ducks into a dish, and pour the sauce over them.

To Roast a Goose.

Boil it half an hour to take out the strong, oily taste, then stuff and roast it exactly like a turkey. If it is a young one, an hour's roasting will be sufficient.

To Boil Partridges.

Put them in a floured cloth into boiling water, and boil them fast fifteen minutes. For sauce, rub a very small piece of butter into some flour, and boil in a teacup of cream. Add cut parsley if preferred.

To Roast Partridges.

Prepare them like chickens, and roast three quarters of an hour.

To Roast Pigeons.

Pick out the pin feathers, or if there are a great many, pull off the skin. Examine the inside very carefully. Soak them half an hour in a good deal of water, to take out the blood. Then boil them with a little salt in the water, half an hour, and take off the scum as fast as it rises. Take them out, flour them well, and lay them into a dripping-pan; strain the water in which they were boiled, and put a part of it into the pan; stir in it a little piece of butter, and baste the pigeons often. Add pepper and sweet marjoram if you prefer. Roast them nearly two hours. Pigeons need to be cooked a long time.

Pigeons in Disguise.

Prepare them just as directed in the receipt above, and boil them long enough to remove all the blood, then pepper and salt them, make a good paste, roll each pigeon close in a piece of it; tie them separately in a cloth, taking care not to break the paste. Boil them gently an hour and a half, in a good deal of water. Lay them in a hot dish, and pour a gravy over them made of cream, parsley, and a little butter.

Pigeon Pie.

Pick, soak, and boil pigeons with the same care as directed in the receipt for roasting them. Make a crust just as for chicken or veal pie. Lay in the pigeons whole, and season with pepper, salt, shavings of butter, and sweet marjoram; flour them thickly, then strain the water in which they were boiled, and fill the dish two thirds with it. Lay the top crust over, and close the edges well. Make many incisions with the point of a knife, or a large fork, and bake an hour and a half.

Woodcocks, Quails, and other small birds.

Pull off the skin, split them down the back with a sharp knife, pepper the breasts, and lay the inside first upon the gridiron. Broil them slowly at first, skewer a small bit of pork upon each one. Turn them after seven or eight minutes. Broil them twenty minutes.

If you wish to make a pie, do just as directed for the pigeon pie.

Calcutta Curry.

Boil and joint two chickens. Fry three or four slices of salt pork, and when they are nearly brown add a large spoonful of butter. Cut three or four onions fine, and fry them a light brown; then remove them, and the pork, and fry the chickens gently in the fat; strew over the meat while it is frying a spoonful and a half of good curry powder, and dredge in flour. Then add hot water to make sufficient gravy; if the gravy is not thick enough, mix a little flour smooth in cold water, and stir in. Add salt to suit your taste. This dish is best when stewed slowly. Garnish with slices of lemon.

Partridges, pigeons, rabbits, sweet-breads, breasts of mutton, lamb, and veal, are all used for curries.

There is a difference in the quality of curry powder. The

above measure, is for the strongest kind, and is enough for a quart of gravy. The East Indians never use flour in thickening the gravy, but depend on the curry powder.

To prepare rice for Calcutta curry, wash a pint in several waters, and put it into a kettle, containing a gallon of warm water, with salt in it. Cook it ten minutes from the time it begins to boil; then pour it into a sieve, and when the water is entirely drained out, shake the sieve, and the particles of rice will separate, and it is ready to serve.

SOUPS.

Soup is economical food, and by a little attention may be made good with very small materials. It should never be made of meat that has been kept too long. If meat is old, or has become tainted in the least, the defect is peculiarly offensive in soup. All meat and bones for soup should be boiled a long time, and set aside until the next day in order that the fat may be entirely removed. Then add the vegetables, rice, and herbs, and boil it from an hour to an hour and a half. The water in which fresh meat is boiled should be saved for soup and broth; and the bones of roast beef should never be thrown away without boiling, as they make excellent soup, and if not used for this purpose, should be boiled in order to save the fat which they contain.

A Rich Soup.

The richest soups are made by using several kinds of meat together; as beef, mutton, and veal. A shank of each of these with very little meat upon it, should be boiled several hours the first day; and vegetables, with various kinds of spice, added the day it is to be served. Nice soups should be strained; and they are good with macaroni, added afterwards, and boiled half or three quarters of an hour. If you have the water, in which chickens have been boiled, the soup will be much better if the beef, mutton, or veal are boiled in this, instead of pure water.

Roast Beef Bone Soup.

Boil the bones at least three hours, or until every particle of meat is loose; then take them out and scrape off the meat and set aside the water; the next day take from it all the fat, cut up an onion, two or three potatoes and a turnip, and put into it. Add, half an hour before dinner, powdered sweet majoram, catsup, and some salt. Boil it an hour.

Shank Soup.

When you buy a shank, have the butcher cut it into several pieces, and split open the thickest part of the bone. Boil it three or four hours and set it aside. The next day, take off the fat, and if you do not wish to eat the meat in the soup, take that out also; add vegetables, etc., as in the preceding receipt. To make a convenient use of the meat, see the receipt for minced meat.

Turtle-Bean Soup.

Soak a teacup and a half of beans in a little water over night. To boil, add two quarts more. When soft, strain through a sieve; add broth, or water in which roast-beef bones have been boiled; also an onion, turnip, carrot, salt, sweet marjoram, thyme, and four cloves. Boil an hour longer. If too thick, add water. Take out the vegetables before serving. It can be made without broth, but needs more seasoning.

Tomato Soup.

Put three pints of tomatoes, stewed, strained, and sweetened, to two quarts of meat liquor (the fat being removed). Add an onion, salt, and pepper, and water if too thick. With more seasoning, and a bit of butter, it is good without meat liquor.

Mock-Turtle Soup.

Add to the foregoing ingredients, red wine, nutmeg, and mace; and force meat balls, made in the following way, — Chop some of the meat fine, and put with it an equal quantity of fine bread crumbs, onions chopped small, cayenne and black pepper, sweet marjoram and powdered clove. Beat two eggs and with them stir the ingredients together, and make into balls, and fry in butter enough to brown them; then put the balls and the butter into the soup.

Turkey Soup.

The remnants of a young turkey make good soup. Put all the bones, and little bits left of a dinner into about three quarts of water. If you have turkey gravy, or the remnants of chickens, add them also, and boil them two hours or more. Skim out the meat and bones, and set the water aside in a cool place till the next day. Then take all the fat from the top; take the bones and pieces of skin out from the meat and return it to the liquor. If some of the dressing has been left, put that in also, and boil all together a few minutes. If more seasoning is needed, add it to suit your taste.

White Soup.

Boil a knuckle of veal to shreds, add a quarter of a pound of vermicelli, half a pint of cream, and lemon peel and mace.

Pea Soup.

Take a pint of split peas, and when carefully picked over and washed, put them into a pint of water to soak over night. Three hours before dinner, put them into a pot with a quart more water, and about half a pound of pork (less if you wish the soup not very rich.) Boil it steadily, and be careful to stir it often, lest it should burn. It may need more water before dinner, and can be made of whatever thickness you prefer.

If you prefer to have the soup without pork (which makes it

too rich for many persons), use the liquor in which beef or other fresh meat has been boiled instead of water, and use no pork. This is a very good way.

Vegetable Soup.

Take two turnips, two carrots, four potatoes, one large onion, one parsnip, and a few stalks of celery or some parsley. Cut them all very fine, or chop them in a tray; put them, with a spoonful of rice, into three quarts of water, and boil the whole three hours. Then strain the soup through a colander or coarse sieve, return it to the kettle, and put it over the fire. Add a piece of butter of the size of a nut, stir the soup till the butter is melted, dredge in a little flour, let it boil up and then serve it.

Mutton or Lamb Broth.

Take the water in which a leg of mutton or lamb was boiled on the previous day, take off the fat and boil it two hours with a turnip, an onion, and a carrot, cut small. Add some minced parsley and a spoonful of rice. All these, except the parsley, should be put in while the water is cold. Any little pieces of the neck, ribs, or shank will make excellent broth.

Veal Broth.

Take a knuckle, or if you have a large family, two knuckles of veal. Put them over the fire, at least three hours before dinner-time; use not more than two quarts of water for two knuckles, and skim it until it is no longer necessary. (Veal requires more attention in this respect than any other meat). When this is done, add a spoonful of rice. A quarter of an hour before it is to be served, put in some minced parsley, salt, and pepper It is a very nutritious dish. Some persons add two or three slices of salt pork.

It is a good way, after having taken off cutlets from the large end of a leg of veal, to boil the entire piece that remains, with the knuckle. Boil it two hours or two hours and a half. Make broth of the liquor by putting in a small gill of rice, and some parsley; add the parsley about ten minutes before it is served.

Melt butter with cut parsley, to eat on the meat.

In families that like salt pork, a piece should be boiled separately to eat with the veal.

EGGS.

Boiled.

NEW laid eggs require half a minute longer to cook than others. The fresher they are the better, and the more healthful. Eggs over a week old should never be boiled; they will do to fry. Put them into water that boils, but not furiously, as it will crack them. If you like them very soft, boil them three minutes. If you wish the yolk hard, boil them five minutes. To be served with salad, they should be boiled twelve minutes.

Fried.

After you have fried ham, drop in the eggs one at a time. In about a minute dip the boiling fat with a spoon over them again and again. This will prevent the necessity of turning them, which it is difficult to do without breaking the yolks. Take them up in about two minutes and a half, with a skimmer. The fat that roasts out of a ham that is browned in an oven, is good for frying eggs.

Poached.

Set a tin pan or pail on the range, containing a pint of milk; then beat six eggs well. When the milk is very nearly boiling, put in a teaspoonful of salt, and half a table-spoonful of butter; then add the eggs, and stir steadily, until it thickens, which will be in a minute or two. Set it off before it becomes very thick, and continue to stir it a minute more. Have ready, in a warm dish, two slices of toasted bread, spread with butter, and pour the egg over them. It should be a little thicker than boiled custard. This is an ample breakfast for six or seven persons.

Dropped.

Drop fresh eggs into a saucepan of boiling water with salt in it. Put them in gently, so as not to break the yolks. Have ready slices of buttered toast, and either take up the eggs with a skimmer or pour off the water, and then turn them out of the saucepan upon the toast. Add more salt, if they are not seasoned enough by that which is in the water.

Omelet (baked, and very simple).

Heat three gills of milk with a dessert spoonful of butter in it; beat four or five eggs thoroughly, wet a table-spoonful of flour with a teaspoonful of salt, smooth, in a little cold milk. Mix the eggs with the flour and cold milk, then add the hot milk, stirring very fast. Put the mixture into a buttered dish just large enough to contain it. It will bake in a quick oven in fifteen or twenty minutes. Besides being very palatable, it is a beautiful-looking dish for the breakfast-table, and a very convenient addition to a small dinner.

The old rule is, eight eggs to a pint of milk; but six is enough.

Omelet (Fried).

Make a batter of three eggs, two gills of milk, and two table-spoonfuls of flour. Beat it well, and add chopped onion, parsley, salt, and nutmeg. Fry brown in nice drippings or butter.

Another.

Make a batter in the same way, and add a gill of grated ham. Fry in nice fat, or the drippings of a roasted ham.

Another.

Wash a piece of salt cod as large as your hand, and soak it

in warm water over night. In the morning take out the bones and chop it very fine ; then put it into two or three gills of milk and boil it up. Stir in a piece of butter half the size of an egg, and a table-spoonful of flour wet smooth in cold milk ; then add three eggs well beaten, and boil it half a minute more.

DIRECTIONS RESPECTING FISH.

Purchase those which have just been caught. Of this you can judge by their being hard under the pressure of the finger. Fish lose their best flavor soon, and a few hours make a wide difference in the taste of some sorts.

Cod are best in cold weather. Mackerel are best in August, September, and October. Halibut, in May and June. Oysters are good from September to April; but are not very good or healthy from the first of May to the last of August. Lobsters are best at the season when oysters are not good.

They must be put alive into boiling water and be boiled from thirty-five to forty minutes. Allow a large spoonful of salt to every quart of water in which they are boiled. The medium sized ones are the best. The shells of old lobsters are apt to be encrusted. On no account should they be eaten later than eighteen hours after being boiled. Some persons never eat them after twelve hours. Pond fish should be soaked in strong salt and water to take out the earthy taste. Fish may be kept good several days, if frozen. All large fish need to be soaked in water that is a little warm, before being cleaned; and they should be cleaned with great care, for even if there are few scales upon them, there is a great deal of slimy substance which a knife will remove. A boiled fish is done when the eyes turn white.

When you broil fish, rub the gridiron with lard or drippings, to prevent its sticking. Do not attempt to turn it like steaks, with a knife and fork, but lay an old dish upon it, and hold it on with one hand, while you turn over the gridiron with the other. Lay the skin side down first.

Fish that is to be fried, should be cut up and laid in a cloth for an hour that the moisture may be absorbed. It should then be rolled in fine bread crumbs, or Indian meal. That which is apt to break in frying may be kept whole by being dipped in a beaten egg, before it is rolled in the bread crumbs. Oysters should be skimmed out of the liquor before being cooked, in order that it may be strained, as there are often bits of shell in it.

To Boil Cod.

Rub a little salt down the bone, and over the thick part. Wrap it in a cloth and put it over the fire in cold water; putting it into hot water at first will cause the outside to break before the centre is done. See that it is covered with water, and throw in a table-spoonful of salt. Take off the froth carefully, and boil it half an hour. Fresh cod is eaten with oyster sauce and melted butter, or with the latter alone, prepared as directed under the head of *Drawn Butter*, with the addition of parsley and if you choose three or four eggs boiled very hard, cut up and put into it.

The head and shoulders of cod are so much thicker than the other part, that it is impossible to boil the fish whole and have all parts equally cooked. It is therefore a good way to buy a large cod, divide it, boil the head and shoulders, and fry the other part, or sprinkle it with salt, and after a day or two, broil it.

Cod Sounds and Tongues.

Soak them in warm water, scrape them thoroughly, and boil them ten minutes in milk and water. To be served with egg sauce.

To Bake a Cod or Black Fish.

The simplest way of baking fish, is very good. Spread little pieces of bread, with butter; pepper and salt them, and lay them inside the fish. Then take a needle and thread and sew it up. Put a small skewer through the lip and tail, and fasten them together with a piece of twine. Lay it into a dish, in which it may be served, put two or three thin slices of salt pork upon it, sprinkle salt over it, and flour it well. Baste it several times with the liquor which cooks out of it. A fish weighing four pounds will cook in an hour.

To make a richer dish.

Chop fine a half a teacupful of fat ham; add a large spoonful of butter, some parsley, thyme, marjoram, a little salt, nutmeg, and pepper. If you have oysters, add a few. Beat two eggs, and put all together with fine bread crumbs enough to compound them. With this, stuff the fish, which should be floured thick, and wind a string around it to keep it together, or else sew it up. Fasten the head and tail together with a skewer. Bake it in a stove an hour. Baste it with butter.

To Fry Cod (or other Fish).

After it has been cleansed, cut it into pieces of the proper size, and lay them in a cloth in order to dry them. Fry four or five slices of salt pork, or use instead, lard or nice beef drippings; but pork is preferable. When the slices are fried crisp, take them out, dip the pieces of fish in a plate of fine Indian meal, and lay them into the spider. Fry them brown. When the fish is done, lay it with the pork into a hot dish. Pour a little water into the spider, boil it up, dredge in browned flour, and pour the whole over the fish.

To make a Chowder.

Fry three slices of salt pork, crisp, in a deep kettle; take them out and lay in slices of potatoes; flour and pepper them; then lay in slices of cod or haddock, which must also be floured and peppered. Put in alternate layers of potatoes and fish, with flour, salt, and pepper, till it is all laid in. Pour over it boiling water enough almost to cover it. When it boils up, dredge in more flour. Dip a few crackers in cold water and lay over the top, and cover the kettle close. Boil it three quarters of an hour. Use ship bread, if it is preferred. Some people add a cup of milk just before it is served. Add part of a fresh lemon, if you like.

Another Way.

Fry three or four slices of salt pork, soak a dozen hard crackers, cut up four or five onions. When the pork is fried brown take it out, and lay in half of the crackers, and half the onions. Cut up the cod, and lay the pieces next, then the rest of the crackers and onions, season it with pepper and salt, pour boiling water enough into the kettle to cover the whole. Let it stew moderately an hour.

The fish should be fresh from the water. Cod's heads and sound bones make the richest chowder.

To Boil Salt Cod.

Lay a piece of salt fish into the cellar a few days before it is to be cooked, that it may become softened by the dampness. The afternoon before it is to be boiled, wash it carefully in several waters. It is well to keep a brush on purpose to cleanse salt fish, and use it repeatedly while it is soaking. Leave it in water till morning, and then put it into a kettle, and set it where it will keep warm, and at length simmer, but not boil. Eat it with beets and potatoes, and drawn butter; or with pork scraps if you prefer.

To prepare the Scraps. Cut salt pork into very small square pieces, put them in a saucepan, and cook them till they are crisped. A quarter of a pound of pork will be enough for a family of five, and it will take half an hour to fry it enough.

There is a great difference in the quality of salt fish. The Dun is considered best.

Minced Salt Fish.

Pick out all the bones and bits of skin the day that the fish is boiled, as it is most easily done while it is warm. Next day chop it fine, and also all the potatoes left of the previous dinner; they are better for this purpose than those that are just boiled. Lay three or four slices of salt pork into a spider, and fry till they are crisped; take them out, and put the chopped fish and potato into the middle, and press it out equally, so that the fat will be at the sides. Cover it close; after about five minutes put into the centre a gill of milk, and cover it again. In a few minutes more stir it, but so carefully as not to disturb the sides and bottom, else a brown crust will not form. Add more milk if it is too dry. When thoroughly heated through, stir in a small piece of butter, loosen the crust from the sides with a knife, and turn it out upon a hot dish. If it is done right, it will come out whole, and nicely browned.

Fish-Balls.

Take equal quantities of chopped fish and potato, enough to nearly fill a tray of medium size. Add a beaten egg, and a table-spoonful of butter, melted. Mix and mash well with a wooden spoon. Roll the balls in flour, and fry them with salt pork and a little lard or beef fat. The whole surface of the balls should be gradually browned.

To Boil or Broil Halibut.

If you wish to boil it, purchase a thick slice cut through the body, or the tail piece, which is considered the richest. Wrap it in a floured cloth, and lay it in cold water with salt in it. A piece weighing six pounds, should be cooked half an hour after the water begins to boil. It is eaten with drawn butter and parsley. If any of it is left, lay it in a deep dish and sprinkle on it a little salt, throw over it a dozen or two of cloves, pour in some vinegar, and add butternut vinegar or catsup. It will, when cold, have much the flavor of lobster.

The *nape* of a halibut is considered best to broil; but a slice through the body a little more than an inch thick, if sprinkled with salt an hour or two before being cooked, will broil without breaking, and is excellent. When taken up, put on butter, pepper, and salt.

To Boil Salmon.

Clean a salmon in salt and water. Allow twenty minutes for boiling every pound. Wrap it in a floured cloth, and lay it in the kettle while the water is cold. Make the water very salt. Skim it well; in this respect it requires more care than any other fish. Serve it with drawn butter and parsley.

If salmon is not thoroughly cooked it is unhealthy. When a piece of boiled fresh fish of any kind is left of dinner, it is a very good way to lay it in a deep dish, and pour over it a little vinegar, with catsup, and add pepper or any other spice which is preferred.

To Broil Salmon.

Cut it in slices an inch and a half thick, dry it in a clean cloth, salt it, and lay it upon a hot gridiron, the bars having been rubbed with lard or drippings. It cooks very well in a stove oven, laid in a dripping-pan.

To Broil Shad.

Procure fresh caught shad. It requires twenty minutes to broil, on moderately hot coals. To turn it, see Directions respecting Fish. Sprinkle it with salt, and spread on a little butter. Fresh fish requires a longer time to broil than meat.

The simplest way of Cooking Oysters.

Take them, unopened, rinse the shells clean, and lay them on hot coals, or the top of a cooking-stove, with the deepest side of the shell down, so as not to lose the liquor. When they begin to open a little, they are done, and the upper shell will be easily removed with a knife, and the oyster is to be eaten from the lower shell. The table should be supplied with coarse napkins, and a large dish to receive the shells.

Oyster Pie.

Make a nice paste and lay into a deep dish, turn a teacup down in the centre. This will draw the liquor under it, and prevent it from boiling over; it also keeps the upper crust from falling in and becoming clammy. Lay in the oysters, add a little pepper, butter, and flour; make a wide incision in the upper crust, so that when the pie is nearly done, you can pour in half a teacup of cream or milk. Secure the edges of the crust according to the directions for making Pastry, and bake it an hour. It should be put into the oven immediately, else the under crust will be clammy. Use but little of the liquor.

To Fry Oysters.

Lay them in a cloth a few minutes to dry them, then dip each one into sifted cracker crumbs, and fry in just enough fat to brown them. Put pepper and salt on them, before you turn them over.

Escaloped Oysters.

Butter a deep dish, and cover the bottom and sides with fine crumbs of bread. Put in half the oysters, with pounded mace, pepper, and salt, and cover them with bread crumbs and small bits of butter; add the rest of the oysters with pepper and mace, and cover as before. Put in but little of the liquor, as oysters part with a good deal of moisture in cooking, and if the mixture is too wet, it is not as good. Bake a quart of oysters half an hour. A plainer dish, with little butter and no spice is very good.

Pickled Oysters.

Boil the liquor of an hundred oysters and pour it over them. When they have stood a few minutes, take them out and boil the liquor again, with a gill of vinegar, a few whole black peppers, and two or three blades of mace. When this is cold, pour it over the oysters, and cover them closely. This is a very good way to keep them.

Stewed Oysters.

Boil them up five minutes, then set them off, in order to take off the scum which rises. Have ready, for a quart of oysters, half a table-spoonful of butter, with as much flour rubbed into it as it will receive. Return the kettle to the fire, and when it begins to simmer, stir in the butter till it is melted, and then serve.

Another Way.

Boil a pint of milk; rub a heaping table-spoonful of flour smooth in cold milk, and stain into it; then strain in the liquor of a quart of oysters, and when it boils up again, add half a spoonful of butter, a little salt, and the oysters, and let the whole boil two minutes more.

[In opening lobsters, care must be taken to remove the poisonous part. This lies in the head, all of which must be thrown away, as well as the vein which passes from it, through the body. All the other parts are good. Break the shells with a hammer. The liquor and the spawn should be saved.]

Lobster Salad.

To the yolks of four eggs, boiled hard, add a little sweet oil, mustard, pepper, salt, and a gill of vinegar. Stir these all together a long time. Cut up celery or lettuce fine, sprinkle it on the lobster in the dish in which it is to be served, and pour the mixture over it.

The simplest way of serving lobsters is very good, and most healthful. Take them from the shells and eat them cold, with vinegar and mustard.

Stewed Lobster.

Take one large or two small lobsters; cut them in pieces, and put into the stew-pan with the liquor two glasses of wine, one teaspoonful of fine allspice, half a teaspoonful of mixed mustard, a little cayenne, and a quarter of a pound of butter rubbed into some flour. If there is not liquor enough for the gravy, add a little water. Simmer the whole a half an hour.

Baked Bass.

Make a stuffing of pounded cracker or crumbs of bread, an egg, pepper, clove, salt, and butter. Fill it very full, and when sewed up, grate over it a small nutmeg, and sprinkle it with pounded cracker. Then pour on the white of an egg, and melted butter. Bake it an hour in the same dish in which it is to be served.

Potted Shad (a very convenient and excellent dish).

Take three or four fresh caught shad, and when nicely dressed, cut them down the middle, and across in pieces about three inches wide; put these pieces into a jar in layers, with salt, whole cloves, pepper-corns, and allspice sprinkled between. When all is laid in, put in sharp vinegar enough just to cover them, and bake in the oven. It is the best way to put the jar into a brick oven after the bread is drawn, if considerable heat still remains, and let it stand two or three hours, or put it into a range oven at night, to stand till morning. This will keep several weeks, even in hot weather. Almost any fish of the size of shad may be done in the same way.

Brook Trout.

If they are small, fry them with salt pork. If large, boil them, and serve with drawn butter.

Clams.

The round clams, sometimes called quahogs, are much the most healthy. The small ones, with thin edges, are to be preferred. They may be roasted upon a gridiron, or laid in an iron pan upon a stove. When the shell begins to open, pour the liquor into a sauce-pan, and cut the clam from the shell and put with it. When all are taken out, set the sauce-pan on the coals, and when the clams boil up, add pepper and a bit of butter, and pour them upon toasted bread.

Clam broth is made by washing them very clean, and boiling till the shells open; then take out the clams and put them into the water again. Boil them a few minutes, add a little butter and flour, and put toasted crackers in the tureen into which you put the broth. This is very healthy for feeble persons.

Smelts.

Soak smelts a little while in warm water; scrape them, and cut the heads so far that you can gently pull them off, and thus draw out the dark vein that runs through the body; then rinse and lay them into a dry cloth while you fry two or three slices of salt pork crisp. Dip the smelts into a plate of fine Indian meal, and fry them brown. If you fry them in lard or drippings, sprinkle them with salt, but not until they are nearly done, as they will not brown as well, if it is put on at first.

To prepare Salt Shad, Mackerel, or Halibut's Fin to Broil.

Shad should be soaked twenty-four hours, the water being changed once or twice. Mackerel often need soaking thirty, or even thirty-six hours; and halibut's fin thirty-six. A gallon of water is the least in which either of them should be soaked. Grease the gridiron, and lay the skin side down. (See Directions at the head of this chapter.)

Smoked Halibut.

It should be washed in warm water, wiped and laid for only three or four minutes on the gridiron. Halibut is so solid a fish that it is not easy to get that which is cured perfectly free from taint.

DIRECTIONS FOR SALTING MEAT, FISH, &c.

To some young housekeepers, the salting of meat, and taking care of it, and of smoked meat, are perplexing. Perhaps the following directions may assist them. The best pieces to corn are the end of the rump, the thin end of the sirloin, and the edge-bone. If you like it with alternate streaks of fat and lean, the pieces at the ends of the ribs, called by butchers the rattle-ran, are very good. The edge-bone affords the most lean meat.

The best piece of pork to corn is the shoulder. It is a good way to divide it, if large, and stuff half of it with sage and bread crumbs, and roast it; and corn the other half.

In winter, hang fresh killed meat up two or three days before putting it into brine, as it will thus become more tender. Make a brine of four quarts of water, three pints of salt, half a table-spoonful of saltpetre, and a pint of molasses, or a pound of coarse brown sugar. Mix it thoroughly without boiling it. In this lay the meat, and see that it is entirely covered. It is well to look at it after a day or two, and if necessary, turn it the other side up. It will be good in a few days, but it is better to let it lie three or four weeks before boiling it. The same brine will do for many successive pieces in winter. But for a family that like salt meat, it is the best way to make a double measure, and put into it at once as much meat as it will cover. It should be kept in a firkin or tub, with a close cover.

After a considerable quantity of meat has thus been cured, scald and skim the brine, add a little more molasses, salt, and saltpetre, and let it become cold before meat is put into it.

A brine like this, only a little more rich with molasses, is very good for salting tongues, and pieces that are to be smoked. But they should lie in it four or five weeks. Meat should never be salted for smoking, later than February or the middle of March.

In warm weather, it will not do to use the same brine more than once, as the blood from the meat will become tainted. Therefore a less expensive mixture, that may be thrown away after being used once, is better. Two quarts of salt to four of water, is a good rule for brine in hot weather.

In the summer, the strong membrane that covers the rib bones, must be cut open with a sharp knife before the meat is put into brine; for, as the salt will not penetrate this membrane, the bones will else become tainted, and the meat soon be spoiled. Meat, at this season, should be cooked within three or four days after being put into brine.

To Salt Pork.

Allow a bushel of salt for a barrel of pork, or a peck for fifty weight. The salt called *coarse-fine*, is commonly used by butchers; but the best way in a private family, where no more than twenty-five or fifty weight is put down for the year's use, is to use fine salt. Put water enough to cover it. Examine it in a few days, and if the salt is all dissolved, add more. The only sure way of keeping pork sweet, is to have the brine so strong that some of the salt remains undissolved. A board, with a stone upon it, should always be kept on the top of pork, as it will soon become rusty if the edges lie above the surface of the brine.

It is not fit for use, until it has been in brine six weeks.

Pickle for one Ham.

To a gallon of water, put a pint of salt, a pint of molasses, and an ounce of saltpetre. Turn the ham over in the brine often, and let it lie in it six weeks; then let it be smoked nearly as long.

To Cure Hams.

[This receipt is furnished by a person whose hams are celebrated in the eastern part of Massachusetts, for their superior quality.]

For curing fifty weight, allow three quarts of coarse salt, half a pound of saltpetre, and two quarts of good molasses. Add soft water enough just to cover the hams. Common sized hams should be kept in this pickle five weeks; larger ones six. They should all be taken out once a week, and those which were on the top laid in first, and the lower ones last. They should be smoked from two to three weeks with walnut wood or with sawdust and corn-cobs, mixed. Meat smoked with cobs is very delicate.

Pieces of beef for smoking, may be laid in this pickle, after the hams are sent to the smoke house; but more salt should be added.

The Knickerbocker Pickle.

To three gallons of soft water, put four pounds and a half of salt, coarse and fine, mixed; a pound and a half of brown sugar, an ounce and a half of saltpetre, half an ounce of saleratus, and two quarts of good molasses.

Boil the mixture, skim it well, and when cold pour it over the hams or beef. Beef laid down in this pickle, does not become hard, and is very fine, when boiled gently and long.

Some persons consider this the best of all methods for curing beef and hams.

How to keep Hams through the Summer.

When they are taken from the smoke house, do not suffer them to lie a single hour where the flies can find them. Sew them up in a coarse cloth or stiff brown paper, and pack them in ashes. There is no method so sure to preserve them from insects, and the effect of the ashes is to improve the meat; but care should be taken that the hams are so secured that the ashes will not touch them. The ashes should be perfectly cold and dry, and the barrel be in a dry, cool place.

To make Sausages.

A common fault is, that the meat is not chopped enough. It should be chopped very fine, and this is most easily done if it is a little frozen. When ready for the seasoning, put in just cold water enough to enable you to mix the ingredients equally; but be careful not to use more than is necessary for this purpose.

The following excellent rule for seasoning sausages is furnished by the same person whose receipt for curing hams I have been allowed to copy.

To twelve pounds and a half of meat put a gill of fine salt, a large gill of powdered sage, and half a gill of ground pepper Let the measures be exact.

Some persons find it most convenient to keep sausage meat in a cloth. It is done by making a long bag of strong cotton cloth, of such a size that, when filled, it will be as large round as a common half pint mug. It should be crowded full, and each end tied up. If you have not a sausage-filler, it can be filled with the hand. Sew up only a quarter of a yard, then fill it tight, so far; then sew another quarter, and fill it, and so on until you reach the end. When the meat is to be used, open one end, rip up the seam a little way, and cut off slices rather more than an inch thick, and fry them. It may be kept good from December to March, in a cold, dry place. Dip the bag in strong salt and water, and dry it, before filling it.

How to salt Shad to keep a Year.

Procure those which are just caught; soak them an hour or two in a plenty of water, in order that the scales may be easily taken off. Take care to remove them all. Cut off the heads and open them down the back. When you have taken out all the refuse parts, remove the greatest part of the spine, as the fish will be more sure to keep sweet. A sharp knife is indispensable. Lay them in fresh water with a good deal of salt in it for an hour or two, in order to extract the blood. Then take them out, and sprinkle them plentifully with fine salt, taking care that it touches all the ends and edges. If most convenient, let them lie over night. In the morning, mingle an ounce of saltpetre and a pound of sugar with a peck of *coarse-fine* salt, and put a layer of salt, and a layer of fish (the skin being down), into the firkin. A peck of salt will cure twenty-five shad.

To try Lard.

The fat should not be suffered to stand long without being *tried*, because, even in cold weather, some parts of it may soon become musty, and nothing can then restore its sweetness. Remove all the lean bits, as they will adhere to the kettle, and cause the fat to burn. Cut it into pieces a little more than an inch square, and take care to have them nearly of a size. Put a little water into the kettle, and keep a steady, good fire, without much blaze, and stir the fat often. Attention to the kettle and the fire will be necessary, through the process. It will require three hours to do it. When the fat no longer bubbles, but is still, it is done enough. It is best to squeeze it through a tow cloth bag, made by folding half a square in such a way that the corner will form the end, and it should be rounded off a little at the bottom, and the seam made exactly as directed for a pudding-bag. Two pieces of wood fastened together, somewhat like a lemon-squeezer, will facilitate the process of straining it. Strain all that flows off without much pressure into one jar, and that which is extracted last, into another. There is no advantage in putting salt into lard. It does not mingle with it, as appears by its being always found at the bottom of the kettle, undissolved. Stone jars are best for keeping lard, but potter's ware does very well. It should stand in a cold place, and in warm weather, a fire-place with a close board, in a cool room, is a very good place to keep it.

Scraps are a favorite dish with many persons. Put salt, pepper, and pulverized sage to them, while they are still warm, break them small, and stir them well that the seasoning may be equally distributed.

TOMATOES.

Stewed.

Scald them in order to remove the skins. Cut them up and put them into a saucepan, with a little salt, a bit of butter, and some fine crumbs of bread or pounded cracker. Let them stew gently an hour; if you like them sweet, add sugar ten minutes before serving.

Baked.

Butter a dish, and when you have skinned the tomatoes lay

them in it, whole. Sprinkle salt and sugar over them, and then fine crumbs of bread or pounded cracker. Bake them forty minutes in a dish in which they may be put upon the table. When they are half baked, dip the syrup over the top, so as to moisten the crumbs.

Broiled.

Cut them in two without skinning, and lay them upon the gridiron. They will not break, and will require six or seven minutes to cook through. Turn them, and when laid in the dish, add salt and butter, and also pepper if you prefer.

Like Cucumbers.

Take fair fruit. The small kind, called love-apples, are the best for this use. Take off the skins, slice them, sprinkle salt over them, add vinegar (rather less than for cucumbers), and put on pepper.

Preserved.

Having skinned them, weigh equal quantities of fruit and sugar. Let the tomatoes lie upon a hair sieve a little while, in order that some of the juice may drain out. Then lay them carefully, so as not to spoil the shape, into a stone jar, in alternate layers with the sugar. Allow one lemon for every four pounds of fruit, and lay slices of lemon between each layer of fruit. Cover the jar close, and set it in a kettle of cold water, where it will boil moderately, but constantly, many hours — all day if possible. See that the water comes up high enough around the jar, and also that none of it boils into the top. When it is boiled enough, let the jar stand until the water has in a measure cooled, as it may be broken by being taken at once out of boiling water.

Soup.

Take two quarts of rich beef soup, — remove the fat and

add an onion. Cut small, tomatoes enough to make three pints, stew them until they can easily be strained through a sieve or cullender, and add to the soup. Put in salt and a little pepper, and, before serving, add a table-spoonful of sugar.

Pickle (an excellent Condiment).

Put eight pounds of skinned tomatoes, and four of brown sugar, into a preserving kettle. Stir often and see they do not burn. Boil them to the consistency of molasses, then add a quart of sharp cider-vinegar, a teaspoonful of mace, another of cinnamon, and half a teaspoonful of clove, and boil five minutes longer.

Stewed Tomato (to keep the year round).

Skin and cut up the fruit, and boil it gently two hours in a porcelain kettle; add nothing to it but a little salt. Have ready enough clean bottles to contain the quantity to be stewed. Olive bottles are very convenient for the purpose, but common junk bottles are also good. Provide a tunnel, good corks, a coarse towel, a hammer, and a tin dish containing equal parts of rosin and shoemaker's wax. After two hours' boiling, set the kettle off; have the bottles ready warmed by standing near the fire so that heat will not crack them; put hot water into three or four at a time, shake it about, and drain it out; then fill the bottles with the hot tomato *nearly* far enough to meet the cork. If it does not readily go through the tunnel, push it down with a stick or skewer. When you have filled these, put in the corks and hammer them down; take the coarse towel to protect your hands from the heat, and dip the mouth of the bottle into the melted sealing-wax. See that the cork is entirely covered by it. Set these aside, and do the rest in the same way. This is a convenient way for those who do not own the cans now so much used; and tomatoes put up thus, are as good months afterwards as if the fruit was just gathered. None but fresh and sound ones should be used. Set the bottles in a cool, dry place.

Catsup.

Slice the tomatoes and sprinkle them with salt. If you intend to let them stand until you have gathered several parcels, put in plenty of salt. After you have gathered all you intend to use, boil them gently an hour, strain them through a coarse sieve; slice two good-sized onions very thin for every gallon; add half a spoonful of ginger, two spoonfuls of powdered clove, two of allspice, and a teaspoonful of black pepper. Boil it twenty minutes after the spices are added. Keep it in a covered jar.

This kind of catsup is specially designed to be used in soups, and stewed meats.

Another Catsup (retaining the color and flavor of the Fruit).

Skin and slice the tomatoes, and boil them an hour and a half. Then put to one gallon not strained, a quarter of an ounce of mace, the same of nutmegs and cloves, one handful of horseradish, two pods of red pepper, or a large teaspoonful of cayenne, and salt as you like it. Boil it away to three quarts, and then add a pint of wine and half a pint of vinegar. Bottle it, and leave the bottles open two or three days; then cork it tight. Make this catsup once, and you will wish to make it every year.

Pickled.

Wash green tomatoes, and slice them rather thin; weigh them, and allow three or four sliced onions, four pounds of sugar, and a gallon of cider-vinegar to eight pounds of tomatoes. Put the vinegar to boil in a porcelain kettle with the sugar, stir it, and when it boils up, set it off, and let it stand a few minutes until you can remove the scum without wasting the vinegar; then add the onions, two teaspoonfuls of salt, a tablespoonful each of powdered cinnamon and clove, and a grated nutmeg; then set it upon the fire and immediately add the tomatoes. When the vinegar begins to simmer press the tomatoes gently down. Let them boil only two or three minutes. Put them into covered jars; or, when cool enough, into wide-mouthed bottles. When the pickles are all used, the vinegar need not be lost, as it is excellent upon baked beans, and cold salt meat, or in mince pies.

ON COOKING VEGETABLES.

After being well washed, they should be laid in water, excepting corn and peas, which should be husked and shelled with clean hands, and not washed, as some of the sweetness is thereby extracted. Put all kinds, except peas and beans, into boiling water, with a little salt in it. Hard water spoils peas, and is not good for any vegetables; a very little saleratus or soda will rectify it. Peas are much best when first gathered, and they should not be shelled long before boiling. If they are old, a salt-spoon of soda in the water will make them tender. Asparagus should not be cut so far below the surface of the ground as it usually is for market; the white end never boils tender. Sweet potatoes require a third longer time to cook than the common ones.

Greens, lettuce, and cucumbers should be gathered before the dew is off in the morning, and put into fresh water. All these, with peas, beans, and asparagus, are unhealthful after they are withered.

To Boil Potatoes.

The best potatoes are good boiled without paring, but even they, are best pared; and poor potatoes are unfit to eat, boiled with the skins on. New potatoes are made watery by being laid in water, but late in the winter and in the spring they should be pared and laid in cold water an hour or two before they are cooked. Put them into boiling water, with salt in it, and allow thirty or forty minutes for boiling, according to the size. When they are done through, pour off the water, and take the kettle to the door or window, and shake them. Doing this in the open air makes them mealy; return them to the fire a minute or two, and then serve. Many persons take a fork and break them up in the kettle, before taking them up, and they make a beautiful looking dish done in this way.

Potatoes require nearly an hour to bake in a cooking stove or range.

Mashed Potatoes.

Boil them according to the directions in the preceding receipt, allowing twenty minutes more time before dinner, than if they were to be put on the table whole. When they are dried, set off the kettle and mash them in it with a wooden pestle. This is better than to take them into a pan, as they will keep hot in the kettle. Have ready a gill or two of hot milk or cream; if you use milk, put a small piece of butter into it. Sprinkle salt into the potato and mash it till it is perfectly fine; then pour in the hot milk and mix it thoroughly. The more it is wrought with the pestle, the whiter it becomes. Put it into the dish for the table, smooth the top into proper shape, and set it into the stove to brown. To prepare it in the nicest manner, beat the yolk of an egg and spread over the top before putting it into the stove. If you do not care to take all this trouble, it is very good without being browned.

Potatoe Balls.

Mash boiled potatoes fine, stir into them the yolk of an egg, and make them into balls; then dip them into a beaten egg, roll them in cracker crumbs, and brown them in a quick oven; or, fry them in a small quantity of nice drippings, and in that case flatten them so that they can be easily turned, and browned both sides.

Old Potatoes.

When potatoes are poor, as they often are in the spring, pare, soak, and boil them as directed in the first receipt. Then take two together in a coarse cloth, squeeze and wring them. You can, with care, turn them into the dish in shape; but if not, it is no matter. The broken pieces will still be far better than before, for they will be dry and mealy. Keep a cloth for the purpose.

To Fry Potatoes.

Pare and slice them thin, and if you have the drippings of a baked ham in which to fry them, it will give them a much better relish than butter or beef drippings. Cold boiled potatoes, if fried, should be sliced thicker than raw ones. The latter require much more time to cook than the others. Sprinkle them with salt while frying.

Potatoes Heated in Milk.

To make a very good dish for breakfast, cut cold potatoes quite small, and put them into a saucepan or spider, with milk enough almost, but not entirely, to cover them. When the milk becomes hot, stir and mash the potatoes with a large spoon until there are no lumps. Add salt, and a small bit of butter, stir it often, until it is as dry as you wish to have it. It is a nicer dish, when prepared with so much milk that a good deal of stirring is necessary to make it dry, than if done in but a small quantity.

Sweet Potatoes.

They are best baked; are very nice boiled till tender, and then pared and laid into the oven to brown. They require more time for being cooked, than the common potato. Cold sweet potatoes are excellent sliced and browned on the griddle. When one side is done, sprinkle salt over before turning them.

Mashed Turnips.

Boil them in salt and water, at least an hour and a half, unless they are of early growth. Take them from the kettle into

15 *

a deep dish, press them a little and pour off the water; mash them like potatoes, but use no milk, as they are moist enough. Add salt and a little butter.

It is a very nice way to put an equal number of potatoes and turnips together, and mash them until they are thoroughly mixed. This is a favorite dish among the Dutch in the State of New York.

Shelled Beans.

Put them into cold soft water, just enough to cover them. Boil them from an hour to an hour and a quarter. Some kinds are more easily boiled than others. Do not put in salt until they are nearly done, as its tendency is to make them hard. Take them up with a skimmer and butter them.

String Beans.

Beans should never be used in this way after the pod has become old enough to have a *string*, or tough fibre upon it. Cut off each end, and cut them up small. Boil them in as little water as will keep them from burning. Just before you take them up, add salt and butter, and dredge in a little flour. They should have only as much liquor in them as you wish to take up in the dish, else the sweetness is wasted. String beans and peas are good boiled together.

Peas.

If peas are young and fresh (and none others are good), they will boil in half an hour or thirty-five minutes. They should be put into cold water, without salt. The same quantity should be used as for string beans, and for the same reason. When they are tender, add salt and butter. It is an improvement to boil a single small slice of pork in them. It need not be laid into the dish, and the same slice will do for another boiling.

Asparagus.

Wash it, trim off the white ends, and tie it up in bunches with a twine or a strip of old cotton. Throw them into boiling water with salt in it. Boil twenty-five minutes or half an hour. Have ready two or three slices of toasted bread, dip them in the water and lay them in the dish. Spread them with butter and lay the bunches of asparagus upon the toast. Cut the strings with a scissors and draw them out without breaking the stalks; lay thin shavings of butter over the asparagus, and send it to the table.

Asparagus and Eggs.

Take cold asparagus, and cut it the size of peas; break four or five eggs into a dish, and beat them with pepper, salt, and the asparagus. Then put it into a stew-pan with a spoonful of butter, set it on the fire, and stir it all the time till it thickens. Put it upon toasted bread in a hot dish.

Mushrooms.

Choose such as are young, having red gills; cut off the part of the stalk which grew in the earth; wash them, remove the skin from the top, stew them with some salt in a little water, and when tender add butter, into which you have rubbed browned flour. They are good fried on a griddle.

Salad.

Gather lettuce and pepper-grass early, before the dew has evaporated; pick them over, and lay them in cold water. If the weather is very warm, change the water before dinner-time, and add ice. Just before it is served, cut it small, and prepare the dressing in the following manner. Boil three eggs twelve minutes, and throw them into cold water; remove the shell, and take out the yolks; mash them fine in a spoonful of water and two of oil; add salt, powdered sugar, made mustard and vinegar; pour the mixture over the salad, cut the whites of the eggs in rings and garnish the top.

Cucumbers.

Cucumbers should be gathered while dew is yet on them, and put immediately into water. Half an hour before dinner, pare and slice them very thin, and let them lie in fresh water till dinner is ready; then drain them, lay them into a dish, sprinkle them with salt, pour on the vinegar, and add the pepper last.

Macaroni.

Procure that which looks white and clean. When it is to be used, examine it carefully, as there are sometimes little insects inside. Wash it, and put it in a stew-pan in cold water enough almost to cover it. Add a little salt. Let it boil slowly half an hour; then add a gill of milk and a small piece of butter, and boil it a quarter of an hour more. Then put it into the dish in which it is to go to the table, grate old cheese over it, and heat a shovel red-hot and hold over the top to brown it. It may be browned in a stove, but if the dish would be injured by it, the better way is to use the shovel.

Parsnips.

Those that have remained in the ground till March, are usually very nice. Boil them three quarters of an hour, and cook enough for two days. Scrape the outside, split them, and lay them on a dish with a little butter, salt, and pepper. Take those that are left the next day, and lay them on a hot griddle or spider, with a little butter, ham fat, or nice drippings, and brown them. These are better than on the first day. They will brown well when first boiled, but not so quickly.

Carrots.

These are not considered by most people very good; but they are so in broth and soup. To eat with meat they should be boiled three quarters of an hour, if fresh from the garden; in the winter, an hour and a half. They make very good pies after the fashion of pumpkin or squash; but they must be boiled very tender, and in a good deal of water, else a strong taste will pervade the pies.

Beets.

When they are washed the little fibres and ragged excrescences should not be broken off, as the juices of the root will thus be lost. Young beets boil in an hour; but in the winter they require from two to three hours. When tender, put them for a minute or two into cold water, take them in your hands and slip the skins off. This is a much easier and better way than to remove the skin with a knife. Lay them into a dish, cut them several times through, sprinkle them with salt and pepper, add a little butter, and, if you choose, vinegar also. It is a very good way to cut up all that remain after dinner, put on salt and vinegar, and set them aside to be used cold another day.

Salsify, or Oyster Plant.

Wash and scrape it very thoroughly, and put it in boiling water with salt in it. When tender, cut it in slices and fry it in hot fat, in a batter made of an egg, milk, flour, and salt. It is very nice, also, dipped in bread-crumbs moistened with a beaten egg, and browned on a griddle.

Summer Squash.

If the rind is tender, boil it whole, in a little bag kept for the purpose. It should be put into boiling water; three quarters of an hour is long enough to cook it. Take the bag into a pan and press it with the edge of a plate or with a ladle, until the water is out; then turn the squash out into a dish, add salt and butter, and smooth over the top.

Winter Squash.

Cut it up and take out the inside. Pare the pieces, and stew them in as little water as possible. If you have a tin with holes in it, which will fit the kettle and keep the squash from touching the water, it is the nicest way to steam it. Be careful it does not burn. It will cook in an hour. Mash it in a dish, or, if it is watery, squeeze it in a coarse cloth like summer squash. Stir in butter and salt. Lay it into the dish, smooth the top, and, if you like, pepper it.

Onions.

Boil them twenty minutes, and pour off the water entirely; then put in equal parts of hot water and milk, or skimmed milk alone, and boil them twenty minutes more. When they are done through, take them up with a skimmer, let them drain a little, and lay them into the dish. Put on butter, pepper, and salt.

Spinage.

Put it into a net, or a bag of coarse muslin, kept for the purpose, and boil it in a plenty of water with salt in it, ten or twelve minutes. All kinds of greens should be boiled in plenty of water, else they will be bitter.

One method of serving spinage is, to press it between two plates, then put it into a saucepan with a small bit of butter, salt, and a little cream, and boil it up. Another is to drain it thoroughly, lay it in the dish, put upon the top hard boiled eggs, sliced, and pour melted butter over it.

Greens.

Cabbage plants, turnip or mustard tops, the roots and tops of young beets, cowslips, dandelions, and various other things, make a good dish in the spring. When boiled enough, they will sink to the bottom of the kettle. Some require an hour, and others less time. Turnip-tops will be boiled enough in twenty minutes. Remember to put salt into the water, unless you boil a piece of pork with them.

Cabbage.

Remove the waste leaves, and divide the stump end as far as

the centre of the cabbage. It is good boiled with salt meat; but if cooked by itself, salt should be added to the water. Cabbage should be put into boiling water, be well skimmed, and boil an hour or hour and a half, according to the size.

Cauliflowers.

Lay them an hour or two in cold salt and water; remove the outside leaves and boil them half an hour in milk and water. If they are strong, pour off the water when they are half done, and put fresh boiling water to them. Brocoli is cooked in the same manner, and should be laid on toast exactly like asparagus.

Egg Plant.

Take fresh purple ones, and pull out the stem; parboil them and cut them in slices about an inch thick. Dip them in a beaten egg, and then in a plate of bread or cracker crumbs, with salt and pepper, and fry them in drippings until they are nicely browned.

Boiled Corn.

Put the ears into boiling water, with salt in it, and boil them half an hour.

Corn Soup.

Cut the corn off the cob, and boil the cobs half an hour in the water; then take them out, put in the corn and boil it twenty minutes or half an hour. If there is a quart of the corn and water, add a pint of new milk, with salt, pepper, and one or two beaten eggs. Continue the boiling a few minutes, and thicken it a little with flour.

Succotash.

Cut off the corn from the cobs, and, an hour and a half before dinner, put the cobs, with a few shelled beans, into cold water to boil. After one hour take out the cobs, put in the corn and boil it half an hour. There should be no more water than will be necessary to make the succotash of the right thickness; as having too much occasions a loss of the richness imparted by the cobs. When you take it up, add a small piece of butter. This is much better than to boil the corn on the cob and then cut it off.

It is a very good way, when a family are tired of fresh meat in hot weather, to boil a piece of pork in another pot until the grossest fat has boiled out, and then put it with the succotash for the remainder of the time. It gives a very good flavor to the corn, and makes an excellent dinner.

Corn Oysters.

Grate young, sweet corn into a dish, and to a pint add one egg, well beaten, a small teacup of flour, half a gill of cream, and a teaspoonful of salt. Mix it well together. Fry it exactly like oysters, dropping it into the fat by spoonfuls about the size of an oyster.

PICKLES.

Pickles should never be kept in potter's ware, as arsenic and other poisonous substances are used in the glazing; and this is sometimes decomposed by vinegar. Whole families have been poisoned in this way; and where fatal effects do not follow, a deleterious influence may be operating upon the health, from this cause, when it is not suspected. Pickles should be made with cider vinegar.

Cucumbers.

Wash and drain them in a sieve, but take care not to break the little prickles upon them, as the effect will be to make them soft. Lay them in a jar, pour boiling vinegar upon them and cover them close. The next time you gather any, take those from the jar, and put them into that in which they are to be kept, in fresh vinegar having a very little salt in it, and a small bag of spices. Take the vinegar from the first jar, boil it again, pour it upon the fresh cucumbers, and transfer them like the first to the larger jar, the next time you have a new quantity to boil. When you have gathered all you wish for, put a brass or bell-metal kettle * over the fire, with the vinegar in it which you have so often boiled, and add a little more to it, — no matter if it is not sharp. Lay in your pickles and scald them a few minutes. Take them out with a large skimmer, draining them, and lay them back into the jar of spiced vinegar. Look at them occasionally; they may need a little more vinegar. Keep them covered close.

Mangoes.

Select small musk-melons (the common kind are much better for this purpose than cantelopes); cut an oval piece out of one side. You must have a sharp knife, and be careful to make a smooth incision. Take out the seeds with a teaspoon. Fill the melons with a stuffing made of cloves, mustard-seed, peppercorns, scrapings of horseradish, and chopped onion if you like it. Sew on the piece with a needle and coarse thread, or bind a strip of old cotton around each one and sew it. Lay them in a jar, and pour boiling vinegar on them with a little salt in it. Do it two or three times, then lay them in fresh vinegar and cover them close.

Peaches.

Select peaches that are ripe, yet not quite soft enough to eat; push a clove into each one at the end opposite the stem. Put two pounds of brown sugar to a gallon of vinegar, and boil it

---

* A kettle lined with porcelain is better than any other for cooking acids. Brass or bell-metal should be thoroughly scoured immediately before it is used for these purposes.

up; skim off the top, boil it up once more, and pour it, hot, upon the peaches. Cover them close.

It may be necessary to scald the vinegar again in a week or two; after that, they will keep any length of time. They retain much of the flavor of a fresh peach.

Nasturtiums.

Gather the seeds while green, let them lie a few days, then throw them into vinegar. They need no spice except a little salt, being themselves sufficiently spicy. Boil the vinegar and pour on them. They are considered by many persons better than capers, and are much like them. They should be kept six months, covered close, before they are used.

Eggs.

Boil them twelve minutes, and throw them immediately into cold water, which will cause the shell to come off easily. Boil some red beets till very soft, peel and mash them fine, and put them into cold vinegar enough to cover the eggs; add salt, pepper, cloves, and nutmeg. Put the eggs into a jar and pour the mixture over them.

Peppers.

Take fresh, hard peppers, soak them in salt and water nine days, changing the brine each day. Let them stand in a warm place. Then put them into cold vinegar. If you wish them very hot, leave in the seeds. If not, take out the seeds of the greatest part of them. If peppers are put into the same jar with cucumbers, the entire strength of them will go into the cucumbers, and they themselves will become nearly tasteless. Half a dozen peppers will improve a jar of cucumbers.

Butternuts.

Gather them between the twenty-fifth and thirtieth of June. Make a brine of boiled salt and water, strong enough to bear up an egg after it is cold. Skim it while it boils. Pour it on the nuts, and let them lie in it twelve days. Then drain them; lay them in a jar, and pour over them the best of cider vinegar, boiled with pepper-corns, cloves, allspice, mustard, ginger, mace, and horseradish. This should be cooled before it is poured on. Cover close, and keep them a year before using them. Walnuts are done in the same way. The vinegar becomes an excellent catsup, by many persons preferred to any other.

Martinias.

Gather them when they are rather small, and so tender that you can run the head of a pin into them. Wipe off the down and put them into a cold, weak brine. Keep them in brine nine days, changing it every other day. Make a pickle of vinegar, allspice, cloves, mace, nutmegs, and cinnamon. Take the martinias out of the brine, wipe them, and lay them into a stone jar; pour the mixture of vinegar and spice, boiling hot, over them; cover them close, and let them stand one month, and they will be fit for use. There can be no finer pickle than this, and the plant is so prolific, that half a dozen seeds will produce enough to fill a large jar.

Tomatoes.

See page 170.

Plums, Peaches, Cherries, or Tomatoes.

Four quarts of cider vinegar, five pounds of sugar, a quarter of a pound of cinnamon, and two ounces of clove, to seven pounds of fruit. Scald the vinegar and sugar together, and take off the scum; add the spices and boil it up again, and pour it immediately upon the fruit. Scald the vinegar twice more at intervals of three or four days, and cover the jar close after it is poured in.

A less expensive way is found to be very good. Put four pounds of sugar to eight of fruit, half the quantity of spice, a spoonful of salt, and one also of powdered allspice.

TEA, COFFEE, CHOCOLATE, COCOA, ETC.

Tea.

SEE that the water boils. Scald the pot, and put in a teaspoonful for each person. Upon green tea, pour a little water, and allow it to stand two or three minutes where it will keep hot; then fill the pot from the teakettle. Green tea should never be boiled, and it is rendered dead by being steeped long.

Of black tea the same measure is used; the pot being filled up at first, and set immediately upon the stove, just long enough to boil up once. Water should be added to the teapot from the teakettle; never from the water pot, as in that case it cannot be boiling hot. Black and green tea are good mixed. If tea is made from a boiling urn at the table, which is, on several accounts, a very good practice, make black tea in the same way as green.

To roast Coffee.

As this must be done well in order to have good coffee, directions for it may not be amiss. There are often little stones in coffee, of the same color with it; therefore, pick it over carefully. If you have no coffee-roaster, put it into a round-bottomed, iron kettle, and let it be where it will be hot an hour or two without burning; then put it where it will brown, and stir it constantly until it is done. If it is left half a minute, the kernels next to the kettle may be burnt black, and this is enough to injure all the rest. It should be a dark, rich brown, but not black. Before taking it up, stir in a piece of butter the size of a small nut. Put it, while steaming hot, into a box with a close cover.

In a small family, not more than two pounds should be roasted at once, as it loses its freshness by being roasted long before use. For the same reason it should be ground as it is wanted. The practice of grinding up a quantity for two or three weeks, is a poor one. The best kinds are the Java and the Mocha, and it is considered an improvement to mix the two. West India coffee, though of a different flavor, is often very good.

To make Coffee.

Put a coffee-cup full into a pot that will hold three pints of water; add the white of an egg, or two or three clean eggshells, or a well cleansed and dried bit of fish-skin of the size of a ninepence. Pour upon it boiling water and boil it ten minutes. Then pour out a little from the spout, in order to remove the grains that may have boiled into it, and pour it back into the pot. Let it stand eight or ten minutes where it will keep hot, but not boil; boiling coffee a great while makes it strong, but not so lively or agreeable. If you have no cream, boil a sauce-pan of milk, and after pouring it into the pitcher, stir it now and then till the breakfast is ready, that the cream may not separate from the milk.

If you use a coffee-biggin, let the coffee be ground very fine and packed tight in the strainer; pour on boiling water, stop the spout of the pot, shut the lid close, and place it upon a heater kept for the purpose. This is made at the table.

Coffee Milk.

Put a dessert spoonful of ground coffee into a pint of milk; boil it a quarter of an hour with a shaving or two of isinglass; then let it stand ten minutes and pour it off.

Chocolate.

For those who use a great deal of chocolate, the following is an economical method. Cut a cake into small bits and put them into a pint of boiling water. In a few minutes set it off the fire and stir it well till the chocolate is dissolved; then boil it again gently a few minutes, pour it into a bowl, and set it in a cool place. It will keep good eight or ten days. For use, boil a spoonful or two in a pint of milk, with sugar.

Another.

Shave fine an inch wide across a cake of chocolate; pour on it a quart of boiling water; boil it twenty minutes; add milk in such proportion as you like, and boil it up again.

Cocoa.

The cracked cocoa is considered the best. Two large spoonfuls put into three pints of cold water, and boiled from one to two hours, is a good rule to make it for four or five persons. It should be boiled over several times, as it is very strong. Boil milk for it by itself.

To make the ground Cocoa.

Boil two large spoonfuls in a quart of water half an hour; skim off the oil, pour in three gills of milk, and boil it up again. It is the best way to make it the day before it is used, as the oily substance can be more perfectly removed when the cocoa is cold.

Shells.

Put a heaping teacupful to a quart of boiling water. Boil them a great while. Half an hour will do, but two or three hours is far better. Scald milk as for coffee. If there is not time to boil shells long enough before breakfast, it is well to put them into the water over night.

Syrup of Cream.

To a pint of fresh cream, put a pound and a quarter of loaf sugar; boil it in an earthen pot or saucepan; pour it into a jar or basin, and let it stand till it is cold; then put it into phials and cork close. It will keep good for several weeks, and is convenient to carry to sea.

To raise a Thick Cream.

Put new milk into an earthen pan, and set it on a stove, or over clear embers till it is quite hot. Then set it aside till the next day, and it will produce excellent cream for coffee or fruit.

CONVENIENT COMMON DISHES, AND WAYS OF USING REMNANTS.

Baked Pork and Beans.

For a family of six or seven, take a quart of white beans, wash them in several waters, and put them into two or three quarts over night. In the morning (when it will be easier to cull out the bad ones, than before they were soaked), pick them over, and boil them until they begin to crack open; then put them into a brown pan, such as are made for the purpose. Pour upon them enough of the water they were boiled in almost to cover them. Cut the rind of about a pound of salt pork into narrow strips; lay it on the top of the beans, and press it down so that it will lie more than half its thickness in the water. Bake several hours; four or five is not too much. Where a brick oven is used, it is well to let beans remain in it over night. If they are baked in a stove, or range, more water may be necessary, before they are done.

Many persons think it a decided improvement to put in a large spoonful or two of molasses. It is a very good way.

Those who object to the use of pork, can have a very good dish of beans, by substituting two table-spoonfuls of nice beef-drippings, and adding two teaspoonfuls of salt.

To heat over baked beans, put them in a spider with a little water; heat them slowly at first, and cover close. If they are too moist, remove the cover and stir them often.

Salt meat and Vegetables, boiled together.

Put in the beef first, and allow twenty-five minutes or half an hour for every pound. Skim the water when it begins to simmer. An hour and a half before the dinner-hour, put in the pork, well scraped and washed, and again skim off the froth. Wash the vegetables with special care, and allow for boiling turnips, carrots, and cabbage, an hour, or an hour and a quarter;

for parsnips three quarters, and for potatoes, half an hour. If the potatoes are not pared, a small piece of the skin should be cut off from each end. When the dinner is served, the pot should be set away in a cool place, and the fat taken from the top the next day, and put aside for soap grease. It will not be good for any other use, as it will have the flavor of the vegetables.

Remnants of Roast Beef.

Take off with a sharp knife all the meat from the bones. If there are a few nice slices, reserve them, if most convenient, to be eaten cold. Chop the rest fine in a tray. Take cold gravy, without the fat, and put into a spider to heat. If you have not this, some of the stock, or water in which meat has been boiled. When it boils up, sprinkle in salt, and put in the minced meat; cover it, and let it stand upon the fire long enough to heat thoroughly, then stir in a small piece of butter. Toast bread and lay in the dish and put the meat over it. The common error in heating over meat, sliced or minced, is the putting it into a cold spider, with too much fat, and cooking it a long time. This makes it oily and tasteless. Almost all meats, when cooked a second time, should be done very quick. The goodness of these dishes depends much upon their being *served hot.*

Another.

When tomatoes are to be had, cut up several, according to the size of your family, and the quantity of cold meat; put them into a covered saucepan or kettle. When it boils put in the remnants, large and small, of cold roast beef, and also of roast mutton and lamb, if you have them. Add half a spoonful of brown sugar, salt, and a small bit of butter unless you have cold gravy. This, with the fat taken off, is nearly as good. Boil it again, fast, but only long enough to heat the meat thoroughly. Five minutes is enough.

Remnants of Boiled Meat.

Chop fine cold pieces of soup meat, or other boiled meat, salt or fresh; then add cold potatoes, and when these are chopped and mixed with the meat, heat in a spider some cold soup, or water in which meat has been boiled. As it boils up, put in the meat and potatoes, add salt, and cover it close for two or three minutes, then stir in a small piece of butter, let it stand a minute or two longer and then serve in a warm dish.

To heat over Beefsteak.

Cut it up small, or chop it; put it into a spider or saucepan with a little hot water. Season it with salt and a little butter.

All these dishes of remnants are much improved by using, instead of water, some of the stock for which a receipt is given on page 123.

Minced Veal.

Chop fine the pieces left of roast veal. Heat the gravy in a spider, or, if you have none left, melt a piece of butter half the size of an egg in a gill of hot water; stir it till it is melted lest it become oily. When it boils, put in the veal and cover it; stir it two or three times in the course of eight or ten minutes; season it with salt and pepper. Toast two or three slices of bread and lay in the dish. Put the veal upon the toast.

Brawn.

Boil a hock of beef, and any little pieces you may have besides, several hours. When the meat is ready to fall from the bones, take it out into an earthen pan, salt it, and season it with pepper, sage, and sweet marjoram. Put it into a coarse linen cloth or towel, twist it up tight and lay a weight upon it. A good deal of fat will thus be pressed out. When it has lain twenty-four hours take off the cloth. Cut thin slices for breakfast. It is very good, and will keep in a cool place several weeks. The water in which it was boiled will make excellent soup, or stock for gravies.

Head Cheese.

Take the head, feet, ears, and tail of a hog, and boil them until every bone falls out. Then take all the meat, both fat and lean, and put into an earthen pan. Season it with salt, pepper, sage, cloves, and summer savory, or any spice and herbs you may prefer. Put it into a coarse cloth, twist it up, and lay a weight upon it. This is a favorite article of food in some parts of the country, and certainly it is very good. Great care is necessary in cleaning such giblets of pork.

Another economical use for them is to take out all the bones, as for head cheese, and then return the meat to the liquor, boil it up, and stir in Indian meal, just as in making hasty-pudding. Put in considerable salt, and let it boil very moderately another hour and a half. Then take it up in deep dishes, and when it is cold cut it in slices and brown it on a griddle. A convenient breakfast article for laborers, but too hearty for persons of sedentary habits.

Souse.

Take off the horny parts of the feet and toes of a pig, and clean the feet, ears, and tail very thoroughly; then boil them till the large bones slip out easily. Pack the meat into a stone jar, with pepper, salt, and allspice sprinkled between each layer. Mix some good cider vinegar with the liquor in which it was boiled, in the proportion of one third vinegar to two thirds liquor, and fill up the jar.

To boil Rice.

Rice should be carefully picked over, and then washed first in warm water, and rubbed between the hands; then, five or six times in a good deal of cold water. It will not be white unless it is well washed.

To cook rice as a vegetable to be eaten with meat, put a pint into three or four quarts of hot water, with a teaspoonful of salt for each quart. Boil it fast fifteen minutes, then pour off the water, and set it, uncovered upon the stove where it will not burn, to dry. Boiled in this way, the kernels are separate, and it is considered, by those who live in the rice growing countries, the best, if not the only proper way of cooking it.

To boil rice in milk, is a very good way for families that keep cows, as it is thus a nice substitute for a pudding. Put a pint of rice into nearly two quarts of cold milk, an hour before dinner. Add two teaspoonfuls of salt. Boil it very slowly, and stir it often. It will cook on the back part of the range or stove, and not be liable to burn. When the supply of milk is small, boil rice in skimmed milk, or milk and water. It should, when boiled in a way to lose the distinct form of the kernels, be taken up in a mould, or bowl, wet in cold water, a short time before it is served.

Cracked Wheat.

Take one or two quarts, according to the size of the family, put it into cold water and after stirring it well, let it settle, then pour off the water, and add more, in the proportion of three quarts to a quart of wheat. Let it stand over night, and the next day boil it very moderately two or three hours. Add salt, and stir it very often lest it should burn. If it becomes too thick, add more water. The evaporation is more rapid at some times than at others. It should be not quite as thick as hasty pudding. Take it up in dishes wet in cold water. To brown it for breakfast, grease a tin or dripping pan, turn the wheat out of the dish upon it, and set it into the stove oven. It will become heated through, and handsomely browned in half an hour or forty minutes, and many people like it thus, better than when it is first boiled. Either way it is very nutritious and healthful.

Hasty Pudding.

Boil in a pot or kettle about six quarts of water, leaving room for the addition of the meal; mix a pint bowl full of Indian meal and cold water with a small spoonful of salt. When the water boils, stir this into it. After thirty or forty minutes, stir in four or five handfuls of dry meal, and let it boil as much longer; then add more dry meal. Taste it to see if it is salt enough. Stir it very often to prevent its burning. Most people make it too thick, and do not cook it half long enough. Boil it, altogether, at least two hours. When taken out, it should be so soft that it will in a few minutes settle down smooth in the dish. If you wish to fry it, put a spoonful of water into each deep pan or dish into which it is to be put, to keep it from sticking.

Hasty Pudding fried.

Cut cold pudding in slices the thickness of your finger, and lay them on the griddle. More fat will be necessary than for buckwheat cakes, but it fries much slower. If the fire is right it will be ready to turn in fifteen minutes, and will be brown. Turn it and let it lie about half as long as on the first side.

This is a very good breakfast for a winter morning. It does very nicely to be laid in the dripping-pan, and set into a stove oven; it will in that case not need turning, and of course will absorb less fat. It will take forty minutes to brown it in the stove.

Pan Pie.

The sour apples that drop from the trees early in the autumn, make an excellent pan pie without being pared. The skin then contains much of the richness of the apple, and is often so thin, that when cooked, it cannot be distinguished from the pulp. There are few articles of diet so healthy and palatable as pan pie, that are prepared with so little trouble and expense.

Where a brick oven is used, the following is a good receipt.

Take a potters ware pan, that will hold a gallon, and fill it with apples, quartered and cored; in winter pare the apples; roll out a piece of light bread dough, and lay upon the top; butter the edge of the pan to prevent the dough from sticking to it; cut an opening in the crust to allow the steam to escape, and put it into the oven. After about two hours draw it out and remove the crust, sweeten it with good molasses, or, if you choose, coarse sugar. Some persons use both. Put in a few sticks of cinnamon or some allspice, and a piece of butter as large as a nut. Stir it up thoroughly from the bottom. Your taste must guide you as to the quantity of sugar or molasses. Break up the bread crust and put into the apple. If it is very moist, return the pan uncovered to the oven; but if dry enough, cover it with an old plate; let it stand four or five hours.

There are various ways of making this dish. Some persons prefer to put in the molasses at first, and others use only sugar. It is very easy to improve it by rolling a little butter into the dough, exactly as in pie-crust; and if this is done once only, it makes the crust much more tender. Some persons put any crusts or pieces of bread they happen to have, into the apple, and if the crust that was baked with it is thin, it is a very good way.

Another.

To make a pan pie to bake in a stove oven, or range, cover the bottom of a deep dish with a layer of stewed apple; spread over it brown sugar enough to make it sweet, scatter in a little powdered cinnamon, and add two or three bits of butter the size of a filbert; then lay in pieces of plain pie crust or biscuit, baked rather brown, or crusts of light bread; spread a thick layer of apple over the pieces, scatter more cinnamon, and pour over the whole molasses enough to sweeten the upper layer of apple, then bake it in a moderate heat an hour and a half, or two hours. It is the best way to make it while the stewed apple is hot.

Crumb Cakes.

Keep a bowl or pitcher with sour milk in it, and from time to time throw in the crumbs of bread which break off when it is sliced, and also the dry pieces left of the table. When you next want griddle-cakes, take this mixture and break up all the pieces with your hand, add an egg, salt, and saleratus, and a few spoonfuls of flour. If the proportion of bread is too great, the cakes will not be good. Experience must teach, as no exact rule can be given.

Milk Toast.

Put a quart of milk, except two or three spoonfuls, to boil; rub smooth a small table-spoonful of flour in the reserved milk; when that in the saucepan begins to boil, stir in a piece of butter, rather larger than an egg, cut up in little bits. Stir steadily until it is all melted; then stir in the flour, and add a tea-spoonful of salt. When it boils up again, set it where it will keep hot, without boiling, while the bread is toasted. Bread is not good when it is dried in the process of toasting; it should be browned quickly, and dipped while it is hot.

If you have cream, boil it without adding any butter; when boiled, put in a little salt, and a very little flour rubbed smooth in a spoonful of milk; dip the slices of toasted bread, and let them remain half a minute; then lay them into a hot dish with a cover, and pour over the remainder of the boiled cream.

Bruiss.

Take crusts of brown bread, and if they are dry and hard, lay them over night in a little water. In the morning add milk and boil them slowly. Take care they do not burn. Sprinkle in salt, and just before you take them up, add a little butter. If there is too much milk, take off the lid the latter part of the time. Take up the pieces as whole as you can.

Crusts of white bread make a good breakfast dish, in the same way, except that they do not need soaking over night.

Uses for pieces of Bread.

In some families there is always an accumulation of pieces of bread, and a good deal of ingenuity is necessary to prevent waste. If bread is good, and proper care is taken, such a thing as a plate of dry pieces is needless. Some families never have them. But for the benefit of those who, from any cause, cannot always prevent it, the following modes for making good use of pieces are suggested. A bread pudding is easily made, by boiling the pieces in milk. You can make as rich a pudding as you choose, by adding sugar, eggs, suet, spice, and raisins; or as plain a one, putting no sugar, two eggs, and a few sliced apples to a quart of milk, and boil or bake it. Make crumb cakes of some of the pieces. Boil a dish of others in milk for breakfast. If you are cooking meat that requires or admits of a stuffing, soften crusts with a very little boiling water, add butter, herbs, and a beaten egg. In summer, when bread becomes mouldy from long keeping, lay the pieces which cannot be used immediately, upon a tin and dry them in the oven; they are as good pounded for puddings and crumb cakes as before drying, and as nice to dress a ham as cracker crumbs. Nice pieces of bread are good in pan pie, and also in stewed tomato.

It is a good way to have a small board upon which to slice bread; and brush the crumbs from it into a box, or dish kept for the purpose. Such things may seem of little consequence, but the beneficial influence of economical habits is not limited to the actual value of the amount saved.

Care of Fat and Drippings.

In a large family, where much meat is consumed, the care of the fat and drippings is an important item; and every housekeeper should know what is done with them.* If she has a young cook, she probably will not be acquainted with the various ways of preventing them from being wasted; if one who is experienced, she may not always care to take the trouble. When meat is of a superior quality, there is usually some fat which should be trimmed off before it is cooked, and more will then roast out, than can be properly used for gravy; therefore, about three quarters of an hour before the meat is done, pour

* The custom of giving them to the cook as her perquisite, besides being wasteful, is productive of various evils.

off all the drippings from the roaster, into a dish, and set them away to cool.* Save all the nice pieces of fat, and put those that are not so into the soap-grease. In warm weather, the good pieces should be clarified once in three or four days; in winter, once a week. If you have boiled lamb, or boiled beef which has been slightly salted, take the fat which cools on the top of the liquor, and add to that poured off from the roaster; scrape off any specks which may be on the under side of it. To clarify, cut small all the pieces saved, and put them into a small kettle; cover it, and put it on the stove or range where it will not burn. It should be tried slowly; stir it occasionally. When it looks clear, the cakes of drippings, the pieces from the top of the pot, &c., should be added. As soon as it again becomes clear, pour it through a little sieve, or colander with very small holes.

Fat thus clarified will save butter. It makes very good plain gingerbread and common pie-crust, or if preferred, can be used in each of these with half butter; it is as good as lard, to fry doughnuts or biscuit, and much more healthful; and though not equal for frying fish, to salt pork, does very well for this purpose. It is well to keep a small stone jar for such fat. A brown earthen one soon becomes saturated with it, and smells disagreeably.

The fat of mutton should not be put with other kinds, as it is very hard and tallow-like, and the taste is not agreeable. It however does very well to use on the griddle, or to grease pans for bread.

The fat which is not nice enough for any of these uses, should (unless it is more convenient to dispose of it to the soap boiler) be tried for the purpose of making soap. It should be kept in a dry place where it will not mould, and be covered so that flies will not visit it. Two receipts are given (see page 197) for making soap with very little trouble.

---

* See the directions for making gravies.

To make Soap with Potash.

Allow sixteen pounds each of grease and potash for a barrel of soap. The grease should be such as has been well taken care of, viz., tried before it became wormy or mouldy. The potash should be about the color of pumice-stone. That which is red, makes dark soap, unfit for washing clothes. Cut up the grease into pieces of two or three ounces, put it into a tight barrel with the potash; then pour in two pailfuls of rain or spring water. The soap will be soonest made by heating the water, but it is just as sure to be good if made with cold water. Add a pailful of soft water every day, until the barrel is half full, and stir it well each day. A long stick with a cross piece at the lower end, is convenient for the purpose. When the barrel is half full, add no more water for a week or ten days, but continue to stir it daily. After that, add a pailful a day, until the barrel is full. It is the best way to keep soap three or four months before beginning to use it. It spends more economically, and is less sharp to the hands. When half of it has been used, put two pails of soft water to the rest, and stir it up well, from the bottom. The lower half of a barrel of home-made soap is always the strongest. Soft soap, made with clean grease and good potash is of a light nankeen color, and is better for washing flannels and white clothes than any other.

It is good economy to make soap, and it is so little work to make it with potash, and the result is so sure, that no one need to be deterred from it by the fear of trouble or ill-success.

To make Soap with Ashes.

The following method of making soap with ashes has been tried and proved good.

Provide a leach cask, that is, one that is large at the top, and small at the bottom. If this is not readily obtained, procure a hogshead that will not leak, have the head taken out at one end, and set it, propped forward a little, upon logs placed right and left, and high enough from the ground to set a pail under the front side. There should be a hole in the bottom, close to the front, with a tight plug in it. Lay in two or three bricks around the plug hole, and across them some bits of board, so as to reserve a space, and keep the ashes from packing close against the plug hole, — also several bricks here and there over the bottom with straw or brush laid on them. Then have the ashes put in and pressed down, till the hogshead is very full. Scoop a hollow in the centre in which to pour the water, and then fill it with cold *soft* water, until it will absorb no more. The next day, see if the water has settled away, if so, add more. When it is full, cover it up. After three weeks, draw off the ley, and put it into the soap barrel. Then pour into it twenty pounds of grease, of all kinds, tried and rough, ham skins, and scraps, boiling hot. Stir it very thoroughly, and every day. Have the hogshead filled again, and after three or four weeks draw off the ley, which will, this time, be comparatively weak; fill up the soap barrel, and continue to stir it daily for a week or two. The first ley being very strong will completely eat up even the coarsest of the grease, and after three or four months you will have a barrel of excellent soap, fit for use.

In order to have strong ley the ashes should be of good wood. Walnut and maple ashes are best for the purpose. If you wish to make the soap immediately, the water for filling the leach should be nearly boiling, and it can be drawn off the next day.

Leached ashes are useful to spread upon grass.

THE CARE OF MILK, AND MAKING BUTTER.

No branch of household economy brings a better reward than the making of butter; and to one who takes an interest in domestic employments, it soon becomes a pleasant occupation.

The following instructions are derived from the personal experience of one of the most skilful dairy-women in New England; and by observing them, the youthful house-keeper, hitherto unpractised in such mysteries, will have the pleasure of furnishing her table with the finest butter, the work of her own hands.

The first requisite is to have a good cow. One that has high hips, short fore-legs and a large udder is to be preferred. The cream-colored and the mouse-colored cows generally give a large quantity and of rich quality. Her feeding should be faithfully attended to. She should have a good pasture not far distant, or if this is impracticable, care must be taken that she is not made to run — a piece of mischief frequently practised. Give her a teacupful of salt once a week. Feed her once a day with the waste from the kitchen, adding to it about a pint of Indian meal. Give her the skimmed milk not wanted in the family. If she does not readily drink it, teach her by keeping her a few days without an ample supply of water. Take care that nothing is given her which will injure the taste of the milk, such as turnips and parsnips. Carrots are a fine vegetable for cows. Have her milked by a person who understands the process, or she will not give it freely, and will soon become dry. But the most abundant supply of the richest milk will avail little, unless all the articles used in the care of it are kept in perfect order. They should not be used for other purposes. Keep a cloth for washing them only, and never wash them in the same water with other dishes. After washing, every article, and the cloth with which they are washed, must be scalded. Wash off thoroughly all the milk from the pans, pail, strainer, churn, dasher, skimmer, spoons, &c., before scalding them. If milk remains in them when scalded, the butter will be injured, as may be supposed, from the fact that a cloth strainer, if scalded a few times with milk in it, becomes yellow, and as stiff as if it were starched.

To scald them the water must actually boil. Have a kettle

of a size to admit the pail and pans, and plunge all the articles into it; as, if the water is only poured on, the edges of the pan and the ears of the pail will not always be well scalded.

If a cloth strainer is used, it should be of thin, coarse linen. A basin having a fine wire strainer is used by many persons. Tin pails and pans are better than wood and earthen; because tin is more easily kept sweet than wood, and the glazing upon brown earthen pans is sometimes decomposed by sour milk.* Large wooden churns, worked by dogs trained to the business, are used in large dairies; but those who keep one or two cows only, will find a stone-ware churn best. No other is so easily kept sweet. For keeping the cream, never use tin, but always stone, cream-colored or fire-proof ware. For working butter, keep a wooden bowl and ladle. This last article is seldom found in New England, but always in the State of New York. Every butter-maker should have it, as the warmth of the hand detracts from the sweetness of the butter.

Have the milk closet on the coolest side of the house, or in the dryest and coolest part of the cellar, and with a window in it covered with wire-net or slats. Good butter cannot be made without a free circulation of fresh air. Allow no drops of cream or milk to remain a day on the shelves. Every inch of such a closet must be kept perfectly clean.

Strain the milk as soon as it is brought in, and set it immediately in its place. To remove milk after the cream has begun to rise, prevents its rising freely. For the same reason the smallest quantity should not be taken from a pan set for raising cream; therefore all that is wanted for the day's use, must be set apart from the other pans. Those who have ice through the summer, have a valuable aid in making good butter. A piece as large as a peach, should be put into a pan containing three quarts of

---

* About two years since four men, while making hay in a warm day, drank buttermilk which had been kept in a jar of potter's ware, and every one died immediately.

milk, as soon as it is placed in the closet. The milk will not sour as soon, and of course will afford more cream. Skim the cream as soon as the milk has become *loppord*, which will, in hot weather, be in about thirty hours. To do this, first pass the fore-finger round the edge of the pan; (this is better than to use the skimmer, because there is a hard, wiry edge of cream adhering to the pan, which if taken off will injure the butter;) then take off the cream, clear as possible from the milk.

In very hot weather, especially in August, which is the least favorable month for making butter, a heaping spoonful of salt should be put into a pailful of milk, after the portion for the ordinary family uses is taken out; and at all seasons, fine salt should be put into the cream from day to day, as it is gathered. The effect of this is excellent, in keeping it sweet and giving a rich flavor to the butter.

The finest butter is made where the number of cows renders it necessary to churn every day. The custom of churning once a week is not to be tolerated. Cream that is kept seven days, unless it be in the coldest weather, cannot be made into good butter. If you keep but one cow, churn twice a week; and in dog-days, three times. Do it in the cool of the morning. If the weather is warm, set the churn into a tub of cold water; add ice if you have it, and put a piece also into the churn. Air is necessary to make butter *come;* therefore, if the cream flies out of the opening around the dasher, do not put any thing round to prevent it. When the butter has come, continue the strokes of the dasher a few minutes to separate all the little particles from the butter-milk. This done, take it out into the wooden bowl with a ladle or skimmer. The bowl and ladle should have boiling water poured on them when you first begin to churn. After a few minutes it should be poured off, and cold water be poured on them, and they should stand till you are ready to use them. This is to prevent the butter from sticking to them.

Work the butter with the ladle, until the buttermilk ceases

to come out; then sprinkle it with clean sifted salt, as that which was put into the cream will not be enough; work it in well, and taste it to see if more should be added. Observation and experience must teach you how much to use. Mould the butter with the ladle into balls or lumps of any form you prefer; put it into a covered jar or tureen and set it in the ice-house or cellar.

Butter is sweetest to be worked but once, and if all which you make is used from week to week, it is sufficient, provided it comes hard; if it is soft at first, it must be worked again the next morning. That which is to be laid down for future use, or to be kept two or three weeks, must be worked again after a day or two, and every particle of buttermilk got out. Never work butter a third time.

From October to June, the best method of raising cream is to set the pans for twelve hours in the milk closet, and then for five hours on a stove, or a furnace having embers in it, where the milk will become hot, *but not scald;* then return it to the closet, and after it is cold, take off the cream, draining it very clear from the milk. Much more cream will be obtained in this, than in the ordinary method; and at least a quarter more butter will be secured from the same quantity of milk. It also comes very quick — ten minutes' churning being often sufficient, This is the method practised in Devonshire, England; and the *clotted cream,* as it is there called, is carried up to the London market; for it is not only good for butter, but also for coffee and other uses. Care must be taken that the milk is not made too hot. If it becomes so hot as almost to scald, the cream will have little skinny flakes in it, which will be visible in the butter.

A good Brine for keeping Butter.

To two quarts of water, put one of clean fine salt, a pound of loaf or crushed sugar, and a teaspoonful of saltpetre. When it has stood an hour, in order that the salt and sugar may dissolve, strain it through a flannel bag, and pour it over the butter.

Less salt may be enough. The object is to have as much as the water will take up.

To keep Butter sweet a Year.

Take care that the butter is made in the best manner, and the buttermilk entirely worked out of it. Lay it in a white-oak firkin. Make a strong brine of salt and water, and put it into another and larger firkin, and set the one containing the butter into the one in which the brine is. Let the brine come up very near to the top of the butter firkin. Lay on the top of the butter a white bag with fine salt in it, cover it close, and then put on the cover of the outside firkin.

ON MAKING CHEESE.

THE articles used in making cheese should be kept sweet and clean as in making butter. They should be scalded daily, and never be set away until perfectly dry. The conveniences wanted are a large pine tub, painted white inside; a cheese basket and a ladder, on which to set the basket over the tub; two cheese-hoops, large or small, according to the size of the dairy; two large square strainers of thin coarse linen; two circular boards called *followers;* and a brass kettle large enough to hold several pails of milk. Presses used are of various constructions. The most convenient one has a lever and weight; and for making very large cheeses, a windlass should be attached to the end of the lever.

To make Cheese.

Strain the night's milk into the tub; in the morning stir in the cream (if you want rich cheese do not let any of it be taken off), and put a part of the milk over a clear fire, in the brass kettle. Heat it enough to make the milk which is still in the tub quite warm, but not hot; pour it back into the tub, and strain in the morning's milk. Put in a spoonful or two of rennet, stir it well, and let it stand half an hour undisturbed. If the curd does not form well by that time put in more rennet.

To prepare rennet. This is the stomach of a calf; and it is often the case that a piece of curd (the last milk eaten by the calf) is found in it. See if there is any thing inside which should be removed, and then return the curd to its place, in the rennet; it is the best part of it. Soak the rennet in a quart of water, then salt it and hang it up to dry where the flies will not find it; keep the water in a jar or bottle. There is a great difference in the strength of rennets; some will make a thousand weight of cheese, while others will scarcely make fifty. Experience alone will teach exactly how much to use.

When the curd is well formed, cut it in squares, making the knife go down to the bottom of the tub at every stroke; let it stand fifteen minutes for the whey to separate. Then break it up very gently, putting the hand down through all parts. It should be done gently, or some of the milk will be lost in the whey. This causes white whey; the greener the whey, the richer the cheese. Lay the strainer on the top of the curd, and dip off the whey that presses up through, until you have dipped about a third of it. Put this immediately over the fire to heat. When hot, but not boiling, pour it back upon the curd and then break up the curd small, and as quickly as possible, with your hand; then lay the strainer into the cheese basket, and pour the curd into it to drain. When this is done, return it to the tub, salt it, put it again into the strainer, and then into the cheese-hoop. Do not twist up the strainer, but lay it over smooth; lay a follower upon it, put it into the press, and press it tight. Let it remain two days, and increase the pressure four or five times meanwhile, turning the cheese over each time. If you make cheese every day, you will need two presses.

After this, turn the cheese out upon a shelf, in a dark closet or room, secure from flies. Rub every day the side that has lain upon the shelf, and turn it over. Rub it *all over* with butter often. These things must be done for six months. Butter made of *whey-cream*, is generally used for this purpose. If cheese is rich, a strip of new American cotton, as wide as the thickness of the cheese, should be sewed tight around it, when first taken from the press. Without this, it would soon melt out of shape. During the season, when flies are about, rub cheese now and then with butter sprinkled with cayenne pepper.

FOOD AND DRINKS FOR THE SICK, AND FOR INFANTS.

Beef Tea.

CUT a piece of lean, juicy beef into pieces an inch square, put them into a wide-mouthed bottle and cork it tight. Set the bottle into a kettle of cold water and boil it an hour and a half. This mode of making beef tea concentrates the nourishment more than any other.

Another (furnished by a physician).

Take a piece of beef cut from the round; take off every particle of fat, then cut it into pieces about an inch square and put into cold water, in the proportion of a pint to the pound. After standing half or three quarters of an hour, set it on the fire and boil it slowly several hours. If the water boils away, add more cold water, so that there will be a pint of tea for every pound of beef. Strain it, add salt, and black pepper also if the case allows it.

Another Way.

Choose a lean and juicy piece of beef, the size of your hand; take off all the fat; broil it only three or four minutes, on very hot coals. Lay it in a porringer or bowl, sprinkle it with salt, and pour upon it two or three gills of boiling water; then cut it into small pieces, as it lies in the water. Cover it close, and let it stand where it will keep hot but not boil. It is fit for use in half an hour, and does well where such nourishment is wanted immediately.

This is more agreeable to the taste than tea made by either of the two preceding rules, but it is not as good for a patient who is so sick as to take but very little nourishment at once.

Chicken Broth.

If the weather is warm, use but half a chicken to make broth for one person. If it is cool take a whole one, as the broth will keep several days. Pull off the skin (because there is a good deal of oil in it) and allow two quarts of water for a chicken. Skim it in the neatest manner when it begins to boil. Put in a large spoonful of rice, and a teaspoonful of salt, and boil it slowly two hours. If onion and parsley are to be added, cut them fine; put in the onion when the broth has boiled an hour, and the parsley five minutes before it is served.

It is the best way to boil the chicken the day before it is wanted, and the next day take off the fat, add the rice, &c., and boil it another hour.

Chicken Tea.

Take a leg and thigh of a chicken, lay it into a pint of cold water, and set it on the fire till it boils up long enough for you to skim it. Put in a little salt.

Chicken Panada.

Boil a young chicken half an hour in a quart of water. Then remove the skin, cut off the white meat, and when cold, put it into a mortar with a spoonful or two of the water in which it was boiled, and pound it to a paste. Season it with salt, and a very little nutmeg; add a little more of the water, and boil it up three or four minutes. It should be of such a consistency that it can be drank, though rather thick.

The bones which remain may be returned to the water in

which the chicken was boiled; and with the addition of rice, a good broth be made of it.

Calf's foot Broth.

Boil two feet in three quarts of water, until it is wasted to three pints. Strain it, and set it aside in a cool place. When cold, take off the fat. Heat a little at a time as it is wanted, and add salt, nutmeg, and, if approved, a spoonful of good wine.

Wine Whey.

To a pint of milk put two glasses of wine; mix it, and let it stand twelve minutes, then strain it through a muslin bag or a very fine sieve. Sweeten it with loaf sugar.

If it is necessary to have the whey weaker, put a little hot water to the milk.

Barley Water.

Boil an ounce of pearl barley a few minutes to cleanse it, pour off the water, and put a quart of cold water and a little salt to it. Simmer it an hour.

Arrow-root.

The best kinds of arrow-root are the Jamaica and Bermuda.

Wet a large teaspoonful in a little cold water, with half a teaspoonful of salt; pour on it half a pint of boiling water, stirring it very fast. Then set it where it will just boil up for one minute. Sweeten it, and add milk if it is allowed. For a drink, make it very thin, and put in lemon juice and sugar.

Pearl Sago, and Tapioca.

The directions, page 90 are appropriate for the preparation of these articles for invalids.

Milk Porridge.

Put to half a pint of boiling water, two teaspoonfuls of flour wet smooth in cold water, and add salt. Then put in half a pint of milk, stir it well, and let it boil up again. Vary the proportions of milk and water as the case requires. Made wholly with milk it is a very hearty dish.

Oatmeal Gruel.

Put two large spoonfuls of oatmeal, wet in cold water, into three pints of boiling water; boil it gently half an hour, skim it, add a little salt, sugar, and nutmeg. If raisins are also used, a large teacupful stoned, will be enough. But gruel with raisins should be boiled longer than without.

Ground Rice Gruel.

Rub a heaping teaspoonful of ground rice in a small quantity of cold water, and stir it into half a pint of boiling water; add a little salt, and let it boil up half a minute. If milk is allowed, it is an improvement to make the gruel with equal parts of milk and water.

Indian Meal Gruel.

This is made in the same way as the ground rice, but requires much longer boiling. It should never be boiled less than half an hour, and an hour is much better. The white froth that rises upon the top should never be skimmed off, as it is the most nutritious part of the gruel. Nutmeg, sugar, and a spoonful of cream may be added, if approved.

Panada.

Set a saucepan with three gills of water upon the fire, add one glass of white wine, a little loaf sugar, and a very little nutmeg, and grated lemon. Meanwhile, grate some white bread, and the moment the mixture boils, put in the bread, keeping it still on the fire. Let it boil fast, and when of a thickness just to allow of drinking it, set it off.

A Nutritious Jelly.

Take of rice, sago, pearl barley, and hartshorn shavings, each an ounce; add three pints of water, simmer it till reduced to one, and then strain it. When cold, it will be a jelly, to be given dissolved in broth, milk, or wine, as directed by the physician.

Caudle.

Into a pint of thin rice gruel put, while it is boiling hot, a mixture made of the yolk of an egg, beaten well with sugar, a large spoonful of cold water, a glass of wine, and some nutmeg. It should be stirred in by degrees.

Rennet Whey.

Wash a piece of rennet an inch or two square, and lay it into half a gill of warm water for an hour. Warm a pint of milk. but do not make it hot; put it into a shallow dish, and stir the rennet-water into it. Let it stand undisturbed half an hour, then cut it across many times with a knife, and after an hour pour off the whey. Let the dish then remain several hours undisturbed, and more whey will be formed.

In cases of great debility of the stomach, consequent upon inflammation, or attended with it, rennet whey will be retained when every thing else is rejected, and may be given, a teaspoonful at the time, very often, in order to prepare the stomach to receive and retain nourishment.

Apple Tea.

Roast sour apples and pour boiling water upon them. Let them stand till the water is cold.

Another.

Pare and slice thin three or four pleasant sour apples, pour a pint of boiling water on them, and boil them six or eight minutes. Let them stand till they are cold, then pour or strain off the water, and sweeten it a little, unless the invalid prefers it without. It is a refreshing drink.

A Refreshing Draught in a Fever.

Wash a few sprigs of sage, burnet, balm, and sorrel, and put them into a jug with half a sliced lemon. Pour in three pints of boiling water, sweeten it, and stop it close.

Crust Coffee.

Take a large crust of bread; brown is to be preferred, but Graham bread will answer. Dry it in the toaster, and at last almost burn both sides; lay it in a saucepan and pour boiling water on it; boil it up a minute or two, and then strain off the coffee; return it to the saucepan with a little milk or cream, and boil it up again. It should be made strong enough to look like real coffee, of which it is a very good imitation when well made.

Toast Water.

Toast a crust of white bread very brown without burning it, and put it into cold water. After an hour, the water will be a refreshing drink; and it is sometimes grateful to the stomach when no other can be taken.

Herb Drinks.

Herb drinks should be made with boiling water in an earthen pitcher or tea-pot, and be drank after standing a few minutes without boiling. Long steeping makes them insipid and disagreeable.

All food and drink for the sick should be prepared with careful attention and perfect neatness, and should be served in as inviting a manner as possible. The appetite of an invalid is excited or checked by things that escape the observation of a person in health.

Food for a Young Infant.

Pour four spoonfuls of boiling water upon one of sweet cream, and add a very little loaf sugar. This receipt was given by an experienced physician, and has been proved, to be entirely suited to the stomach of the youngest infant. But care must be taken to secure *good* cream; and this can be done only by providing new milk every day, from *one* cow. Mixed milk cannot be safely used for a little infant.

For a child just weaned.

There is always danger, especially in warm weather, that the stomach, even of a healthy child, will become disordered by being weaned; and it is important to guard against the evil, by careful attention to the diet, for a little while. Boil every morning new milk enough to last twenty-four hours, and stir into it the best of arrow-root wet in cold water, in the proportion of a large teaspoonful to a quart. Add a very little salt, and boil it up again for one minute, then set it in a cold place.

Flour Gruel (for children sick with teething complaints).

Tie up in a piece of thick cotton cloth a coffee-cup of white flour. Put it into boiling water, and keep it boiling steadily three hours. Then remove the cloth and lay the lump where it will become perfectly dry. To use it, grate it and thicken two gills of boiling milk with a dessert spoonful of it wet in cold water. Put a little salt in the milk. This is excellent food for feeble children.

[The value of the following receipts has been proved in the successful rearing of very feeble infants by the use of them. Several mothers have gratefully testified to their excellence, especially for children reduced to extreme debility by teething complaints. After weighing the articles a few times it will be easy to proportion the ingredients by measure].

Food for an Infant at successive periods.

For the first three months: — 5 grains of gelatine; 25 grains of arrow-root; 2 gills of milk; 1 gill of cream; 1½ pints of water.

From three to six months: — gelatine, arrow-root, and water, as above; 3 gills of milk; 1 gill of cream.

From six to nine months: — gelatine, arrow-root, and water, as above; 1 pint of milk; 1½ gills of cream.

From nine to twelve months: — gelatine, arrow-root, and water, as above; $1\frac{1}{4}$ pints of milk; $1\frac{1}{2}$ or 2 gills of cream.

If the child is feeble, use in each case one quart of water.

Put the gelatine into $1\frac{1}{4}$ pints of hot water, and when it boils add the arrow-root dissolved in a gill of cold water. When this has boiled five minutes, add the milk, and when it boils again pour in the cream. Take it from the fire, and sweeten with loaf sugar until it is slightly sweeter than cow's milk. Strain if necessary, through fine muslin, and stir occasionally while cooling. If the child is constipated, use a little more cream, or sweeten with brown sugar. In the opposite case, use a little less cream. This food should be prepared once in twenty-four hours; in warm weather, twice, unless kept in a very cool place.

MISCELLANEOUS RECEIPTS AND DIRECTIONS.

Lemon Syrup.

One pound of loaf or crushed sugar to every half pint of lemon juice. Let it stand twenty-four hours, or till the sugar is dissolved, stirring it very often with a silver spoon. When dissolved, wring a flannel bag very dry in hot water, strain the syrup, and bottle it. This will keep almost any length of time.

Another without lemons.

Put six pounds of white sugar to three pints of water, and boil five minutes. Have ready the beaten white of an egg mixed with half a pint of water, and stir it into the boiling mixture. In a few minutes a scum will arise, and the kettle must be set off from the fire, and stand five minutes; then remove the scum. When it is almost cold, measure it, and to a gallon of syrup put three ounces of tartaric acid, dissolved in half a pint of hot water; add at the same time a large teaspoonful of the oil of lemon. When it is cold, bottle it. The goodness of the syrup (and it is an excellent imitation of the genuine), depends on the oil of lemon being fresh. If this is in the least rancid, it will spoil the syrup.

Raspberry Vinegar.

To two quarts of raspberries, put a pint of cider vinegar. Let them lie together two or three days; then mash them up and put them in a bag to strain. To every pint, when strained, put a pound of best sugar. Boil it twenty minutes, and skim it. Bottle it when cold.

Currant Wine.

Use sugar, water, and currant juice in these proportions, viz., one quart each of juice and the best of sugar, and two of water. Put the mixture into a tight keg with a faucet. Leave out the bung for two or three weeks, and then put it in loosely, so that if it continues to ferment longer, the keg will not burst. After a few days more put in the bung tight. Let it stand a year, and then draw it off and bottle it.

Another.

To one gallon of currant juice, put nine pounds of the best of sugar, and two gallons of water. Set it where it won't be disturbed, and bottle it at the end of the year.

Currant Shrub.

Boil currant juice five minutes with loaf or crushed sugar—a pound of sugar to a pint of juice. Stir it constantly while cooling, and when cold, bottle it. A spoonful or two in a tumbler of water affords a refreshing beverage.

Sarsaparilla Mead.

Three pounds of sugar, three ounces of tartaric acid, one ounce of cream tartar, one of flour, one of essence of sarsaparilla, and three quarts of water. Strain and bottle it, then let it stand ten days before using it.

English Ginger Beer

Pour four quarts of boiling water, upon an ounce and a half of ginger, an ounce of cream of tartar, a pound of clean brown sugar, and two fresh lemons, sliced thin. It should be wrought twenty-four hours, with two gills of good yeast, and then bottled. It improves by keeping several weeks, unless the weather is hot, and it is an excellent beverage. If made with loaf instead of brown sugar, the appearance and flavor are still finer.

Maple Beer.

To four gallons of boiling water, add one quart of maple syrup and a small table-spoonful of essence of spruce. When it is about milk warm, add a pint of yeast; and when fermented, bottle it. In three days it is fit for use.

Spring Beer.

Take a handful of checkerberry (wintergreen), a few sassafras roots cut up, a half a handful of pine-buds, while they are small and gummy, and a small handful of hops.* Put all these into a pail of water over night, and in the morning boil them two or three hours; fill up the kettle when it boils away. Strain it into a jar or firkin that will hold a half a pailful more of water. Stir in a pint and a half of molasses, then add the half pailful of water, and taste it. If not sweet enough add more molasses. It loses the sweetness a little in the process of fermentation, and should therefore be made rather too sweet at first. Add two or three gills of good yeast, set it in a warm place, and let it remain undisturbed till it is fermented. When

---

* If dried in the ordinary way. But a small pinch of the hops put up in pound packages by the Shakers is enough.

the top is covered with a thick dark foam, take it off; have ready clean bottles and good corks; pour off the beer into another vessel, so gently as not to disturb the sediment; then bottle it, and set it in a cool place. It will be ready for use in two days. The sediment should be put into a bottle by itself, loosely corked, and kept to ferment the next brewing.

Spruce and Boneset Beer.

Boil a small handful each of hops and boneset for an hour or two, in a pailful of water; strain it, and dilute it with cold water till it is of the right strength. Add a small table-spoonful of essence of spruce, sweeten, ferment and bottle it, like the spring beer.

The essences of hops, checkerberry, ginger, and spruce, put into warm water in suitable proportions, then sweetened, fermented, and bottled, make good beer.

Rennet Wine.

Wash a third, or half of a salted rennet; wipe it dry and put it into a bottle of wine. The wine will be fit to use for custard the next day. To keep the remainder of the rennet till more is needed, put it into a strong brine and cover it close.

To Boil Cider.

Take cider which has been made but a day or two, and boil it nearly half away. Skim it often. It will keep good a long time, and is useful in making mince pies, and to flavor pudding sauce. Bottle it and cork it well. A mould will form over the top, but will not injure the cider.

Cologne Water.

To one gallon of alcohol, put twelve drachms each, of oil of lavender, oil of bergamot, and essence of lemon; four drachms of oil of rosemary, and twelve drops of oil of cinnamon.

Indelible Ink.

To make the ink, put into the small bottle six cents worth of lunar caustic, and fill it with rain water.

To make the wash, nearly fill the largest bottle with soft water, and add gum arabic enough to make a thin solution — about a teaspoonful of the lumps. Then put in a drachm of salt of tartar. If the ink spreads, add more gum-arabic to the wash.

To prevent Books, Ink, Paste, &c., from moulding.

A drop or two of oil of lavender on a book, and a single one in a pint bottle of ink, will prevent mould.

Tooth Powder.

Two ounces of Peruvian bark, two of myrrh, one of chalk, one of Armenian bole, and one of orris root.

Rose Butter (a good substitute for rose water).

Gather every morning the leaves of the roses that blossomed the day before, and put them in a stone jar in alternate layers with fine salt. After all the leaves are gathered, put a saucer or small plate into the jar, and lay in a pound of butter, for cake or pudding sauce. It is a very good way of obtaining the flavor of roses, without expense.

To keep Parsley.

Gather fresh sprigs, and after washing them, chop them fine, and work them into as much butter as will be needed for boiled poultry, lamb, and fish, before the next summer. Put the butter into a stone jar, and cover it with a brine made with nice salt.

To keep Suet.

Pull off the skin or membrane from fresh suet, sprinkle salt upon it, tie it up in a cloth or bag, and hang it in a cool, dry place. It will keep sweet the year round.

To keep Eggs.

To four quarts of air-slacked lime, put two ounces of cream of tartar (that is, two table-spoonfuls), two of salt, and four quarts of cold water. Put fresh eggs into a stone jar, and pour the mixture over them. This will keep nine dozen, provided they are all good when laid down; and after many months, the yolks will be still whole, and the whites stiff and clear as at first. The water may settle away so as to leave the upper layer uncovered. If so, add more. Cover them closely and keep them in a cool place.

Eggs should be laid down when they are at the lowest market price.

To cleanse a Calf's Head and Feet.

Take them as soon as the animal is killed, wash them clean, and in order to remove the hair, sprinkle pulverized rosin over them and dip them for an instant in scalding water. The rosin will dry immediately, and they can be easily scraped clean. Soak them from one to three days in cold water, changing it repeatedly.

To kill Cockroaches and Beetles.

Strew the roots of black hellebore, at night, in the places infested by these vermin, and they will be found in the morning dead, or dying. Black hellebore grows in marshy grounds, and may be had at the herb shops.

To drive away Ants.

The little red ants will leave closets where sea-sand is sprinkled, or where oyster shells are laid.

Scatter sprigs of wormwood in places infested with black ants.

To secure Woollens, Furs, Furniture, etc., from Moths.

Carefully shake and brush woollens early in the spring, so as to be certain that no eggs are in them; then sew them up in cotton or linen wrappers, putting a piece of camphor gum, tied up in a bit of muslin, into each bundle, or into the chests and closets where the articles are to lie. When the gum is evaporated it must be renewed.

A lady put up her blankets and carpets in this way before going to Europe, and on her return, three or four years after, found every article safe from moths.

Furs should not be hung out in the sun in the spring before being put away for the season. The moth miller will be likely to visit them when thus exposed. They should be put into a close box with a piece of camphor, and the box tied up in a pillow case or bag.

Blankets that are in use only occasionally during the summer, should be laid when not wanted, under a mattress in constant use, or in a trunk where there are pieces of camphor gum, or cedar chips. It would be a most convenient arrangement for housekeepers to have a closet with shelves and draws made of cedar boards.

It is more difficult than it used to be, to preserve woollens, furs, carpets, and furniture from being injured by moths. Thirty years since it was regarded as an indication of very negligent housekeeping to have a moth-eaten carpet. Now, the utmost care will not always preserve carpets from being injured in this way. Perhaps the reason may be, that in general, warehouses and dwellings are warmed throughout, during the winter, by furnaces. New stuffed and cushioned furniture is sometimes found to contain moths. To destroy them, pour burning fluid plentifully upon the cushions, sofas, &c. If it is fresh, it will leave no stain, and the disagreeable odor will soon pass away. To preserve a carpet that cannot be often shaken, draw out the tacks twice a year, turn back the edges a quarter of a yard all around, brush out the dust, and then with a painter's brush put new spirits of turpentine upon the boards as far as the carpet is turned back; then return it immediately to its place, and put in the tacks.

The floors of some houses have moths in the cracks. In this

case, cedar saw-dust sprinkled over the floor before laying down the carpet, will protect it from these diligent mischief-workers. If this cannot be had, use tar-paper.

To kill Moths.

Take furs or pillows infested with moths, and put them into a brick oven which has just been used for baking. Let them remain over night, and the next day beat them well in the open air.

To remove the Bad Odor from New Feathers.

Make a cover for the bed of some coarse material, or a couple of old sheets; get a baker to put it into his oven one or two nights. A better way, when it can be done, is to send the feathers in bags to a baker's oven, before they are put into the tick.

To purify a Sink or Drain.

Dissolve half a pound of copperas in two gallons of water, and pour in half one day, and the remainder the next.

To take out Mildew.

(This and the next receipt were furnished by a chemist.)

Obtain the dryest chloride of lime that can be bought, and for strong fabrics dissolve four table-spoonfuls in a half a pint of water. Let the mildewed article lie fifteen minutes in this solution. Then take it out, wring it gently, and put it immediately into weak muriatic acid — one part of the acid and four parts soft water.

For delicate fabrics, laces, muslins, &c., the solution of lime should be diluted by the addition of three or four times the measure of water. Let the article lie in it five minutes; then put it into the muriatic acid.

To take out Iron Mould.

Dissolve a teaspoonful of salts of tin in two table-spoonfuls of water. Dip the iron-mould into the solution, and let it remain five minutes. Then dip it into a mixture of equal parts of muriatic acid and water. Dip the mould spots alternately into these mixtures, or make the first one stronger with the salts of tin, and apply it with a soft rag on the end of a stick. Last of all, rinse the articles very thoroughly in cold water.

A simpler method of removing iron-mould succeeds well, provided it is recent, and not very dark. Tie up a teaspoonful of cream of tartar in the moulded place, and put it into cold water without soap, and boil it half an hour.

To take out Ink.

Turn boiling water upon it immediately, in this way: spread the cloth over a pitcher or basin, with the ink-spots in the centre, and while you hold it in its place, let another person turn the boiling water on the spots. This is better than to put the article into boiling water, as the whole will then be tinged with the ink. If the spots are still visible, tie up a teaspoonful of cream of tartar in the places where they are — more for a large stain, less for a very small one — then put the cloth into cold water without soap, and boil it half an hour. If it is not convenient to put boiling water at once on the stains, put them in cold water; do not let them become dry.

Articles that have been stained with ink or fruit, should not be put into soap suds until the stains are removed. Soap will tend to make them permanent.

To take out Fruit Stains.

Tie up cream of tartar in the spots, and put the cloth in cold water, to boil; or if the stains are much spread, stir the cream of tartar into the water. If they are still visible, boil the cloth in a mixture of subcarbonate of soda, a small table-spoonful to a pail of water.

To take out Grease or Fresh Paint.

Rub grease spots with chloric ether. To remove paint, the

ether should be applied on the other side. The ether carries off the oil by evaporation, and leaves the lead of which the paint was composed, dry. New turpentine will remove fresh paint.

To remove rust from Iron Ware and Stoves.

New stove or range furniture is sometimes so much rusted as to make the use of it very inconvenient. Put into a rusty kettle as much hay as it will hold, fill it with water and boil it many hours. At night set it aside, and the next day boil it again. If it is not entirely fit for use, repeat the process. It will certainly be effectual.

Rub the rusty spots on a stove with sand-paper, and then with sweet oil.

To take off starch or rust from Flat-irons.

Tie up a piece of yellow beeswax in a rag, and when the iron is almost, but not quite hot enough to use, rub it quickly with the wax, and then with a coarse cloth.

To prevent Glass, Earthen, Potter's and Iron Ware from being easily broken.

Put dishes, tumblers, and other glass articles into a kettle; cover them entirely with cold water, and put the kettle where it will soon boil. When it has boiled a few minutes, set it aside, covered close. When the water is cold, take out the glass.

Treat new earthen ware in the same way. When potter's ware is boiled, a handful or two of bran should be thrown into the water, and the glazing will never be injured by acids or salt.

Cast-iron stoves, and iron ware should be heated gradually the first time they are used.

A permanent Cement for Glass, China, and Wood.

Steep Russian Isinglass twenty-four hours in white brandy, gently boil and stir the mixture until it is well compounded, and a drop of it, cooled, will become a very thick jelly; then strain it through a linen cloth, and cork it up closely. A gentle heat will dissolve it into a colorless fluid. Broken dishes united with it, will break elsewhere, rather than separate in the old fracture. To apply it, rub the edges, place them together, and hold them two or three minutes.

To preserve steel Knives from Rust.

Never wrap them in woollen cloths. When they are not to be used for some time, have them made bright, and perfectly dry; then take a soft rag, and rub each blade with dry wood-ashes. Wrap them closely in thick brown paper and lay them in a drawer or dry closet. A set of elegant knives, used only on great occasions, were kept in this way more than an hundred years without a spot of rust.

To prevent Ivory Knife Handles from being cracked.

Never let knife blades stand in hot water as is sometimes done to make them wash easily. The heat expands the steel which runs up into the handle a very little, and this cracks the ivory. Knife handles should never lie in water. A handsome knife, or one used for cooking is soon spoiled in this way.

To remove spots from Furniture.

Paint, or white spots occasioned by spilling medicine, or setting something hot upon furniture, can be removed by rubbing them with camphene.

To remove Mortar or Paint from Windows.

Rub the spots of mortar with a stiff brush dipped in sharp, hot vinegar, and paint spots with burning fluid or camphene and sand.

To clean Paint with Pumice-stone.

Use powdered pumice-stone instead of whiting or sand. It cleans paint very quickly, and without injuring it. But very little should be put on the cloth at once. A pint of it is enough to clean the paint of a large house. It is well to keep it on hand, as it is often needed for removing spots from paint, and for cleaning closet shelves.

To polish unvarnished Mahogany Furniture.

First take out ink stains, if there are any, by touching them with spirits of salt. Do it with a sponge tied upon the end of a stick; then wash the spots instantly with vinegar, and make the whole surface to be polished, clean with it. Then rub on the following preparation with a woollen cloth: —

Melt together in an earthen pot two ounces of beeswax, and half an ounce of alconet root; then take it from the fire and add two ounces of spirits of wine, and half a pint of spirits of turpentine. Polish with a soft silk cloth.

To clean Silver and Plated Ware.

Use fine whiting, and wet it with hartshorn instead of water. The spots that make their appearance upon silver or plated-ware that is not in constant use, are quickly removed by this mixture. Silver is injured by coarse whiting; therefore it is well to sift it through a piece of muslin.

It is a good way to boil half an ounce of hartshorn powder in a pint of water, and put into it clean linen or cotton rags enough to absorb the whole of the mixture; then dry them, and keep them to clean silver and plate. Wash leather should be used afterwards.

To clean Paper Hangings.

Put a clean soft bag, or an old pillow-case over a new broom, and gently brush the dust from the paper; then take crusts of stale bakers' bread, and wipe it down lightly, beginning at the top. If you rub it, the dirt will adhere to the paper. After thus brushing all around the upper part of the walls with the bread, begin just above where you left off, and go round again. Do thus until you have finished the paper. The dust and crumbs will fall together. Whenever a room is cleaned it is a good way, before the paint and windows are washed, to wipe the paper with a covered broom as above directed.

To prepare earth for House Plants.

Put together equal parts of the three following things — soil from the sides of a barn-yard, well-rotted manure, and leaf mould from the woods, or earth from the inside of an old tree or stump. Add a small quantity of sand. For Cactuses, put as much sand as of the other materials and a little fine charcoal.

To raise Hyacinths in Winter.

When they are put into the glasses or earth, set them into a dark closet until they sprout. If they are in glasses, do not let the water touch the bulb, by an inch. When the roots have shot down to the water, fill the glass, put in a piece of charcoal, and set them in the sun.

Soot Tea for Roses.

Get soot from a stove or chimney where wood is used for fuel, put it into an old pitcher, and pour hot water upon it. When cool, use it to water your plants every few days. When it is all used, fill up the pitcher again with hot water. The effect upon plants, especially upon roses that have almost hopelessly deteriorated, is wonderful in producing a rapid growth of thrifty shoots, with large thick leaves, and a great number of richly-tinted roses. Never despair of a decayed rose till this has been tried.

To destroy Grass in Gravel Walks.

Scatter the cheapest coarse salt along the edges, and whereever the grass is springing.

Even the Canada thistle can be rooted out by cutting off the stalks very near, but not below the surface of the ground, and putting salt on them. Old brine, not fit for any other purpose, is good for this.

Use to be made of Ashes, Saw-dust, etc.

To spread ashes upon grass makes it thrifty, and of a richer green. Those which have been first used for making soap, are as good for the purpose as new ashes. Let them be scattered just before a rain.

If you cultivate raspberries and blackberries, have saw-dust from the wood-house put around them once a year. Where these berries grow wild, the largest ones are found near decayed stumps and logs.

To purify a Well.

When a well is cleared out, if any offensive substance is found in it, have the bottom sprinkled with two or three quarts of quick-lime.

As a general rule, it is most economical to buy the best articles. The price is, of course, always a little higher; but good articles *spend* best. It is a sacrifice of money to buy poor flour, meat, sugar, molasses, butter, cheese, lard, &c., to say nothing of the injurious effect upon the health.

Of West India sugar and molasses, the Santa Cruz and Porto Rico are considered the best. The Havana is seldom clean. White sugar from Brazil is sometimes very good. Refined sugars usually contain most of the saccharine substance, therefore there is probably more economy in using loaf, crushed, and granulated sugars, than we should at first suppose.

Butter that is made in September and October is best for winter use. Lard should be hard and white, and that which is taken from a hog not over a year old, is best.

Rich cheese feels soft under the pressure of the finger. That which is very strong is neither good or healthy. To keep one that is cut, tie it up in a bag that will not admit flies, and hang it in a cool, dry place. If mould appears on it, wipe it off with a dry cloth.

Flour and meal of all kinds should be kept in a cool, dry place.

The best rice is large, and has a clear, fresh look. Old rice sometimes has little black insects inside the kernels.

The small white sago, called pearl sago, is the best. The large brown kind has an earthy taste. These articles, and tapioca, ground rice, &c., should be kept covered.

The cracked cocoa is the best, but that which is put up in pound papers is often very good.

Shells are apt to be musty. Try a quarter of a pound before buying a quantity.

To select nutmegs, prick them with a pin. If they are good, the oil will instantly spread around the puncture.

Keep coffee by itself, as its odor affects other articles. Keep tea in a close chest or canister.

Oranges and lemons keep best wrapped close in soft paper, and laid in a drawer of linen.

When a cask of molasses is bought, draw off a few quarts, else the fermentation produced by moving it will burst the cask.

Bread and cake should be kept in a tin box or stone jar.

Salt cod should be kept in a dry place, where the odor of it will not affect the air of the house. The best kind is that which is called Dun, from its peculiar color. Fish-skin for clearing coffee should be washed, dried, cut small, and kept in a box or paper bag.

Soft soap should be kept in a dry place in the cellar, and should not be used till three months old.

Bar soap should be cut into pieces of a convenient size, and laid where it will become dry. It is well to keep it several weeks before using it, as it spends fast when it is new.

Cranberries will keep all winter in a firkin of water in the cellar.

Potatoes should be put into the cellar as soon as they are dug. Lying exposed to the sun turns them green, and makes them watery. Some good housekeepers have sods laid over barrels of potatoes not in immediate use. To prevent them from sprouting in the spring, turn them out upon the cellar-bottom.

To thaw frozen potatoes, put them in hot water. To thaw

frozen apples, put them in cold water. Neither will keep long after being frozen.

Cabbages should be buried in sand, with the roots upward.

Celery should also be buried in sand.

Turnips and beets should be put in a dry part of the cellar. Carrots keep anywhere. Onions keep best spread, and in a cool place, but should not freeze. Parsnips are best buried in a pit in the garden, and not opened till March or April, in cold parts of the country.

Squashes should be kept in a dry place, and as cold as may be without freezing.

Apples should remain out of doors in barrels till the weather becomes too cold. They should not be headed up immediately after being gathered, as a moisture accumulates upon them which causes them to decay. When brought in, set them in a back room, until the weather requires their being put into the cellar. A linen cloth laid over them will keep them from frost till very cold weather. Many good housekeepers prefer not to have apples headed up at all. There is an advantage in being able to pick them over several times in the course of a winter, as one defective apple injures all its neighbors. If they are moist, wipe them.

Herbs should be gathered when just beginning to blossom; as they are then in their perfection. Medicinal herbs should be dried, put up in paper bags, and labelled. Those used in cooking should be pounded, sifted, and put into labelled boxes or bottles. Herbs retain their virtue best, to be dried by artificial heat. The warmth of an oven a few hours after the bread is drawn, is sufficient.

Inspect every part of your house often, and let every place be neatly kept. Habits of order in housekeeping save a great deal of time and trouble, and the most thorough way of doing every thing, is the most economical of labor and money, in the end.

Every thing used in the preparation of food should be kept clean. A half washed pot or saucepan, or a dingy brass kettle, will spoil the articles cooked in them. A lady should accustom herself to such habits of attention to her household concerns, that careless ways on the part of those who serve her, will not escape her observation. Unfaithfulness in servants is the sure result of ignorance or negligence in the housekeeper.

DIRECTIONS ABOUT WASHING, &c.

The design of these directions is to assist the inexperienced; to teach those who are unacquainted with the business of washing, how to do it, and those who can afford to employ others, how to direct them; and also to discover where the fault lies when it is not done well.

As I write only for the uninitiated, I shall be excused for being very minute; and for giving some preliminary hints, needed only by learners.

For the family wash, good water, and good soap are indispensable. Rain, river, or spring water is best, but in some places the well-water is soft, and good for washing. Clothes washed repeatedly in hard water with common soap, will soon become too yellow to be worn, and can never be made white again. As the supply of soft water sometimes fails where a cistern is depended on, it may be well to mention that hard water can be made to answer the purpose, temporarily, by dissolving in it the sub-carbonate of soda, commonly called washing-soda. Put a large table-spoonful into three or four pails of water while it is heating, and then use the olive-soap both for rubbing and boiling the clothes. Remember that soda must not be used in washing calicoes or flannels. It will spoil both. Here it may be well to say that white clothes which are constantly washed with soda, will, when laid aside a few months become of a deep yellow color, not easily removed by any ordinary bleaching process.

Provide a wash bench of convenient height, three tubs, one a large one for rinsing,* a water ladle, a pail to be kept for use about the washing alone, a washing board, a clothes stick, clothes pins, a line and two baskets; one cheap coarse one in which to drain the clothes, when taken from the boiling-kettle, and a better one for taking them to the line, and for laying them in to when folded for the ironing. Have good soft soap, which, if you cannot readily procure at the manufactory, you can make with very little trouble.† Bar-soap is not necessary for white clothes, provided the soft is of a nice quality. The olive soap is a great improvement on the common yellow soap. If it is several months old, it spends economically, cleanses quickly, and is not sharp to the hands.

When clothes are very much soiled, they should be put into a tub of warm suds over night.

Borax soap is so effectual in cleansing soiled clothes, that the use of it essentially diminishes the labor of washing. To prepare it, put together bar soap, borax, and hot water in the following proportions, — a pound of the soap, cut into small pieces, an ounce of powdered borax, and a quart of hot water. Mix the ingredients together over the fire, but see that it does not boil. When it is cold, cut it up in cakes, and use it like common hard soap. Put the clothes which are most soiled, or if you choose, all the white clothes of the wash into quite a warm suds made with this soap, and let them remain from Saturday evening until

---

* A large painted wash-tub is expensive, and it may be convenient to some persons to know that a very good rinsing tub can be made of a flour barrel. Take one that is clean and well made; have the upper part sawed off about nine inches. See that there are no nails sticking through. Make three holes large enough to admit the fingers, in two opposite staves, to serve for handles. If there are cracks, caulk them, and fill the tub with water. The water will soon swell the staves so as to close the cracks; and when it has once done leaking, keep it always turned down in the cellar when not in use. All kinds of tubs and firkins should be turned down on the cellar floor, to prevent them from leaking.

† See two receipts, p. 197.

Monday morning. This method is recommended by very good housekeepers.

To do the Washing. Sort the clothes, putting the finest and cleanest by themselves, to be washed first, and the coarse and more soiled ones together. Where there are white clothes enough to make two or three boilings, sort them accordingly; always boil coarse towels by themselves. If there are fine calicoes, nice ginghams, or delicate printed muslins, separate them from the common ones, and also the white flannel, angola, or merino articles from the colored woollens.

The tub should be a third full of water, not hot, but very warm. Stir in soap enough to make a weak suds, and put in the nicest clothes. Rub handkerchiefs, night-caps, and other fine articles between the hands, using a little soap. Never rub them on a washboard. As fast as they are washed, wring and shake them open, and put them into an old pillow case or white bag, else they will be liable to be torn by the weight of the larger articles when taken out of the boiling kettle. Some persons keep a large bag in which they boil all the white clothes together; if the kettle is a nice one, so that there is no danger of iron mould, or any kind of stain, it is better to boil them without it. Use a wash-board for the large articles, and for those which are not easily made clean, and use more soap than for the fine things, taking special pains with places that are most soiled. All articles worn upon the person should be washed on both sides, and special pains taken with seams and hems. If there are streaks which you cannot entirely wash out, rub soap on them after you have wrung out the article ready for the boiling.

Lay all the washed clothes together in an empty tub or the draining basket, until you have enough for the first boiling. Then dip out all the hot water from the kettle into a tub, and cover it over with a thick cloth, in order to keep it hot for washing more clothes. Put a pail or two of cold water into the kettle, and a large spoonful of soft soap — more if the kettle is a large one. Shake open and lay in the clothes, and add enough more water to cover them. Do not crowd the boiler very full;

the clothes will not look as well, and beside, the water will be continually boiling over. Have a good fire, push the clothes down often with the stick, and let them boil steadily, half an hour. Set the draining basket upon a tub, with two or three strips of board laid across, to keep it up. A little frame, somewhat like the cheese ladder used in a dairy, is more convenient. Place the tub near the boiler, and take out the clothes with the stick. When this is done, dip out part of the boiling suds, cover it, and set it aside to be used as occasion requires. Add cold water to the kettle, and put in more clothes. Continue washing until all the white clothes are rubbed, remembering to dip out part of the dirty water from the tub now and then, and add some of the boiling suds which you have kept covered. When the clothes in the basket are well drained, put them into a tub of clean cold water, and take more clothes from the boiler into the draining basket. When all the white clothes are rubbed, and while the last of them are still boiling, get the second rinsing water ready in the largest tub. (Some people have an idea that clothes look best rinsed in hard water, because rain-water is not so white as the other. But rain-water is the best, because it takes out the soap more thoroughly.) Fill the rinsing tub two thirds full of water, squeeze the blue-bag in it two or three times, and stir till the water is equally blue.*

When you wring the clothes from the first rinsing-water, see whether the streaks you could not rub out have disappeared. If not, they can probably be removed quickly now. Wring the clothes dry, else the suds remaining in them will make the last rinsing water soapy. If the wash is large, dip off part of

* *To make a blueing-bag*, take a very thick piece of cotton or a doubled piece, and stitch a close seam near the edge, on three sides, then turn it and stitch it round again; put in a piece of indigo as large as an egg, sew the end twice across, and put on a loop. If it is slightly made, too much of the indigo will come out into the water. Keep it hung up where it will not become dusty.

The Spanish indigo is best. It is hard, and of a rich deep color. Poor indigo breaks easily, and shows a slightly greenish tinge in the sunlight.

the water, when half of the clothes are wrung out, and add clean water, and a little more blueing. Strength, and some practice are necessary, to wring large articles dry, and the appearance of the clothes will but poorly pay for the labor bestowed, if this part of the work is not well done. Perhaps it is the most fatiguing part of washing. The inventor of a good machine for wringing clothes will deserve and have, the thanks of many a a toil-worn woman.

When the white clothes are upon the line, take boiling suds and wash the coarse towels; boil them in a clean water, or in some of the last rinsing-water. Wash them thoroughly as the table-cloths; not negligently because they are coarse. If the weather is wet, let the clothes lie in the rinsing-water till a fair day, but omit the blueing, as it will be apt to settle in streaks upon them; or some of the articles will be very blue, while others will not be so at all. If the weather threatens to be rainy, better not put them out, as they cannot be taken in half dry, and carried out while damp to be put on the line again, without getting more or less soiled. If the wind is violent, let them lie in the water even if it is fair (unless they can be hung up in an attic or wood-house chamber or in a yard sheltered from the wind), as the hems will very likely be snapped from the corners of the sheets and table-cloths, and all the clothes will be more worn (even if they are not torn) by being blown half a day, than by two months' use from week to week. In the winter when they will freeze stiff in a few minutes, and there is a strong wind, they are liable to be torn. I have known a large and new table-cloth, cracked completely across, in a few minutes after being hung out. Small and fine articles, like caps, collars, handkerchiefs, and baby's dresses should be dried in the house in severe winter weather. Clothes are made very white by the night frosts, and where the yard is sheltered from the wind it is well to leave them out sometimes for that reason, provided there is no danger of their being stolen.

When the last boiling is done, dip out all the water and save it as before. Heat clean water for the flannels and other woollens. These should be washed in quite warm water with good soft soap. Bar-soap makes woollens hard and wiry. Wash the finest and most delicate articles first. If they are much soiled, use considerable soap so as to get them clean quickly without much rubbing, for it is this which fulls up flannels, as we may know from the fact that it is by a similar process cloth is made thick at the fulling-mill. As fast as they are done throw them into a plenty of scalding water. If they lie in a pile until all are washed, they will shrink. When you can bear your hands in the water, wring them and throw them into another; from this last water wring them dry, snap them well, and hang them out. Few people rinse flannels twice, but they look enough better to pay for the trouble. If the soap is not rinsed out, they will shrink, and also become yellow. The water used for the white flannels is fit for the colored ones, and for mixed footings, or calicoes. All sorts of stockings should be washed first on the right side, and then upon the other.

Red flannel preserves the color best, and is softest, washed in hard water. A sailor's red flannels, that have been, during a long voyage, often tied to a rope and towed through the waves, look better and feel softer than those washed at home. A word here in regard to the purchase of flannels, will not be out of place. It is the best economy to buy those made of soft wool. They will shrink very little, while coarse wool flannels will grow small and thick every week, and no pains-taking can prevent it.

After hanging out the woollens, wash the calicoes in clean water, with hard soap, and rinse them twice. Have the starch* ready, and dip them before they are hung up. Calicoes should be thrown into the rinsing water as fast as they are washed. Even firm colors are injured by lying. If the weather is not fair leave them in the second rinsing, but put the light and dark ones into separate tubs, unless the colors are perfectly

---

* To make starch, see page 240.

fast. Put a little salt into the water. They will not be injured any more than white clothes, by lying in the water over night. Nice calicoes and ginghams should be dried in the shade, and so put upon the line as to dry quickly. Hang a dress in an angle of the line near the post, with the waist down; put one pin at the turn of the line, and one on each side, a few feet from the angle, so that the hem of the skirt will form a triangle. When the skirt is dry, except near the waist, shake open the waist and sleeves, and reverse the dress, pinning the shoulders to the line.

Calicoes should not be sprinkled till the morning of the day they are ironed. The colors sometimes run together when they are folded over night, and in very warm weather, the starch in a dress that is sprinkled in the evening will become sour by the next morning. In July and August, damp clothes that lie folded together two nights, are very liable to become mildewed. Care should be taken that soiled articles are not put aside in a damp state, during the week, for the next wash. Sad accidents have occurred through want of care in this particular.

For the assistance of ladies who are not able to detect the reasons, if their clothes do not come from the laundry in good order, I will specify a few particulars as to the causes.

If good water and soap are provided, and yet the white clothes look badly, it is owing to one, or possibly, all, of the following things — their not being well assorted, the coarse clothes, and those most soiled being washed and boiled with the best ones; or perhaps those places which required special care, had no more rubbing than other parts. If the seams of under-clothes are not clean, it is because they are not turned, after being washed on the right side, and well rubbed on the other. If the clothes look yellow, perhaps the washer uses too small a quantity of water, and neglects to dip off, often, that which is cool and dirty, and add more which is hot; and very likely too many are crowded into the boiler at once. If they are not wrung dry from the first rinsing-water, before being thrown into the second, they will be yellow; and lastly, if they are not well wrung out of the second, they will have soapy streaks in the gathers and hems. If spots of iron mould appear, perhaps the washer is not careful to avoid touching the clothes while wet, to the wire handles of the tubs or pails. If the calicoes fade more than you had reason to expect, very likely they are washed in boiling suds. The soft soap in it will spoil them; and besides, it is never clean enough for nice calicoes. It is a good way to have calico dresses washed on some other day by themselves; it will be easier to have them done well. If the flannels are becoming dingy, it may be that they too are washed in the water in which the white clothes were boiled, and then rinsed but once. If they shrink, although made of fine wool, probably the soap is not all rinsed out, and that they were laid together in a pile, and became cold before they were thrown into scalding water. If they retain the wrinkles after being ironed, they were not well shaken out (or snapped) before being put out to dry. They should not be sprinkled; but if laid in the basket over night with the folded white clothes, they will be just damp enough to iron smooth. If the toes of the footings, and woollen stockings feel stiff, they were not washed clean.

Some domestics bestow great care upon the nicest articles, and take no pains with common ones. This is neither neat or economical. All clothes that are both washed and ironed well, keep clean longest.

There are some advantages in a lady's taking the clothes from the bars, after they are ironed, herself. She sees at once whether they are well washed without the trouble of unfolding them to examine, and all those which need mending can then be most conveniently laid apart from the rest. I will only add to these minute directions, that the boiler should be left perfectly dry, and the tubs, &c., rinsed and put away clean. It is good economy after the usual cleaning is done, to save all the suds to water the garden and trees. The good effects will soon reward the trouble.

Starching, Ironing, and Polishing Gentlemen's Linen.

To make the Starch — Dissolve three table-spoonfuls of the best of starch in cold water, and stir it very fast into a quart of boiling water, and boil it half an hour. Five minutes before it is done, put in a piece of spermaceti the size of a large walnut, and stir until it is well mixed. Dip the linen as soon as you can bear your hands in the starch, and see that every part is thoroughly wet, or you will have what are called blisters. Fold the collars in a dry towel. Fold the shirts through the middle up and down, so as to bring the two parts of the bosom together, that the starch may not get on any other part of the shirt. Let them lie over night.

A bosom board is indispensable. Have a piece of board eight inches by eighteen; cover one side with three thicknesses of flannel; fasten it at the edges with small tacks. Then cover both sides with three thicknesses of cotton, sewed on tight and perfectly smooth.

Iron a shirt completely (the bosom upon the side of the board where the flannel is), then hang it on the bars to air. After about an hour, lay the bosom on the hard side of the board, dip a soft towel in cold water, wring it dry, and brush the bosom until it looks a little damp. Then lay it upon the softest side and use the polishing iron quickly, pressing with all your strength. The polishing iron is very different from the common flat-iron, and far better for this use. It is oblong, and rounded at each end. They are to be found at all the hardware stores, and are not expensive. If there is any roughness upon the iron, touch it when nearly hot with bees-wax tied up in a rag.

A porcelain, or tin saucepan should be kept for making starch, and used for nothing else. The linen ironed by the lady who furnished these directions, was an ample recommendation of them.

To wash Calicoes, the colors of which are not Fast.

Pare and cut up a dozen or fifteen potatoes, and boil them in five or six quarts of water. Strain off the water through a hair sieve, and when it is cool enough to put your hands in it, wash the dress without soap. The starch imparted to the water by the potatoes will cleanse it, and also make it stiff enough without other starch even after passing through the rinsing water. If there is green in the calico, dissolve a piece of alum half as large as an egg, in a pailful of water to rinse it. If there are grease spots upon a dress, a thread should be run around them before it is washed, so that those places may receive special care, else they will be as distinct as ever, after being ironed. If washing does not remove them, use chloric ether, or new spirits of turpentine. Some very nice managers use beef's gall in washing calicoes to prevent their being faded. It is good for the purpose, but the odor is unpleasant, and will be perceptible when the dress is worn, unless it is used sparingly. A table-spoonful of the gall, to a pailful of suds is enough. Put what you do not use into a bottle, with a large table-spoonful of salt, and cork it tight. It is very useful in removing grease from woollens, and cleaning the collars of coats.

To wash Mourning Calicoes, Muslins, and Lawns.

Wash them in perfectly clean water; and if the color comes out, soak them until the water is clear, even if it should require two or three days, changing the water twice a day. A black calico that parts with much of the dye in washing, will have rusty streaks in it, and look like an old thing, if it is dried without being soaked. But in the way directed, a dress of good quality can be done up many times without losing its beauty, as experience amply proves. Such dresses should not be sprinkled over night, before being ironed.

To Wash, Starch, and Iron Muslins, Laces, etc.

Soiled muslins should be looked over and mended before being washed. Embroidered articles should be basted in exact shape upon a piece of flannel or other soft cloth. The muslin will be less liable to be frayed or torn by the weight of the needlework. Common laces should be folded evenly together into many thicknesses, and then basted through and through around the edges, with a fine needle and thread. Soak these various articles in warm water with Castile or olive soap in it. After a few hours, or the next day, squeeze them dry (never rub or wring them); put on more soap, pour on hot water, and let them stand another day. Then squeeze them dry, and examine them. If they are not white, lay them loosely into a broad dish or platter, with warm suds in it, and set them in the sun a day or two; or, put them into a large white glass bottle, with a wide mouth, fill it with warm suds and set it in the sun. Turn the muslins over now and then, and also turn the bottle round, so as to give every side the benefit of the sun. This is a very good way where there is no grass-plot which can be used for bleaching. There can be no better way of whitening muslins than to dip the articles in soap suds, spread them on clean grass and let them lie two or three days and nights, wetting them once or twice a day with suds. When you take them from the grass, rinse them twice in a plenty of water, the last time with blueing in it. Squeeze them dry as possible, then dip all in fine starch, except those articles which should be very stiff, and they should be dried before being starched. Sort them, dip those which need most stiffness first, then add hot water enough to make the starch thinner for the next, and lastly still more, for dipping those which need very little stiffness. Hang them all out of doors to dry, unless the weather is cold enough to freeze. When dry, sprinkle them very wet, or squeeze them in cold water, pull them out a little, and lay them two or three double in a sheet — a linen one if they are to be ironed in an hour or two; a cotton one if they are not to be done till the next day — this, because they keep damp much longer in cotton than in linen. To wash elegant, expensive laces, sew a piece of white flannel closely around a common junk bottle, and wind the lace round and round perfectly smooth, and with a fine needle and thread, baste it enough to keep it in place. If the lace is pointed, pass the needle and thread through each point; put the bottle into a jar or deep pitcher filled with warm suds. Change the water once a day for two or three days; then put the bottle into the boiler with the finest white clothes on washing day; as soon as it is taken from the boiler, and cooled a little, rinse it again and again in a plenty of cold water, then wrap a soft, dry towel around it to press out the water, and set it in the sun. When the lace has become entirely dry, take out all the threads, unwind it, and wear it without starching.

Our grandmothers would have thought an elegant lace nearly spoilt by being washed in any other way than this, and a very nice way it is. Having once tried it, you will prefer to wash your laces yourself, rather than pay a French laundress for doing them not half as well.

When you iron muslins, pull them gently into shape, fold and lay them on a plate, and cover them with a bowl, to keep the edges from getting too dry. Have clean irons, and rub each one before using it with a bit of wax or spermaceti tied up in a piece of cotton, and wipe it on a clean rag. This is to prevent the starch from sticking to the iron. Lay the muslin upon the ironing board, the wrong side up, and always move the iron in the direction of the threads. The article will be out of shape, and look badly, if ironed diagonally. Bobbinet laces, if ironed at all, should be ironed diagonally, as in this way only can the mesh retain its shape. Dip them in stiff starch, and after drying them, dip them again, then pin them out upon a bed. They will dry soon, and will need only to be folded even, and a warm iron set upon them to press the folds flat. Whether pressed or not, they will look like new bobbinet, and this is a very convenient way when a lady is so situated that she cannot iron her own kerchiefs, or get them done to her liking by others.

To iron lace or edging, carefully pull into shape the points or scollops, and pearling; lay it the wrong side up with the wrought edge from you, pass the iron along the edge nearest you, and then, beginning at the right hand end, move it out from you. Do this the whole length, or a yard at a time, then adjust every part even, and pass the iron over it again and again until it is dry. Lay every piece, as you finish it, upon a waiter or dish, so that you will not have occasion to handle it again till you lay it in its place.

Needlework should be ironed upon clean flannel, and be long enough under the iron to dry it, as it will look ill if laid away damp. Iron it on the wrong side.

Wrought collars, so much worn as to be easily torn by being washed, if they are not badly soiled, may be squeezed out of cold water, rolled in a dry cloth for a few minutes, and then ironed. The same may be done with plain muslins that are only tumbled. Sometimes it is convenient to be able to produce a clean collar in a few minutes.

It is convenient to have a board expressly for ironing caps, collars, cuffs, laces, and other small articles. It should be about two feet long, a foot and a half wide, covered on one side with four or five thicknesses of cotton cloth sewed on tight and perfectly smooth, and covered with white flannel.

To make fine Starch.

There is a great difference in the quality of starch. It is but labor lost to make use of that which is not good. There is so much difference in the quantity of *gluten* in this article, that no precise measure can be given. Those who are least experienced will soon learn the proportion needed for any given number of articles.

A small sauce-pan or porringer should be kept for boiling starch, and used for nothing else. Boil the water in the porringer, wet the starch smooth in a little cold water, and pour it in slowly, stirring steadily till it has become of equal thickness. Leave it to boil moderately eight or ten minutes. If starch is pure, and well made, it need not be strained. The leg of a fine cotton stocking makes a very good strainer.

To make Flour Starch.

Wet white flour smooth in cold water, and pour it into boiling water, just like the fine starch. Some people do not boil it; others think dresses retain the stiffness longer if it is boiled. It should be so made as to have no lumps in it, and if it is not, it should be strained through a fine colander. Allow a table-spoonful of flour, and nearly three pints of water for a dress. If there are several dresses and skirts to be dipped, divide the starch into two or three parcels, because the first article put into it will take too large a proportion of the stiffness, and leave what remains too thin for the rest. Reserve those which need least stiffness to be starched last.

To Whiten or Bleach.

The best time in the year is the month of May. The dew at that period has a peculiar efficacy for bleaching. In the country, where clean grass plots are accessible, it is a good way to take all the white clothes of the week's wash, from the first rinsing water, or from the boiling suds, and lay them on the grass. After two or three nights take them up before they are dry in the morning, rinse them well, and put them on the line. Their improved appearance will pay for the trouble. In August, clothes should never be more than one day and night upon the grass, lest they become mildewed. In the winter, they will whiten fast, in sunny weather, upon clean snow; and leaving them on the line in the frost over night, after being washed, makes them white.

To wash Thibet Cloths, Bombazines, Mouslin de Laines, and Plaids.

If you wish to make over a dress before it is badly worn or soiled, rip it, and sponge it in warm water with Castile soap in it. Sponge a piece at a time, on the side which is to be out, and iron it on the other side, until perfectly dry. The irons should be quite hot but not so as to change the color. If it is hung upon the bars or laid away, damp, it will curl and look old.

Thibet cloths of good quality last so long that they are worth being done up twice. After doing good service, till parts of the waist and sleeves are worn out, the dress should be ripped and washed (sponging will not answer), and if it is of a color that fades at all, wash with it any new pieces that you may have to use in making it over. Wash it just as you would a nice flannel, with Castile or olive soap, and then rinse it in two clear warm waters. Remember not to wring it either time, as it is almost impossible to iron out the wrinkles. Squeeze out the suds a little before you rinse it. Let it drip as it hangs upon the clothes line, for twenty minutes or half an hour; and before the upper edge begins to dry, and while the lower edge is still wet, turn the lower edge up over the line, and the dry edge down, and let it hang a few minutes, then fold each piece, and lay them in a pile with a damp cloth round them. Have a steady good fire, and several irons, and press them upon the wrong side until dry.

Bombazines if not badly soiled, can be sponged, in the same way as the Thibet cloths. If they are to be made up the same side out as before, sponge that side, and iron on the other. If they need to be washed, it is usually best that they should be made up the inside out, and of course should be ironed on what has been the right side. Wash them just like Thibet cloth. The black bombazines, and other similar fabrics worn in mourning, all wash well, and can be done repeatedly, and each time look so well as to reward the trouble.

Wash de laines and plaids in the same way. It is safe to use the genuine olive soap for those of the most beautiful colors; they will remain unchanged.

To wash Shawls.

Almost all kinds of shawls bear washing; and they should be done as the Thibet cloths and de laines, except that when there is much white in them, or they are composed chiefly of delicate colors, there should be a very little blueing in the last rinsing water, and after being fifteen minutes on the clothes line, they should be laid perfectly smooth into a sheet, which should then be folded up (not *rolled*, because that will make wrinkles), and as soon as the water is absorbed, so that the shawl remains only very damp, iron it on the wrong side, until it is dry, then fold it, making the creases as when it was new.

To wash Colored, Plaid, Black, and Raw Silks and Ribbons.

For a single dress, pare four or five good-sized potatoes, slice them thin and lay them in a quart of cold water for a few hours; then, if the silk is much soiled, sponge both sides freely, rubbing the soiled places with most care. Sponge one piece at a time, and iron it dry upon the side that is to be the inside, moving the iron up and down, or straight across — never diagonally. Have the irons quite hot, yet not so as to scorch, or change the color. If they are too cool, they will draw up or *crimp* the silk in very minute gathers, and it will be nearly impossible to make such places smooth again. The effect of the starch from the potatoes is to cleanse the silk, and also give it a little stiffness, and even plaid silks of the most delicate colors are made to look new in this way. If a silk is not much soiled, sponge it only on what is to be the outside, and iron it on the other. A good black silk may be made to look "amaist as weel 's the new," again and again by this process, and those who have never tried it, would be surprised at the renovating effect.

Good ribbons, black, white, or colored, are made fresh and handsome in precisely the same way. To iron them, set the iron across one end, on the wrong side, and while you press it hard, draw the whole length of the ribbon under it with the other hand.

Raw silks should be washed in potato water, as directed for calicoes that are liable to fade; and after being rinsed once, and hung without wringing upon the line, long enough for the water to drip off, they should be rolled for fifteen minutes in a sheet, and then ironed dry, on the wrong side.

To renovate black Veils and Lace.

Make a very weak solution of gum arabic, so that it will barely be distinguishable from pure water; lay the veil or lace upon an ironing, or other smooth board, and apply the gum-water with a sponge. See that the article to be sponged lies straight and even; and when you have wet it perfectly smooth, let it remain untouched till the next day. This is the way that ladies who embroider their own veils give them their finish. If the gum water is too thick, there will be danger of tearing the lace in taking it off.

To renovate Velvet.

Wet a clean sponge in warm soap suds, squeeze it very dry in a cloth, and wipe the velvet with it. Then pass the velvet over the edge of a hot iron, turned down side-ways — the wrong side of it next to the iron.

Another very good way is to hold the velvet in the steam of boiling water, and then pass it over the edge of an iron.

To wash English Blankets.

If care is taken to keep them clean, they will seldom need to be washed. New ones ought not to need washing for several years. Those which are not in constant use, should be kept where they will not be exposed to moths or dust, in a closet, pinned close in a cloth, or under a mattress. A chamber-maid or a domestic who does the general house-work, should keep a large apron to be worn only while she makes beds. Blankets, counterpanes, and even bed-ticks sometimes have to be washed in consequence of negligence on this point.

If there are soiled spots on a blanket, baste a thread around them, or else wash those places before it is put into the tub. Then put a handful of soft soap into the water, and begin to rub at one end of the blanket, using more soap, and slipping it along as fast as it is washed, from one end to the other; and as it is not possible to rub the whole width of a large blanket at once, — after it is washed along one side, taking it up to the middle, wash along the other side, just as in washing sheets. It takes two persons to wring a blanket or counterpane well. Have ready a large tub of as hot water as you can bear your hands in, and put them as soon as they are washed into it; rinse them in this, and still in another warm water; and after wringing them dry as possible, have the person who assists you take one end, and taking the other yourself, open and snap them several times. This will take out the wrinkles, so that if the day is fair with a good breeze, the blankets will look almost as smooth as if they were pressed. If there are several to be washed, cover the rinsing tubs, so as to keep the water warm, and have some hot water ready to add, when that in the tubs becomes cool.

To wash white Counterpanes and Calico Quilts.

Wash them in the same way as blankets only with hard soap, and rinse them in cold water. If convenient, it is the best way to take them to a pump; and pump upon them and pour off the water again and again, till it is clear; then wring them and hang them on the line. In this way one wringing is saved, which is well, for it is some of the hardest work that is done. The heaviest kind of counterpanes, especially if they are large, should be rinsed at a pump, and taken in the tub to the clothes line, and put upon it without wringing.

To wash the Tick of a Feather-bed, or Pillow.

Have it washed very thoroughly and rinsed in a plenty of water. When it is entirely dry, melt together bar soap and beeswax in the proportion of two parts soap, and one of wax. Mix it well, and then, having laid the tick, inside out, upon a large table or ironing board, spread the soap and wax on it with a knife, as thinly as possible. Even a thick tick, when it is washed, does not hold the feathers as securely as before, and the use of this mixture is to remedy the defect.

The odor of the soap soon passes away.

To wash Worsted Table-covers.

Wash them in quite warm water with olive soap. If this is not to be had, soft soap, if it is of the best kind, is better than common bar soap. This last, always has rosin in it, and sometimes there is so much as to make woollens washed with it feel *gummy;* and no pains-taking will entirely remove the bad effect. If there are grease spots, they should be first taken out with chloric ether or spirits of turpentine. Make a suds, wash the cloth very thoroughly in it, and then in another; then rinse it twice in warm water. Do not wring it when you put it from one water into another, but drain it, and very gently press the water out. Hang it a short time upon the line, until the water has almost ceased dripping from the lower edge; then reverse it, putting the lower edge up on the line. Have the irons hot, and the ironing-board ready, and make up your mind to iron patiently a long time. A medium-sized broadcloth table cover, such as used to be in fashion, required to be ironed two hours and a half. A less time is necessary for the thinner fabrics; but whatever the texture is, if it has wool in it, it must be pressed until it is dry, else it will not look well. Faded table-covers, having one color only, mingled with white, may be dyed with advantage. I have seen one that was originally green and white, that after being in constant use many years, was sent to a dye-house, and came back transformed into a maroon and white cloth, and was as good as when it was new.

To wash Carpets.

According to the experience of many persons, the Kidderminster carpets, and others of like fabric, are as well washed at a fulling-mill as at a dye-house, or by a professed carpet-cleanser. They are washed whole, and if the colors are good, they are returned with a good degree of their original beauty; and I have never known one to be torn or injured in any way. The charge for washing a large carpet, does not exceed a dollar and a quarter, and for medium-sized and small ones, proportionately less. After a carpet has been in hard service, if it is worth being made over, or thoroughly repaired, it is also worth being washed; and a person who has spent two or three days in mending an old, unwashed carpet, will appreciate the assertion.

The directions for removing oil and grease from carpets not having been inserted in the appropriate place, they are given here.

When oil is spilled on a carpet, put on a plenty of white flour, and do it as quickly as possible, in order to prevent it from spreading. If the oil is near a seam, but does not reach it, rip the seam in order to stop it. Put flour on the floor under the oil spot. The next day take up all the flour from the carpet and floor, with a dust-pan and a very stiff clothes broom, and put on fresh flour, and a plenty of it. It will not be necessary to do it a third time. To take out grease spots, rub them with a bit of white flannel, dipped in new spirits of turpentine; and if they again become visible, rub the spots again, on both sides of the carpet, when it is taken up and shaken. If there are oil or grease spots on the floor, they should be covered with thick paper before the carpet is again laid down. Scouring will not entirely remove them.

GENERAL INDEX.

Page

Ants 217
Arrow-root Gruel 207
Articles, Various, to keep . . . 225
Apple Island 91
" Snow 91
" Sauce, common family . . 116
" " Boiled cider . . . 114
" Tea 209
Apples, Steamed, Sweet. . . . 113
" Baked 114
" " Sour 114
" Coddled 115
" Dried, or Peaches, stewed 116
Ashes, Sawdust, &c., use to be made of. 224
Asparagus 175
" and Eggs 175

Barley Water 207
Bass, Baked 161
Beef, to roast. 126
" to use remnants of. . . . 188
" " " " boiled . 189
" Steak 126
" " to heat over 189
" " Stuffed 127
" " Tomato 127
" Alamode 128
" Stewed 129
" Stewed Brisket of 129
" Corned, to boil 130
" Smoked Frizzled 188
" " to shave 189
" Tea 205
Beans and Pork, baked 187
" Shelled 174
" String 174
Beer, English Ginger 214
" Maple 214
" Spring 214
" Spruce and Boneset . . . 215

Page

Beets, boiled 117
Biscuit, raised 33
" Butter-milk 33
" Cream 33
" Cream of Tartar . . . 34
" Fried 61
Blanc-mange, Arrow-root . . . 92
" Calf's Foot . . . 92
" Gelatine 93
" Isinglass 92
" Moss 93
Bleach, to, or Whiten. 241
Bread, good family 26
" made without a Sponge . 28
" " with milk 29
" " " water. . . . 28
" Diet 50
" Rice 29
" Third 29
" Graham 30
" " one loaf 30
" Boston Brown 30
" Steamed " 31
" Indian Loaf. 31
" Rye 32
" to make stale fresh . . . 32
" dough, various convenient uses of. 32
" uses for pieces of. . . . 194
Brawn 189
Brine, a good, for keeping butter 202
Broth, Lamb 150
" Mutton 150
" Veal 150
Bruiss 194
Butter, Drawn 124
" to keep sweet a year . . 203

Cabbage 178
Cake, Barnard 49
" Bread 48

Cake, Berwick (Sponge) . . . 51
" Bridgeport 49
" Brooklyn (Sponge) . . . 51
" Commencement 47
" Composition 49
" Cream 54
" Federal 52
" Gold 52
" Howard 48
" Harrison 54
" Jelly (or Washington Pie) . 53
" Lemon 54
" Loaf 47
" Lyman (Sponge) 51
" Mount Pleasant 49
" Measure (Sponge) . . . 51
" Plum, Maine 46
" " one loaf, plainer . 46
" Pound 54
" Provence 49
" Queen's 52
" Rice 54
" Snow or Bride's 52
" Silver 53
" Superior 49
" Tunbridge 49
" Washington 46
" Wedding 45
" White Mountain 53
Carrots 176
Cauliflowers 179
Caudle 209
Calcutta Curry 146
Calf's Head 184
" Foot Broth 207
" Head and Feet, to cleanse . 217
Catsup, Tomato 170
Cement, to make a Permanent . 221
Charlotte Russe 98
Chicken Broth 206
" Panada 206
" Pie 144
" Salad 148
" Tea 206
Chickens, to roast 142
" boil 148
" broil 148
" Fricassee 148
Chocolate, to make 185
Cider, to boil 215
Clams 161
Cookies 56
Cockroaches and Beetles, to kill . 217
Cocoanut Drops 57
Cocoa 186
" Ground 186
Coffee, to roast 184
" make 185
" milk 185
" Crust 210
Cologne Water 215
Corn Cake 40, 41
" Oysters 180
" Soup 179
" Boiled 179
" and Beans (Succotash) . . 179
Crackers, Litchfield 34
Cracked Wheat 191
Crumb Cakes 193
Cream, Syrup of 186
" to raise a thick 186
" Ice 97
" Imperial 98
" Snow 98
" Cakes 55
Crullers 60
" Cream of Tartar 60
Crust Coffee 210
Cucumbers 176
Currant Shrub 218
" Wine 218
Custards, Almond 94
" Boiled 95, 96
" Baked 96
" Wine 99

Draught, refreshing in a fever . . 210
Drop Cakes 37
" " Rye 38
Doughnuts, raised 61
Dumplings, Apple, Boiled . . . 87
" " Baked . . . 88
" " Steamed . . 87
" Blackberry 88
Ducks, to roast 144
" boil 144

Earthen ware, to prevent being broken 221
Egg Plant 179
Eggs, to keep 217
" pickled 182
" boiled 151
" dropped 152
" fried 151
" poached 151
" to beat the whites of . . . 43

Farina 90
Fat and Drippings, care of . . . 195
Feathers, to remove the bad odor from 219
Figs, Tomato 168
Fish, Cod, to boil 154
" " Sounds and Tongues . 154
" " or Blackfish, baked . 155
" " to fry 155
" " Chowder . . . 155, 156
" " Salt, to boil 156

Fish, Cod, Salt, minced 157
" " Balls 157
Flat-Irons, to remove Starch or Rust from 221
Floating Island 92
Flummery, Ground Rice . . . 89
" Potato Starch . . . 89
Food for a young Infant 210
" for an Infant at successive periods 211
" for a Child just weaned . . 211
Froth, Stained 99
Fruit, to Preserve, in cans . . . 112
" Jumbles 57
" Ices 97
" stains, to take out . . . 220
Fritters or Pancakes 40
" Snow 40
Frosting 44, 46
Frying Cakes, on 59
Furniture, to remove spots from . 222

Gingerbread, hard sugar 57
" soft sugar 57
" soft, without eggs . 58
" Molasses, hard . . 59
" Molasses, soft . . . 58
Ginger Crackers 58
" Snaps 58
Glass ware, to prevent being broken 221
Goose, to roast 145
Gravies, to make 128
Grease, to take out 220
" to remove, from carpets . 246
Greens, to boil 178
Griddle Cakes, white flour raised . 88
" " Butter-milk or Sour milk 88
" " without an egg . . 89
" " Indian Meal . . . 89
" " Rice 89
" " Rice, ground . . 89
" " Buckwheat . . . 89
Gruel, flour 211
" Arrow-root 207
" Oatmeal 208
" Ground Rice 208
" Indian Meal 208

Ham or Shoulder, to boil or bake . 137
" to fry 138
" to boil 138
" Pickle for one 164
Hams, to cure 164
" to keep, through the Summer 165
" Knickerbocker, pickle for, or for beef 165
Halibut, boiled or broiled . . . 157

Head Cheese 190
Herb drinks 210
House Plants, to prepare earth for 223
Hyacinths, to raise, in winter . . 224

Ice, Apricot 97
" Creams 97
" Currant 98
" Lemon 98
" Strawberry or Raspberry . . 98
Infant, Food for 210
" " for, at successive periods 211
" " for a child just weaned 211
Ink, to take out 220
" Indelible, to make 216
Iron Ware, to prevent being broken 221
Iron mould, to take out 219

Jam, Apple 109
" Grape 109
" Pine Apple 109
" Quince 109
" Raspberry 110
" Strawberry 110
Jelly, Apple 110, 111
" Barberry 111
" Calf's foot 94
" Crab Apple 111
" Cranberry 111
" Currant 111
" Currant, without boiling . 112
" English Gelatine 94
" A Nutritious 208
" Quince 112

Kisses 56
Knife handles, Ivory, to prevent being cracked 222
Knives, to preserve from rust . . 222

Lamb, boiled 130
" steaks 130
" roast 131
" stewed or Alamode . . . 131
Lard, to try 166
Lemon Syrup 212
" " without Lemons . 212
Lind, Jenny 35
Lobster in the simplest way . . 160
" Salad 160
" Stewed 160
Lunn, Sally 35

Macaroni 176
Mackerel, to prepare to broil . . 162
Mahogany Furniture, to polish . 228

Marmalade, Quince 108
" Sweet Apple . . . 115
Milk Porridge 207
" Toast 194
Mildew, to take out 219
Mortar, to remove from windows 222
Moths, to secure woollens, furs, furniture, &c., from . 217
" to kill 219
Mould, Iron, to take out . . . 219
Moulding, to prevent from 216
Muffins. raised 37
" Sour Milk 37
" Cream of Tartar . . . 37
" Top-Overs 37
Mushrooms 175
Mutton, to roast 130
" Steaks 130

Oil, to take out, from carpets . . 246
Omelets 152
Onions 178
Ovens 21
Oyster Pie 159
" Plant. 177
Oysters in the simplest way . . 158
" to fry 159
" pickled 159
" Escaloped 159
" stewed 160
" Corn 180

Panada 208
" Chicken 206
Pan-Cakes or Fritters 40
Pan Pie 192, 198
Paint, to clean, with Pumice-stone 222
" to remove, from windows . 222
" fresh, to take out 220
Paper hangings, to clean . . . 228
Parsley, to keep 216
Parsnips 176
Partridges, to roast 145
" to boil 145
Pears, baked 114
" boiled 116
Pearl Sago and Tapioca . . . 82, 83
Peas 174
Pig, to roast 135
Plated and Silver ware, to clean . 222
Plants, House, to prepare earth for 226
Pork, a shoulder, to roast or corn 136
" steaks 136
" Spare-rib or Chine . . . 136
" Salt, to fry 138
Pickled Cucumbers 180
" Mangoes 181
" Peaches 181
" Nasturtiums 182
" Eggs 182
Pickled Peppers 182
" Butternuts 182
" Martinias 183
" Tomatoes 170
" Peaches, Plums, Cherries, or Tomatoes 183
Pie Crust, good common . . . 65
" " bread dough 65
" " potato 65
Pies, Apple, stewed 65
" " without an upper-crust 65
" " of uncooked . . . 66
" " sweetened with molasses 66
" " dried 116
" Berry 67
" Cherry 67
" Chicken 144
" Cranberry 67
" Currant and Gooseberry . . 67
" Lemon 68
" Mince, rich 68
" " not as rich 68
" " Temperance . . . 69
" " very plain 69
" " without Suet . . . 69
" " without Meat . . . 70
" Oyster 159
" Peach 70
" Pigeon 146
" Rhubarb 70
" Squash or Pumpkin . . 70, 71
" Veal pot 132
" " baked 133
Pigeons, to roast 145
" in disguise 145
Pone, Sweet Potato 80
Potato balls 172
Potatoes, to boil 171
" mashed 172
" fried 173
" heated in milk 173
" old 172
" Sweet 173
Preserved Apples 102
" " Crab 102
" " Pine 103
" " " without boiling . . . 103
" Blackberries 103
" Cranberries 104
" Currants 104
" Damsons 104
" Egg Plums 105
" Peaches 105
" Pears 106
" Quinces 106
" " with Sweet Apple . . . 107

Preserved Quinces, without boiling the Syrup . . . 107
" Strawberries 108
" Tomatoes 168
Pudding, Hasty 191
" " fried 192
" Sauce, elegant 74
" " plainer . . . 74
" " cold 74
" " of Sour cream . 74
Puddings, Almond 75
" Apple 74
" " (Marlborough) . 75
" " (Pemberton) . 75
" Batter, baked 76
" " boiled or steamed 76
" Rye 77
" Bird's Nest 77
" Bread 77
" Bread and Butter . . 78
" Cocoanut 78
" Cottage 78
" Cracker 78, 79
" Farina 79
" Potato 79
" " Sweet 80
" Plum 80, 81
" Rice 81
" " White top . . . 81
" " Ground 81
" Sago 82
" Squash or Pumpkin . 82
" Tapioca 83

Puddings without Eggs.

Pudding, Berry 84
" Indian, baked 84
" " with sweet apples 84
" Plum, boiled 85
" Railroad 85
" Rice 85
" Sago 86
" Salem 86
" Suet 86
Puff Paste, rich 64
" " plainer 64
Puffs 71

Raspberry Vinegar 213
Rennet Whey 209
" Wine 215
Rice, to boil 190
Roley Poley 88
Rose Butter (a good substitute for Rose water) 216
Roses, Soot Tea for 224
Rusk 35, 36
Rye Drop Cakes 38

Sago, Apple 90
Salad 175
Salmon, to boil 158
" broil 158
Salsify, or Oyster Plant 177
Salt Meat and Vegetables, boiled together 187
Sarsaparilla Mead 213
Sausages, to make 165
" fry 137
Shad, Fresh, to broil 158
" to salt, to keep a year . . 166
" Salt, to prepare to broil . . 158
" Potted 161
Shells 186
Silver or Plated Ware, to clean . 223
Sink or Drain, to purify 219
Smelts 162
Soap, to make with ashes . . . 197
" " " potash . . . 197
" Borax 229
Soup, a rich 147
" Roast Beef Bone 148
" Turtle Bean 148
" Mock Turtle 149
" Tomato 148
" Shank 148
" Turkey 149
" White 149
" Vegetable 150
" Pea 149
" Corn 179
Souse 190
Spinage 178
Squash, Summer 177
" Winter 177
Stains, Fruit, to take out . . . 220
Starch, to take off, from flat-irons 221
" Fine, to make 240
" Flour, to make 240
Starching, Ironing, and Polishing Gentlemen's Linen 236
Stoves, to remove Rust from . . 221
Succotash 179
Suet, to keep 216
Syrup of Cream 186
Syrup, to make, for Preserves . 101

Tapioca, Boiled 90
" Pudding 83
Tea 184
Tooth Powder 216
Toast Water 210
Tomato Catsup 170
" Pickle 169
" Figs 165
Tomatoes, baked 167
" broiled 168
" like Cucumbers . . . 168
" preserved 168
" stewed 167

Tomatoes, stewed to keep a year 169
" pickled 170, 188
Tongue, stewed 167
Trout 161
Turkey, to roast 141
" to boil 142
" Soup 149
Turnips, mashed 173

Veal, to roast a Fillet 181
" " Loin 182
" Pot Pie 182
" Pie, baked 133
" Stewed, breast 133
" Cutlets 133
" Broiled 134
" Minced 189
" Cake, or Melton 187
Vegetables and Salt Meat boiled together 187
Venison 135
Velvet, to renovate 244
Veils and Lace, to renovate . . 248

Wafers 56
Waffles 86
Wash, to 228
" Calicoes, the colors of which are not fast . . 236
Wash, to, Mourning calicoes, Muslins, and Lawns . . . 237
" Starch, and Iron Muslins, Laces, &c. 237
" Thibet Cloths, Bombazines, Mouslin de Laines, and Plaids . . 241
" Shawls 242
" Colored, Black, Plaid, and Raw Silks and Ribbons 243
" English Blankets . . . 244
" White Counterpanes and Calico Quilts 245
" The Tick of a Featherbed or Pillow . . . 245
" Worsted Table-covers . 245
" Carpets 246
Well, to purify 225
Whigs 86
Whiten or Bleach, to 241
Wine Whey 207
" Custard 99
Woodcocks, Quails, and other small birds 146
Yeast, Soft Hop 24
" dry " 25
" Potato Hop 25

www.ingramcontent.com/pod-product-compliance
Lightning Source LLC
LaVergne TN
LVHW011202110826
845150LV00006B/1289

9781425572549